Samuel Smiles

Round the World

Including a residence in Victoria and a journey by rail across North America

Samuel Smiles

Round the World

Including a residence in Victoria and a journey by rail across North America

ISBN/EAN: 9783744796095

Printed in Europe, USA, Canada, Australia, Japan

Cover: Foto ©Andreas Hilbeck / pixelio.de

More available books at **www.hansebooks.com**

THE "YORKSHIRE."

ROUND THE WORLD;

INCLUDING

A RESIDENCE IN VICTORIA, AND A JOURNEY BY RAIL ACROSS NORTH AMERICA.

BY A BOY.

Edited by SAMUEL SMILES,

AUTHOR OF
"CHARACTER," "SELF-HELP," "LIFE OF THE STEPHENSONS," "THE HUGUENOTS," ETC.

WITH ILLUSTRATIONS.

NEW YORK:
HARPER & BROTHERS, PUBLISHERS,
FRANKLIN SQUARE.
1872.

PREFACE.

I HAVE had pleasure in editing this little book, not only because it is the work of my youngest son, but also because it contains the results of a good deal of experience of life under novel aspects, as seen by young, fresh, and observant eyes.

How the book came to be written is as follows: The boy, whose two years' narrative forms the subject of these pages, was at the age of sixteen seized with inflammation of the lungs, from which he was recovering so slowly and unsatisfactorily, that I was advised by London physicians to take him from the business he was then learning and send him on a long sea voyage. Australia was recommended, because of the considerable time occupied in making the voyage by sailing ship, and also because of the comparatively genial and uniform temperature while at sea.

He was accordingly sent out to Melbourne by one of Money Wigram's ships in the winter of 1868-9, with directions either to return by the same ship, or, if the opportunity presented itself, to remain for a time in the colony. It will be found, from his own narrative, that, having obtained some suitable employment, he decided to adopt the latter course, and for a period of about eighteen months he resided at Majorca, an up-country township situated in the gold-mining district of Victoria.

When his health had become re-established, he was directed to return home about the beginning of the present year, and he decided to make the return voyage by the Pacific route, *viâ* Honolulu and San Francisco, and from thence to proceed by railway across the Rocky Mountains to New York.

While at sea the boy kept a full log, intended for the perusal of his relatives at home, and while on land he corresponded with them regularly and fully, never missing a mail. He had not the remotest idea that any thing which he saw and described during his absence would ever appear in a book. But since his return it has occurred to the Editor of these pages that the information they contain will probably be found of interest to a wider circle of readers than that to which the letters were originally addressed, and in that belief the substance of them is here reproduced, the Editor's work having consisted mainly in arranging the materials, leaving the writer to tell his own story as much as possible in his own way, and in his own words.

London, November, 1871.

CONTENTS.

CHAPTER I.
DOWN CHANNEL.

At Gravesend.—Taking in Stores.—First Night on Board.—"The Anchor's up."—Off Brighton.—Change of Wind.—Gale in the Channel.—The Abandoned Ship.—The Eddystone.—Plymouth Harbor.—Departure from England..Page 13

CHAPTER II.
FLYING SOUTH.

My Fellow-passengers.—Life on board Ship.—Progress of the Ship.—Her Handling.—A fine Run down by the Line.—Passing Ships.—Amusements.—Climbing the Mizzen.—The Cape de Verd Islands.—San Antonio.. 21

CHAPTER III.
WITHIN THE TROPICS.

Increase of Temperature.—Flying Fish.—The Morning Bath on board.—Paying my "Footing."—The Major's wonderful Story "capped."—St. Patrick's Day.—Grampuses.—A Ship in Sight.—The "Lord Raglan."—Rainfall in the Tropics.—Tropical Sunsets.—The Yankee Whaler.. 31

CHAPTER IV.
THE "BLUE JACKET."

April Fools' Day.—A Ship in Sight.—The "Pyrmont."—The Rescued "Blue Jacket" Passengers.—Story of the burnt Ship.—Suffering of the Lady Passengers in an open Boat.—Their Rescue.—Distressing Scene on board the "Pyrmont".. 40

CHAPTER V.
IN THE SOUTH ATLANTIC.

Preparing for Rough Weather.—The "George Thompson" Clipper.—A Race at Sea.—Scene from "Pickwick" acted.—Fishing for Albatross.—Dissection and Division of the Bird.—Whales.—Strong Gale.—Smash in the Cabin.—Shipping a Green Sea.—The Sea-birds in our Wake.—The Crozet Islands... 48

CHAPTER VI.

NEARING AUSTRALIA—THE LANDING.

Acting on Board.—The Cyclone.—Clearing the Ship for Port.—Contrary Winds.—Australia in Sight.—Cape Otway.—Port Phillip Heads.—Pilot taken on Board.—Inside the Heads.—Williamstown.—Sandridge.—The Landing..Page 60

CHAPTER VII.

MELBOURNE.

First Impressions of Melbourne.—Survey of the City.—The Streets.—Collins Street.—The Traffic.—Newness and Youngness of Melbourne.—Absence of Beggars.—Melbourne an English City.—The Chinese Quarter.—The Public Library.—Pentridge Prison.—The Yarra River.—St. Kilda.—Social Experiences in Melbourne.—A Marriage Ball.—Melbourne Ladies.—Visit to a Serious Family.................... 66

CHAPTER VIII.

UP-COUNTRY.

Obtain a Situation in an Up-country Bank.—Journey by Rail.—Castlemaine.—Farther Journey by Coach.—Maryborough.—First Sight of the Bush.—The Bush Tracks.—Evening Prospect over the Country.—Arrival at my Destination...................................... 81

CHAPTER IX.

MAJORCA.

Majorca founded in a Rush.—Description of a Rush.—Diggers camping out.—Gold-mining at Majorca.—Majorca High Street.—The People.—The Inns.—The Churches.—The Bank.—The Chinamen.—Australia the Paradise of Working-men.—"Shouting" for Drinks.—Absence of Beggars.—No Coppers up-country.............................. 89

CHAPTER X.

MY NEIGHBORHOOD AND NEIGHBORS.

"Dining out."—Diggers' Sunday Dinner.—The old Workings.—The Chinamen's Gardens.—Chinamen's Interiors.—The Cemetery.—The High Plains.—The Bush.—A Ride through the Bush.—The Savoyard Wood-cutter.—Visit to a Squatter............................... 99

CHAPTER XI.

AUSTRALIAN WINTER—THE FLOODS.

The Victorian Climate.—The Bush in Winter.—The Eucalyptus, or Australian Gum-tree.—Ball at Clunes.—Fire in the main Street.—The Buggy saved.—Down-pour of Rain.—Going Home by Water.—The Floods out.—Clunes submerged.—Calamity at Ballarat.—Damage done by the Flood.—The Chinamen's Gardens washed away............ 109

CHAPTER XII.
SPRING, SUMMER, AND HARVEST.

Spring Vegetation.—The Bush in Spring.—Garden Flowers.—An Evening Walk.—Australian Moonlight.—The Hot North Wind.—The Plague of Flies.—Bush Fires.—Summer at Christmas.—Australian Fruits.—Ascent of Mount Greenock.—Australian Wine.—Harvest.—A Squatter's Farm.—Harvest-Home Celebration.—Aurora Australis. —Autumn Rains..Page 117

CHAPTER XIII.
BUSH ANIMALS—BIRDS—SNAKES.

The 'Possum.—A Night's Sport in the Bush.—Musquitoes.—Wattel Birds.—The Piping Crow.—"Miners."—Parroquet Hunting.—The Southern Cross.—Snakes.—Marsupial Animals.................... 131

CHAPTER XIV.
GOLD-BUYING AND GOLD-MINING.

How the Gold is found.—Gold-washing.—Quartz-crushing.—Buying Gold from Chinamen.—Alluvial Companies.—Broken-down Men.—Ups and Downs in Gold-mining.—Visit to a Gold Mine.—Gold-seeking.—Diggers' Tales of lucky Finds.............................. 139

CHAPTER XV.
ROUGH LIFE AT THE DIGGINGS—"STOP THIEF!"

Gold-rushing.—Diggers' Camp at Havelock.—Murder of Lopez.—Pursuit and Capture of the Murderer.—The Thieves hunted from the Camp. —Death of the Murderer.—The Police.—Attempted Robbery of the Collingwood Bank.—Another supposed Robbery.—"Stop Thief!"—Smart Use of the Telegraph...................................... 151

CHAPTER XVI.
PLACES ABOUT.

Visit to Ballarat.—The Journey by Coach.—Ballarat founded on Gold. —Description of the Town.—Ballarat "Corner."—The speculative Cobbler.—Fire Brigades.—Return Journey.—Crab-holes.—The Talbot Ball.—The Talbot Fête.—The Avoca Races.—Sunrise in the Bush.. 160

CHAPTER XVII.
CONCLUSION OF MAJORCAN LIFE.

Victorian Life English.—Arrival of the Home Mail.—News of the Franco-German War.—The German Settlers in Majorca.—The single Frenchman.—Majorcan Public Teas.—The Church.—The Ranters.—The Teetotalers.—The Common School.—The Roman Catholics.—Common School Fête and Entertainment.—The Mechanics' Institute.—Funeral of the Town Clerk.—Departure from Majorca.—The Colony of Victoria.. Page 175

CHAPTER XVIII.
ROUND TO SYDNEY.

Last Christmas in Australia.—Start by Steamer for Sydney.—The "Great Britain."—Cheap Trips to Queenscliffe.—Rough Weather at Sea.—Mr. and Mrs. C. Mathews.—Botany Bay.—Outer South Head.—Port Jackson.—Sydney Cove.—Description of Sydney.—Government House and Domain.—Great future Empire of the South.................. 185

CHAPTER XIX.
TO AUCKLAND, IN NEW ZEALAND.

Leaving Sydney.—Anchor within the Heads.—Take in Mails and Passengers from the "City of Adelaide."—Out to Sea again.—Sight New Zealand.—Entrance to Auckland Harbor.—The "Galatea."—Description of Auckland.—Founding of Auckland due to a Job.—Maori Men and Women.—Drive to Onehunga.—Splendid View.—Auckland Gala.—New Zealand Delays.—Leave for Honolulu.................... 196

CHAPTER XX.
UP THE PACIFIC.

Departure for Honolulu.—Monotony of a Voyage by Steam.—Desagrémens.—The "Gentlemen" Passengers.—The one Second-class "Lady."—The Rats on Board.—The Smells.—Flying Fish.—Cross the Line.—Treatment of Newspapers on Board.—Hawaii in Sight.—Arrival at Honolulu.. 205

CHAPTER XXI.
HONOLULU AND THE ISLAND OF OAHU.

The Harbor of Honolulu.—Importance of its Situation.—The City.—Churches and Theatres.—The Post-office.—The Suburbs.—The King's Palace.—The Nuuanu Valley.—Poi.—People coming down the Valley.—The Pali.—Prospect from the Cliffs.—The Natives (Kanakas).—Divers.—The Women.—Drink Prohibition.—The Chinese.—Theatricals.—Musquitoes... 212

CHAPTER XXII.
HONOLULU TO SAN FRANCISCO.

Departure from Honolulu.—Wreck of the "Saginaw."—The "Moses Taylor."—The Accommodation.—The Company on Board.—Behavior of the Ship.—Death of a Passenger.—Feelings on Landing in a new Place.—Approach the Golden Gate.—Close of the Pacific Log.—First Sight of America... 228

CHAPTER XXIII.
SAN FRANCISCO TO SACRAMENTO.

Landing at San Francisco.—The Golden City.—The Streets.—The Business Quarter.—The Chinese Quarter.—The Touters.—Leave San Francisco.—The Ferry-boat to Oakland.—The Bay of San Francisco.—Landing on the Eastern Shore.—American Railway Carriages.—The Pullman's Cars.—Sleeping Berths.—Unsavory Chinamen.—The Country.—City of Sacramento.................................Page 235

CHAPTER XXIV.
ACROSS THE SIERRA NEVADA.

Rapid Ascent.—The Trestle-bridges.—Mountain Prospects.—"Placers." —Sunset.—Cape Horn.—Alta.—The Sierras by Night.—Contrast of Temperatures.—The Snow-sheds.—The Summit.—Reno.—Breakfast at Humboldt.—The Sage Brush.—Battle Mount.—Shoshonie Indians. —Ten-mile Cañon.—Elko Station.—Great American Desert.—Arrival at Ogden.. 245

CHAPTER XXV.
ACROSS THE ROCKY MOUNTAINS.

Start by Train for Omaha.—My Fellow-passengers.—Passage through the Devil's Gate.—Weber Cañon.—Fantastic Rocks.—"Thousand-mile Tree."—Echo Cañon.—More Trestle-bridges.—Sunset amid the Bluffs. —A Wintry Night by Rail.—Snow-fences and Snow-sheds.—Laramie City.—Red Buttes.—The Summit at Sherman.—Cheyenne City.—The Western Prairie in Winter.—Prairie Dog City.—The Valley of the Platte.—Grand Island.—Cross the North Fork of the Platte.—Arrival in Omaha.. 254

CHAPTER XXVI.
OMAHA TO CHICAGO.

Omaha Terminus.—Cross the Missouri.—Council Bluffs.—The Forest.— Cross the Mississippi.—The cultivated Prairie.—The Farmsteads and Villages.—Approach to Chicago.—The City of Chicago.—Enterprise of its Men.—The Water Tunnels under Lake Michigan.—Tunnels under the River Chicago.—Union of Lake Michigan with the Mississippi. —Description of the Streets and Buildings of Chicago.—Pigs and Corn. —The Avenue.—Sleighing.—Theatres and Churches............. 263

CHAPTER XXVII.
CHICAGO TO NEW YORK.

Leave Chicago.—The Ice Harvest.—Michigan City.—The Forest.—A Railway Smash.—Kalamazoo.—Detroit.—Crossing into Canada.— American Manners.—Roebling's Suspension Bridge.—Niagara Falls in Winter.—Goat Island.—The American Fall.—The Great Horse-shoe

Fall.—The Rapids from the Lovers' Seat.—American Cousins.—Rochester.—New York.—A Catastrophe.—Return Home .... Page 274

INDEX.. 287

ILLUSTRATIONS.

	Page
"The Yorkshire," Outward Bound	Frontispiece.
Map of the Ship's Course, Plymouth to Melbourne................	56–7
View of Melbourne, Victoria...	66
Map of the Gold-mining District, Victoria.......................	83
View of Sydney, Port Jackson.....................................	185
View of Auckland, New Zealand...................................	196
Map of the Ship's Course up the Pacific........................	206
Maps of Auckland, and Sydney, Port Jackson...................	206
View of Honolulu, Sandwich Islands.............................	212
Map of Oahu, Sandwich Islands....................................	214
Maps of Atlantic and Pacific Railways..................	238–9, 264–5
View of Niagara Falls—American side............................	274

ROUND THE WORLD.

CHAPTER I.

DOWN CHANNEL.

At Gravesend.—Taking in Stores.—First Night on Board.—"The Anchor's up."—Off Brighton.—Change of Wind.—Gale in the Channel.—The Abandoned Ship.—The Eddystone.—Plymouth Harbor.—Departure from England.

20th February: At Gravesend.—My last farewells are over, my last adieus are waved to friends on shore, and I am alone on board the ship "Yorkshire," bound for Melbourne. Every thing is in confusion on board. The decks are littered with stores, vegetables, hen-coops, sheep-pens, and coils of rope. There is quite a little crowd of sailors round the capstan in front of the cabin door. Two officers, with lists before them, are calling over the names of men engaged to make up our complement of hands, and appointing them to their different watches.

Though the ship is advertised to sail this evening, the stores are by no means complete. The steward is getting in lots of cases; and what a quantity of pickles! Hens are coming up to fill the hen-coops. More sheep are being brought; there are many on board already; and here comes our milk-cow over the ship's side, gently hoisted up by a rope. The animal seems amazed; but she is in skillful hands. "Let go!" calls out the boatswain, as the cow swings in mid-air; away rattles the chain round the wheel of the donkey engine, and the break is put on just in time to land Molly gently on the deck. In a minute she is snug in her stall "for'ard," just by the cook's galley.

Passengers are coming on board. Here is one mounting the ship's side, who has had a wet passage from the shore. A seaman lends him a hand, and he reaches the sloppy, slippery deck with difficulty.

It is a dismal day. The sleet and rain come driving down. Every thing is raw and cold; every body wet or damp. The passengers in wet mackintoshes, and the seamen in wet tarpaulins; Gravesend, with its dirty side to the river, and its dreary mudbank exposed to sight; the alternate drizzle and down-pour; the muddle and confusion of the deck—all this presented any thing but an agreeable picture to look at. So I speedily leave the deck, in order to make a better acquaintance with what is to be my home for the next three months.

First, there is the saloon — long and narrow — surrounded by the cabins. It is our dining-room, drawing-room, and parlor, all in one. A long table occupies the centre, fitted all round with fixed seats and reversible backs. At one end of the table is the captain's chair, over which hangs a clock and a barometer. Near the after end of the saloon is the mizzen mast, which passes through into the hold below, and rests on the keelson.

The cabins, which surround the saloon, are separated from it by open wood-work, for the purposes of ventilation. The entrances to them from the saloon are by sliding doors. They are separated from each other by folding doors, kept bolted on either side when one cabin only is occupied; but these can be opened when the neighbors on both sides are agreeable.

My own little cabin is by no means dreary or uninviting. A window, with six small panes, lets in light and air; and outside is a strong board, or "dead-light," for use in rough weather, to protect the glass. My bunk, next to the saloon, is covered with a clean white counterpane. A little wash-stand occupies the corner; a shelf of favorite books is over my bed-head, and a swing-lamp by its side. Then there is my little mirror, my swing-tray for bottles, and a series of little bags suspended from nails, containing all sorts of odds and ends. In short, my little chamber, so fitted up, looks quite cheerful and even jolly.

It grows dusk, and there is still the same bustle and turmoil on deck. All are busy; every body is in a hurry. At about nine the noise seems to subside, and the deck seems getting into something like order. As we are not to weigh anchor until five in the morning, some of the passengers land for a stroll on shore. I decide to go to bed.

And now begins my first difficulty. I can not find room to extend myself, or even to turn. I am literally "cribbed, cabined, and confined." Then there are the unfamiliar noises outside—the cackling of the ducks, the baa-ing of the sheep, the grunting of the pigs—possibly discussing the novelty of their position. And, nearly all through the night, just outside my cabin, two or three of the seamen sit talking together in gruff undertones.

I don't think I slept much during my first night on board. I was lying semi-conscious, when a loud voice outside woke me up in an instant—"The anchor's up! she's away!" I jumped up, and, looking out of my little cabin window, peered out into the gray dawn. The shores seemed moving, and we were off. I dressed at once and went on deck. But how raw and chill it felt as I went up the companion-ladder! A little steam-tug ahead of us was under weigh, with the "Yorkshire" in tow. The deck was now pretty well cleared, but white with frost, while the river banks were covered with snow.

Other ships were passing down stream, each with its tug; but we soon distanced them all, especially when the men flung the sails to the wind, now blowing fresh. At length, in about three quarters of an hour, the steamer took on board her tow-rope, and left us to proceed on our voyage with a fair light breeze in our favor, and all our canvas set.

When off the Nore, we hailed the "Norfolk" homeward bound—a fast clipper ship belonging to the same firm (Money Wigram's line)—and a truly grand sight she was under full sail. There were great cheerings and wavings of hats—she passing up the river and we out to sea.

I need not detain you with a description of my voyage down Channel. We passed in succession Margate, Ramsgate, and Deal. The wind kept favorable until we sighted Beachy Head about half past five in the evening, and then it nearly died away. We were off Brighton when the moon rose. The long stretch of lights along shore, the clear starlit sky, the bright moon, the ship gently rocking in the almost calm sea, the sails idly flapping against the masts, formed a picture of quiet during my first night at sea which I shall not soon forget.

But all this, I was told, was but "weather-breeding;" and it was predicted that we were to have a change. The glass was falling, and we were to look out for squalls. Nor were the squalls long in coming. Early next morning I was roused by the noise on deck and the rolling of things about my cabin floor. I had some difficulty in dressing, not having yet found my sea-legs; but I succeeded in gaining the companion-ladder and reaching the poop.

I found the wind had gone quite round in the night, and was now blowing hard in our teeth from the southwest. It was to be a case of tacking down Channel—a slow and, for landsmen, a very trying process. In the midst of my first *mal de mer*, I was amused by the appearance on board of one of my fellow-passengers. He was a small, a very small individual, but possessed of a large stock of clothes, which he was evidently glad to have an opportunity of exhibiting. He first came up with a souwester on his head, the wrong end foremost, and a pair of canvas shoes on his feet—a sort of miniature Micawber, or first-class Cockney "salt" about to breast the briny. This small person's long nose, large ears, and open mouth added to the ludicrousness of his appearance. As the decks were wet and the morning cold, he found the garb somewhat unsuitable, and dived below, to come up again in strong boots and a straw hat. But, after further consideration, he retired again, and again he appeared in fresh head-gear—a huge sealskin cap with lappets coming down over his ears. This important and dressy little individual was a source of considerable amusement to us; and there was scarcely an article in his wardrobe that had not its turn during the day.

All night it blew a gale, the wind still from the same quarter. We kept tacking between the coast of England and the opposite coast of France, making but small way as regards mileage, the wind being right in our teeth. During the night, each time that the ship was brought round on the other tack there was usually a tremendous lurch, and sometimes an avalanche of books descended upon me from the shelf overhead. Yet I slept pretty soundly. Once I was awakened by a tremendous noise outside—something like a gun going off. I afterward found it had been occasioned by the mainsail being blown away to sea, right out of the bolt-ropes, the fastenings of which were immediately outside my cabin window.

When I went on deck the wind was still blowing hard, and one had to hold on to ropes or cleats to be able to stand. The whole sea was alive, waves chasing waves and bounding over each other, crested with foam. Now and then the ship would pitch her prow into a wave even to the bulwarks, dash the billow aside, and buoyantly rise again, bowling along, though under moderate sail, because of the force of the gale.

The sea has some sad sights, of which one shortly presented itself. About midday the captain sighted a vessel at some distance off on our weather bow, flying a flag of distress—an ensign upside down. Our ship was put about, and as we neared the vessel we found she had been abandoned, and was settling fast in the water. Two or three of her sails were still set, torn to shreds by the storm. The bulwarks were pretty much gone, and here and there the bare stanchions, or posts, were left standing, splitting in two the waves which broke clear over her deck, lying almost even with the sea. She turned out to be the "Rosa," of Guernsey, a fine barque of 700 tons, and she had been caught and disabled by the storm we had ourselves encountered. As there did not seem to be a living thing on board, and we could be of no use, we sailed away; and she must have gone down shortly after we left her. Not far from the sinking ship we came across a boat bottom upward, most probably belonging to the abandoned ship. What of the poor seamen? Have they been saved by other boats, or been taken off by some passing vessel? If not, alas for their wives and children at home! Indeed it was a sad sight.

But such things are soon forgotten at sea. We are too much occupied by our own experiences to think much of others. For two more weary days we went tacking about, the wind somewhat abating. Sometimes we caught sight of the French coast through the mist, and then we tacked back again. At length Eddystone Light came in view, and we knew we were not far from the entrance to Plymouth Sound. Once inside the Breakwater, we felt ourselves in smooth water again.

Going upon deck in the morning, I found our ship anchored in the harbor, nearly opposite Mount Edgecumbe. Nothing could be more lovely than the sight that presented itself. The noble bay, surrounded by rocks, cliffs, cottages—Drake's Island, bristling with cannon, leaving open a glimpse into the Hamoaze studded with great hulks of old war-ships—the projecting points of Mount Edgecumbe Park, carpeted with green turf down to the water, and fringed behind by noble woods, looking like masses of emerald cut into fret-work—then, in the distance, the hills of Dartmoor, variegated with many hues, and swept with alternations of light and shade—all these presented a picture the like of which I had never before seen, and feel myself quite incompetent to describe.

As we had to wait here for a fair wind, and the gale was still blowing right into the harbor's mouth, there seemed no probability of our setting sail very soon. We had, moreover, to make up our complement of passengers and provisions. Those who had a mind accordingly went on shore, strolled through the town, and visited the Hoe, from which a magnificent view of the harbor is obtained, or varied their bill of fare by dining at a hotel.

We were, however, cautioned not to sleep on shore, but to return to the ship for the night, and even during the day to keep a sharp lookout for the wind; for, immediately on a change to the nor'ard, no time would be lost in putting out to sea. We were farther informed that, in the case of nearly every ship, passengers, through their own carelessness and dilly-dallying on shore, had been left behind. I determined, therefore, to stick to the ship.

After three days' weary waiting, the wind at last went round; the anchor was weighed with a willing "Yo! heave ho!" and in a few hours, favored by a fine light breeze, we were well out to sea, and the brown cliffs of Old England gradually faded away in the distance.

CHAPTER II.

FLYING SOUTH.

My Fellow-passengers.—Life on board Ship.—Progress of the Ship.—Her Handling.—A fine Run down by the Line.—Passing Ships.—Amusements.—Climbing the Mizzen.—The Cape de Verd Islands.—San Antonio.

3d March.—Like all passengers, I suppose, who come together on board ship for a long voyage, we had scarcely passed the Eddystone Lighthouse before we began to take stock of each other. Who is this? What is he? Why is he going out? Such were the questions we inwardly put to ourselves and sought to answer.

I found several, like myself, were making the voyage for their health. A long voyage by sailing ship seems to have become a favorite prescription for lung complaints, and it is doubtless an honest one, as the doctor who gives it at the same time parts with his patient and his fees. But the advice is sound, as the long rest of the voyage, the comparatively equable temperature of the sea air, and probably the improved quality of the atmosphere inhaled, are all favorable to the healthy condition of the lungs as well as of the general system.

Of those going out in search of health, some were young and others middle-aged. Among the latter was a patient, gentle sufferer, racked by a hacking cough when he came on board. Another, a young passenger, had been afflicted by abscess in his throat and incipient lung disease. A third had been worried by business and afflicted in his brain, and needed a long rest. A fourth had been crossed in love, and sought for change of scene and occupation.

But there were others full of life and health among the passengers, going out in search of fortune or of pleasure. Two stalwart, outspoken, manly fellows, who came on board at Plymouth, were on their way to New Zealand to farm a large tract of land. They seemed to me to be models of what colonial farmers should be. Another was on his way to take up a run in Victoria, some 250 miles north of Melbourne. He had three fine Scotch colley dogs with him, which were the subject of general admiration.

We had also a young volunteer on board, who had figured at Brighton reviews, and was now on his way to join his father in New Zealand, where he proposed to join the colonial army. We had also a Yankee gentleman, about to enter on his governorship of the Guano Island of Maldon, in the Pacific, situated almost due north of the Society Islands, said to have been purchased by an English company.

Some were going out "on spec." If they could find an opening to fortune, they would settle; if not, they would return. One gentleman was taking with him a fine portable photographic apparatus, intending to visit New Zealand and Tasmania as well as Australia.

Others were going out for indefinite purposes. The small gentleman, for instance, who came on board at Gravesend with the extensive wardrobe, was said to be going out to Australia to grow—the atmosphere and climate of the country being reported as having a wonderful effect on growth. Another entertained me with a long account of how he was leaving England because of his wife; but, as he was of a somewhat priggish nature, I suspect the fault may have been his own as much as hers.

And then there was the Major, a military and distinguished-looking gentleman, who came on board, accompanied by a couple of shiny new trunks, at Plymouth. He himself threw out the suggestion that the raising of a colonial volunteer army was the grand object of his mission. Anyhow, he had the manners of a gentleman; and he had seen service, having lost his right arm in the Crimea, and gone all through the Indian Mutiny War with his left. He was full of fun, always in spirits, and a very jolly fellow, though rather given to saying things that would have been better left unsaid.

Altogether, we had seventeen saloon passengers on board, including the captain's wife, the only lady at the poop end. There were also probably about eighty second and third class passengers in the forward parts of the ship.

Although the wind was fair and the weather fine, most of the passengers suffered more or less from sea-sickness; but at length, becoming accustomed to the motion of the ship, they gradually emerged from their cabins, came on deck, and took part in the daily life on board. Let me try and give a slight idea of what this is.

At about six every morning we are roused by the sailors holystoning the decks, under the superintendence of the officer of the watch. A couple of middies pump up water from the sea by means of a pump placed just behind the wheel. It fills the tub until it overflows, running along the scuppers of the poop, and out on to the main deck through a pipe. Here the seamen fill their buckets, and proceed with the scouring of the main deck. Such a scrubbing and mopping!

I need scarcely explain that holystone is a large soft stone, used with water, for scrubbing the dirt off the ship's decks. It rubs down with sand; the sand is washed off by buckets of water thrown down, all is well mopped, and the deck is then finished off with India-rubber squilgees.

The poop is always kept most bright and clean. Soon after we left port it assumed a greatly-improved appearance. The boards began to whiten with the holystoning. Not a grease-mark or spot of dirt was to be seen. All was polished off with hand-scrapers. On Sundays, the ropes on the poop were all neatly coiled, man-of-war fashion—not a bight out of place. The brass-work was kept as bright as a gilt button.

By the time the passengers dressed and went on deck, the cleaning process was over, and the decks were dry. After half an hour's pacing the poop, the bell would ring for breakfast, the appetite for which would depend very much upon the state of the weather and the lurching of the ship. Between breakfast and lunch, more promenading on the poop; the passengers sometimes, if the weather was fine, forming themselves in groups on deck, cultivating each other's acquaintance.

During our first days at sea we had some difficulty in finding our sea-legs. The march of some up and down the poop was often very irregular, and occasionally ended in disaster. Yet the passengers were not the only learners; for one day we saw one of the cabin-boys, carrying a heavy ham down the steps from a meat-safe on board, miss his footing in a lurch of the ship, and away went our fine ham into the lee scuppers, spoiled and lost.

We lunched at twelve. From thence, until dinner at five, we mooned about on deck as before, or visited sick passengers, or read in our respective cabins, or passed the time in conversation, and thus the day wore on. After dinner the passengers drew together in parties and became social. In the pleasantly-lit saloon, some of the elders subsided into whist, while the juniors sought the middies in their cabin on the main deck, next door to the sheep-pen; there they entertained themselves and each other with songs, accompanied by the concertina and clouds of tobacco-smoke.

The progress of the ship was a subject of constant interest. It was the first thing in the morning and the last at night; and all through the day, the direction of the wind, the state of the sky and the weather, and the rate we were going at, were the uppermost topics of conversation.

When we left port the wind was blowing fresh on our larboard quarter from the northeast, and we made good progress across the Bay of Biscay; but, like many of our passengers, I was too much occupied by private affairs to attend to the nautical business going on upon deck. All I know was that the wind was fair, and that we were going at a good rate. On the fourth day I found that we were in the latitude of Cape Finisterre, and that we had run 168 miles in the preceding twenty-four hours. From this time forward, having got accustomed to the motion of the ship, I felt sufficiently well to be on deck early and late, watching the handling of the ship.

B

It was a fine sight to look up at the cloud of canvas above, bellied out by the wind, like the wings of a gigantic bird, while the ship bounded through the water, dashing it in foam from her bows, and sometimes dipping her prow into the waves, and sending aloft a shower of spray.

There was always something new to admire in the ship, and the way in which she was handled; as, for instance, to see the topgallant sails hauled down when the wind freshened, or a staysail set as the wind went round to the east. The taking in of the mainsail on a stormy night was a thing to be remembered for life; twenty-four men on the great yard at a time, clewing it in to the music of the wind whistling through the rigging. The men sing out cheerily at their work, the one who mounts the highest, or stands the foremost on the deck, usually taking the lead—

> Hawl on the bowlin,
> The jolly ship's a-rollin;
> Hawl on the bowlin,
> And we'll all drink rum.

In comes the rope with a "Yo, heave ho!" and a jerk, until the "belay" sung out by the mate signifies that the work is done. Then there is the scrambling on the deck when the wind changes quarter, and the yards want squaring as the wind blows more aft. Such are among the interesting sights to be seen on deck when the wind is in her tantrums at sea.

On the fifth day the wind was blowing quite aft. Our run during the twenty-four hours was 172 miles. Thermometer 58°. The captain is in hopes of a most favorable run to the Cape. It is our first Sunday on board, and at 10 30 the bell rings for service, when the passengers of all classes assemble in the saloon. The alternate standing and kneeling during the service is rather uncomfortable, the fixed seats jamming the legs, and the body leaning over at an unpleasant angle when the ship rolls, which she frequently does, and rather savagely.

Going upon deck next morning, I found the wind blowing strong from the north, and the ship going through the water at a splendid pace. As much sail was on as she could carry, and she dashed along, leaving a broad track of foam in her wake. The captain is in high glee at the speed at which we are going. "A fine run down to the Line!" he says, as he walks the poop, smiling and rubbing his hands, while the middies are enthusiastic in praises of the good ship, "walking the waters like a thing of life." The spirits of all on board are raised by several degrees. We have the pleasure of feeling ourselves bounding forward, on toward the sunny South. There is no resting, but a constant pressing onward, and, as we look over the bulwarks, the waves, tipped by the foam which the ship has raised, seem to fly behind us at a prodigious speed. At midday we find the ship's run during the twenty-four hours has been 280 miles—a splendid day's work, almost equal to steam!

We are now in latitude 39° 16′, about due east of the Azores. The air is mild and warm; the sky is azure, and the sea intensely blue. How different from the weather in the English Channel only a short week ago! Rugs are now discarded, and winter clothing begins to feel almost oppressive. In the evenings, as we hang over the taffrail, we watch with interest the bluish-white sparks mingling with the light blue foam near the stern

—the first indications of that phosphorescence which, I am told, we shall find so bright in the tropics.

An always interesting event at sea is the sighting of a distant ship. To-day we signaled the "Maitland," of London, a fine ship, though she was rolling a great deal, beating up against the wind that was impelling us so prosperously forward. I hope she will report us on arrival, to let friends at home know we are so far all right on our voyage.

The wind still continues to blow in our wake, but not so strongly; yet we make good progress. The weather keeps very fine. The sky seems to get clearer, the sea bluer, and the weather more brilliant, and even the sails look whiter, as we fly south. About midday on the eighth day after leaving Plymouth we are in the latitude of Madeira, which we pass about forty miles distant.

As the wind subsides, and the novelty of being on shipboard wears off, the passengers begin to think of amusements. One can not be always reading; and as for study, though I try Spanish and French alternately, I can not settle to them, and begin to think that life on shipboard is not very favorable for study. We play at quoits—using quoits of rope—on the poop, for a good part of the day; but this soon becomes monotonous, and we begin to consider whether it may not be possible to get up some entertainment on board to make the time pass pleasantly. We had a few extempore concerts in one of the middie's berths. The third-class passengers got up a miscellaneous entertainment, including recitals, which went off very well. One of the tragic recitations was so well received that it was encored. And thus the time was whiled away, while we still kept flying south.

On the ninth day we are well south of Madeira. The sun is so warm at midday that an awning is hung over the deck, and the shade it affords is very grateful. We are now in the trade winds, which blow pretty steadily at this part of our course in a southwesterly direction, and may generally be depended upon until we near the equator. At midday of the tenth day I find we have run 180 miles in the last twenty-four hours, with the wind still steady on our quarter. We have passed Teneriffe, about 130 miles distant — too remote to see it, though I am told that, had we been twenty miles nearer, we should probably have seen the famous peak.

To while away the time, and by way of a little adventure, I determined at night to climb the mizzen mast with a fellow-passenger. While leaving the deck I was chalked by a middy, in token that I was in for my footing, so as to be free of the mizzen-top. I succeeded in reaching it safely, though, to a green hand as I was, it looks and really feels somewhat perilous at first. I was sensible of the feeling of fear or apprehension just at the moment of getting over the cross-trees. Your body hangs over in mid-air at a terrible incline backward, and you have to hold on like any thing for just one moment, until you get your knee up into the top. The view of the ship under press of canvas from the mizzen-top is very grand, and the phosphorescence in our wake, billow upon billow of light shining foam, seemed more brilliant than ever.

The wind again freshens, and on the eleventh day we make another fine run of 230 miles. It is becoming rapidly warmer, and we shall soon be in the region of bonitos, albatrosses, and flying fish—only a fortnight after leaving England!

Our second Sunday at sea was beautiful exceedingly.

We had service in the saloon as usual, and after church I climbed the mizzen, and had half an hour's nap on the top. Truly this warm weather and monotonous sea life seems very favorable for dreaming, and mooning, and loafing. In the evening there was some very good hymn-singing in the second-class cabin.

Early next morning, when pacing the poop, we were startled by the cry from a man on the forecastle of "Land ho!" I found, by the direction of the captain's eyes, that the land seen lay off our weather-beam. But, though I strained my eyes looking for the land, I could see nothing. It was not for hours that I could detect it, and then it looked more like a cloud than any thing else. At length the veil lifted, and I saw the land stretching away to the eastward. It was the island of San Antonio, one of the Cape de Verds.

As we neared the land, and saw it more distinctly, it looked a grand object. Though we were then some fifteen miles off, yet the highest peaks, which were above the clouds, some thousands of feet high, were so clear and so beautiful that they looked as if they had been stolen out of the "Arabian Nights," or some fairy tale of wonder and beauty.

The island is said to be alike famous for its oranges and pretty girls. Indeed the Major, who is very good at drawing the long bow, declared that he could see a very interesting female waving her hand to him from a rock! With the help of the telescope we could certainly see some of the houses on shore.

As this is the last land we are likely to see until we reach Australia, we regard it with all the greater interest, and I myself watched it in the twilight until it faded away into a blue mist on the horizon.

CHAPTER III.

WITHIN THE TROPICS.

Increase of Temperature.—Flying Fish.—The Morning Bath on board.—Paying my "Footing."—The Major's wonderful Story "capped."—St. Patrick's Day.—Grampuses.—A Ship in Sight.—The "Lord Raglan."—Rainfall in the Tropics.—Tropical Sunsets.—The Yankee Whaler.

17th March.—We are now fairly within the tropics. The heat increases day by day. This morning, at eight, the temperature was 87° in my cabin. At midday, with the sun nearly overhead, it is really hot. The sky is of a cloudless azure, with a hazy appearance toward the horizon. The sea is blue—dark, deep blue—and calm.

Now we see plenty of flying fish. Whole shoals of the glittering little things glide along in the air, skimming the tops of the waves. They rise to escape their pursuers, the bonitos, which rush after them, showing their noses above the water now and then. But the poor flying fish have their enemies above the waters as well as under them, for they no sooner rise than they risk becoming the prey of the ocean birds which are always hovering about and ready to pounce upon them. It is a case of "out of the frying-pan into the fire." They fly farther than I thought they could. I saw one of them to-day fly at least sixty yards, and sometimes they mount so high as to reach the poop, some fifteen feet from the surface of the water.

One of the most pleasant events of the day is the morning bath on board. You must remember the latitude we are in. We are passing along, though not in sight of, that part of the African coast where a necklace is considered full dress. We sympathize with the natives, for we find clothes becoming intolerable; hence our enjoyment of the morning bath, which consists in getting into a large tub on board, and being pumped upon by the hose. Pity that one can not have it later, as it leaves such a long interval between bath and breakfast; but it freshens one up wonderfully, and is an extremely pleasant operation. I only wish that the tub were twenty times as large, and the hose twice as strong.

The wind continues in our favor, though gradually subsiding. During the last two days we have run over 200 miles each day, but the captain says that by the time we reach the Line the wind will have completely died away. To catch a little of the breeze, I go up the rigging to the top. Two sailors came up mysteriously, one on each side of the ratlines. They are terrible fellows for making one pay "footings," and their object was to intercept my retreat downward. When they reached me I tried to resist, but it was of no use. I must be tied to the rigging unless I promised the customary bottle of rum; so I gave in with a good grace, and was thenceforward free to take an airing aloft.

The amusements on deck do not vary much. Quoits, cards, reading, and talking, and sometimes a game of romps, such as "Walk, my lady, walk!" We have tried to form a committee, with a view to getting up some Penny Reading or theatrical entertainment, and to ascertain whether there be any latent talent aboard, but the heat occasions such a languor as to be very unfavorable for work, and the committee lay upon their oars, doing nothing.

One of our principal sources of amusement is the Major. He is unfailing. His drawings of the long bow are as good as a theatrical entertainment. If any one tells a story of something wonderful, he at once "caps it," as they say in Yorkshire, by something still more wonderful. One of the passengers who had been at Calcutta, speaking of the heat there, said it was so great as to make the pitch run out of the ship's sides. "Bah!" said the Major, "that is nothing to what it is in Ceylon; there the heat is so great as to melt the soldiers' buttons off on parade, and then their jackets all get loose."

It seems that to-day (the 17th) is St. Patrick's Day. This the Major, who is an Irishman, discovered only late in the evening, when he declared he would have "given a fiver" if he had only known it in the morning. But, to make up for lost time, he called out forthwith, "Steward! whisky!" and he disposed of some seven or eight glasses in the saloon before the lamps were put out, after which he adjourned to one of the cabins, and there continued the celebration of St. Patrick's Day until about two o'clock in the morning. On getting up rather late, he said to himself, loud enough for me to overhear in my cabin, "Well, George, my boy, you've done your duty to St. Patrick, but he's left you a horrible bad headache!" And no wonder.

At last there is a promised novelty on board. Some original Christy's Minstrels are in rehearsal, and the theatrical committee are looking up amateurs for a farce. Readings from Dickens are also spoken of. An occasional whale is seen blowing in the distance, and many grampuses come rolling about the ship—most inelegant brutes, some three or four times the size of a porpoise. Each in turn comes up, throws himself round on the top of the sea, exposing nearly half his body, and then rolls off again.

To-day (the 20th of March) we caught our first fish from the forecastle — a bonito, weighing about seven pounds. Its color was beautifully variegated: on the back dark blue, with a streak of light blue silver on either side, and the belly silvery white. These fish are usually caught from the jibboom and the martingale, as they play about the bows of the ship. The only bait is a piece of white rag, which is bobbed upon the surface of the water to imitate a flying fish.

But what interests us more than any thing else at present is the discovery of some homeward-bound ship, by which to dispatch our letters to friends at home. The captain tells us that we are now almost directly in the track of vessels making for England from the south, and that, if we do not sight one in the course of a day or two, we may not have the chance of seeing another until we are far on our way south—if at all. We are, therefore, anxiously waiting for the signal of a ship in sight; and, in the hope that one may appear, we are all busily engaged in the saloon giving the finishing touches to our home letters.

Shortly after lunch the word was given that no less than three ships were in sight. Immense excitement on board! Every body turned up on deck. Passengers who had never been seen since leaving Plymouth now made their appearance to look out for the ships. One of them was a steamer, recognizable by the line of smoke on the horizon, supposed to be the West India mail-boat; another was outward-bound, like ourselves; and the third was the homeward-bound ship for which we were all on the lookout. She lay right across our bows, but was still a long way off. As we neared her, betting began among the passengers, led by the Major, as to whether she would take letters or not. The scene became quite exciting. The captain ordered all who had letters to be in readiness. I had been scribbling my very hardest ever since the ships came in sight, and now I closed my letter and sealed it up. Would the ship take our letters? Yes. She is an English ship, with an English flag at her peak; and she signals for newspapers, preserved milk, soap, and a doctor!

I petitioned for leave to accompany the doctor, and, to my great delight, was allowed to do so. The wind had nearly gone quite down, and only came in occasional slight gusts. The sea was, therefore, comparatively calm, with only a long, slow swell; yet, even though calm, there is some little difficulty in getting down into a boat in mid-ocean. At one moment the boat is close under you, and at the next she is some four yards down, and many feet apart from the side of the ship; you have, therefore, to be prompt in seizing an opportunity, and springing on board just at the right moment.

As we moved away from the "Yorkshire" with a good bundle of newspapers and the other articles signaled for, and looked back upon our ship, she really looked a grand object on the waters. The sun shone full upon her majestic hull, her bright copper now and then showing as she slowly rose and sank on the long swell. Above all were her towers of white canvas, standing out in relief against the leaden-colored sky. Altogether, I don't think I have ever seen a more magnificent sight. As we parted from the ship, the hundred or more people on board gave us a ringing cheer.

Our men now pulled with a will toward the still-distant ship. As we neared her, we observed that she must have encountered very heavy weather, as part of her foremast and mainmast had been carried away. Her sides looked dirty and worn, and all her iron-work was rusty, as if she had been a long time at sea. She proved to be the "Lord Raglan," of about 800 tons, bound from Bankok, in Siam, to Yarmouth.

The captain was delighted to see us, and gave us a most cordial welcome. He was really a very nice fellow, and was kindness itself. He took us down to his cabin, and treated us to Chinese beer and segars. The place was cheerful and comfortable looking, and fitted up with Indian and Chinese curiosities, yet I could scarcely reconcile myself to living there. There was a dreadful fusty smell about, which, I am told, is peculiar to Indian and Chinese ships. The vessel was laden with rice, and the fusty heat which came up from below was something awful.

The "Lord Raglan" had been nearly two years from London. She had run from London to Hong Kong, and had since been engaged in trading between there and Siam. She was now eighty-three days from Bankok. In this voyage she had encountered some very heavy weather, in which she had sprung her foremast, which was now spliced up all round. What struck me was the lightness of her spars and the smallness of her sails compared with ours. Although her mainmast is as tall, it is not so thick as our mizzen, and her spars are very slender above the first top. Yet the "Raglan," in her best days, used to be one of the crack Melbourne clipper ships.

The kindly-natured captain was most loth to let us go. It was almost distressing to see the expedients he adopted to keep us with him for a few minutes longer. But it was fast growing dusk, and in the tropics it darkens almost suddenly; so we were at last obliged to tear ourselves away, and leave him with his soap, milk, and newspapers. He, on his part, sent by us a twenty-pound chest of tea as a present for the chief mate (who was with us) and the captain. As we left the ship's side we gave the master and crew of the "Raglan" a hearty "three times three." All this while the two ships had been lying nearly becalmed, so that we had not a very long pull before we were safely back on board our ship.

For about five days we lie nearly idle, making very little progress, almost on the Line. The trade winds have entirely left us. The heat is tremendous—130° in the sun; and at midday, when the sun is right overhead, it is difficult to keep the deck. Toward evening the coolness is very pleasant; and when rain falls, as it can only fall in the tropics, we rush out to enjoy the bath. We assume the thinnest of *bizarre* costumes, and stand still under the torrent, or vary the pleasure by emptying buckets over each other.

We are now in lat. 0° 22', close upon the equator. Though our sails are set, we are not sailing, but only floating—indeed, we seem to be drifting. On looking round the horizon, I count no fewer than sixteen ships in sight, all in the same plight as ourselves. We are drawn together by an under-current or eddy, though scarcely a breath of wind is stirring. We did not, however, speak any of the ships, most of them being comparatively distant.

We cross the Line about 8 P.M. on the twentieth day from Plymouth. We have certainly had a very fine run thus far, slow though our progress now is, for we are only going at the rate of about a mile an hour; but when we have got a little farther south we expect to get out of the tropical calms and catch the southeast trade winds.

On the day following, the 24th of March, a breeze sprang up, and we made a run of 187 miles. We have now passed the greatest heat, and shortly expect cooler weather. Our spirits rise with the breeze, and we again begin to think of getting up some entertainments on board; for, though we have run some 4800 miles from Plymouth, we have still some fifty days before us ere we expect to see Melbourne.

One thing that strikes me much is the magnificence of the tropical sunsets. The clouds assume all sorts of fantastic shapes, and appear more solid and clearly defined than I have ever seen before. Toward evening they seem to float in color—purple, pink, red, and yellow alternately—while the sky near the setting sun seems of a beautiful green, gradually melting into the blue sky above. The great clouds on the horizon look like mountains tipped with gold and fiery red. One of these sunsets was a wonderful sight. The sun went down into the sea between two enormous clouds—the only ones to be seen—and they blazed with the brilliant colors I have described, which were constantly changing, until the clouds stood out in dark relief against the still delicately tinted sky. I got up frequently to see the sun rise, but in the tropics it is not nearly so fine at its rising as at its setting.

A ship was announced as being in sight, with a signal flying to speak with us. We were sailing along under a favorable breeze, but our captain put the ship about and waited for the stranger. It proved to be a Yankee whaler. When the captain came on board, he said "he guessed he only wanted newspapers." Our skipper was in a "roaring wax" at being stopped in his course for such a trivial matter, but he said nothing. The whaler had been out four years, and her last port was Honolulu, in the Sandwich Islands. The Yankee captain, among other things, wanted to know if Grant was President, and if the "Alabama" Question was settled; he was interested in the latter question, as the "Alabama" had burnt one of his ships. He did not seem very comfortable while on board, and when he had got his papers he took his leave. I could not help admiring the whaleboat in which he was rowed back to his own vessel. It was a beautiful little thing, though dirty; but it had doubtless seen much service. It was exquisitely modeled, and the two seamen in the little craft handled it to perfection. How they contrived to stand up in it quite steady, while the boat, sometimes apparently half out of the water, kept rising and falling on the long ocean swell, seemed to me little short of marvelous.

CHAPTER IV.

THE "BLUE JACKET."

April Fools' Day.—A Ship in Sight.—The "Pyrmont."—The Rescued "Blue Jacket" Passengers.—Story of the burnt Ship.—Suffering of the Lady Passengers in an open Boat.—Their Rescue.—Distressing Scene on board the "Pyrmont."

1st April.—I was roused early this morning by the cry outside of "Get up! get up! There is a ship on fire ahead!" I got up instantly, dressed, and hastened on deck, like many more. But there was no ship on fire; and then we laughed, and remembered that it was All-Fools' Day.

In the course of the forenoon we descried a sail, and shortly after we observed that she was bearing down upon us. The cry of "Letters for home!" was raised, and we hastened below to scribble a few last words, close our letters, and bring them up for the letter-bag.

By this time the strange ship had drawn considerably nearer, and we saw that she was a barque, heavily laden. She proved to be the "Pyrmont," a German vessel belonging to Hamburg, but now bound for Yarmouth from Iquique, with a cargo of saltpetre on board. When she came near enough to speak us, our captain asked, "What do you want?" The answer was, "'Blue Jacket' burnt at sea; her passengers on board. Have you a doctor?" Here was a sensation! Our April Fools' alarm was true, after all. A vessel *had* been on fire, and here were the poor passengers asking for help. We knew nothing of the "Blue Jacket," but soon we were to know all.

A boat was at once lowered from the davits, and went off with the doctor and the first mate. It was a hazy, sultry, tropical day, with a very slight breeze stirring, and very little sea. Our main yard was backed to prevent our farther progress, and both ships lay-to within a short distance of each other. We watched our boat until we saw the doctor and officer mount the "Pyrmont," and then waited for farther intelligence.

Shortly after we saw our boat leaving the ship's side, and as it approached we observed that it contained some strangers as well as our doctor, who had returned for medicines, lint, and other appliances. When the strangers reached the deck we found that one of them was the first officer of the unfortunate "Blue Jacket," and the other one of the burnt-out passengers. The latter, poor fellow, looked a piteous sight. He had nothing on but a shirt and a pair of trowsers; his hair was matted, his face haggard, his eyes sunken. He was without shoes, and his feet was so sore that he could scarcely walk without support.

And yet it turned out that this poor suffering fellow was one of the best-conditioned of those who had been saved from the burnt ship. He told us how that the whole of the fellow-passengers whom he had just left on board the "Pyrmont" wanted clothes, shirts, and shoes, and were in a wretched state, having been tossed about at sea in an open boat for about nine days, during which they had suffered the extremities of cold, thirst, and hunger.

We were horrified by the appearance, and still more

by the recital, of the poor fellow. Every moment he astonished us by new details of horror. But it was of no use listening to more. We felt we must do something. All the passengers at once bestirred themselves, and went into their cabins to seek out any clothing they could spare for the relief of the sufferers. I found I could give trowsers, shirts, a pair of drawers, a blanket, and several pocket-handkerchiefs; and as the other passengers did likewise, a very fair bundle was soon made up and sent on board the "Pyrmont."

Of course, we were all eager to know something of the details of the calamity which had befallen the "Blue Jacket." It was some time before we learned them all; but as two of the passengers—who had been gold-diggers in New Zealand—were so good as to write out a statement for the doctor, the original of which now lies before me, I will endeavor, in as few words as I can, to give you some idea of the burning of the ship and the horrible sufferings of the passengers.

The "Blue Jacket" sailed from Port Lyttleton, New Zealand, for London on the 13th of February, 1869, laden with wool, cotton, flax, and 15,000 ounces of gold. There were seven first-cabin passengers and seventeen second-cabin. The ship had a fine run to Cape Horn and past the Falkland Islands. All went well until the 9th of March, when, in latitude 50° 26′ south, one of the seamen, about midday, observed smoke issuing from the fore-hatch-house. The cargo was on fire! All haste was made to extinguish it. The fire-engines were set to work, passengers as well as crew working with a will, and at one time it seemed as if the fire would be got under. The hatch was opened, and the second mate attempted to go down, with the object of getting up and throwing overboard the burning bales, but he was drawn back insensible. The hatch was again closed, and holes were cut in the deck to pass the water down; but the seat of the fire could not be reached. The cutter was lowered, together with the two life-boats, for use in case of need. About 7 30 P.M. the fire burst through the decks, and in about half an hour the whole forecastle was enveloped in flames, which ran up the rigging, licking up the foresail and fore-top. The mainmast being of iron, the flames rushed through the tube as through a chimney, until it became of a white heat. The lady passengers in the after part of the ship must have been kept in a state of total ignorance of the ship's danger, otherwise it is impossible to account for their having to rush on board the boats at the last moment with only the dresses they wore. Only a few minutes before they left the ship, one of the ladies was playing the "Guards' Waltz" on the cabin piano!

There was no hope of safety but in the boats, which were hurriedly got into. On deck, every thing was in a state of confusion. Most of the passengers got into the cutter, but without a seaman to take charge of it. When the water-cask was lowered, it was sent bung downward, and nearly half the water was lost. By this time the burning ship was a grand but fearful sight, and the roar of the flames was frightful to hear. At length the cutter and the two life-boats got away, and as they floated astern the people in them saw the masts disappear one by one, and the hull of the ship a roaring mass of fire.

In the early gray of the morning the three boats mustered, and two of the passengers, who were on one of the life-boats, were taken on board the cutter. It now contained thirty-seven persons, including the captain, first officer, doctor, steward, purser, several able-bodied seamen, and all the passengers; while the two life-boats had thirty-one of the crew. The boats drifted about all day, there being no wind, and the burning ship was still in sight. On the third day the life-boats were not to be seen; each had a box of gold on board by way of ballast.

A light breeze having sprung up, sail was made on the cutter, the captain intending to run for the Falkland Islands. The sufferings of the passengers increased from day to day; they soon ran short of water, until the day's allowance was reduced to about two table-spoonfuls for each person. It was pitiful to hear the little children calling for more, but it could not be given them: men, women, and children had to share alike. Provisions failed. The biscuit had been spoiled by the salt water; all that remained in the way of food was preserved meat, which was soon exhausted, after which the only allowance, besides the two table-spoonfuls of water, was a table-spoonful of preserved soup every twenty-four hours. Meanwhile the wind freshened, the sea rose, and the waves came dashing over the passengers, completely drenching them. The poor ladies, thinly clad, looked the pictures of misery.

Thus seven days passed—days of slow agony, such as words can not describe—until at last the joyous words "A sail! a sail" roused the sufferers to new life. A man was sent to the mast-head with a red blanket to hoist by way of signal of distress. The ship saw the signal, and bore down upon the cutter. She proved to be the "Pyrmont," the ship lying within sight of us, and between which and the "Yorkshire" our boat kept plying for the greater part of the day.

Strange to say, the rescued people suffered more after they had got on board the "Pyrmont" than they had done during their period of starvation and exposure. Few of them could stand or walk when taken on board, all being reduced to the last stage of weakness. Scarcely had they reached the "Pyrmont" ere the third steward died; next day the ship's purser died insane; and two days after, one of the second-cabin passengers died. The others, who recovered, broke out in sores and boils, more particularly on their hands and feet; and when the "Yorkshire" met them, many of the passengers, as well as the crew of the burnt "Blue Jacket," were in a most pitiable plight.

I put off with the third boat which left our ship's side for the "Pyrmont." We were lying nearly becalmed all this time, so that passing between the ships by boat was comparatively easy. We took with us as much fresh water as we could spare, together with provisions and other stores. I carried with me a few spare books for the use of the "Blue Jacket" passengers.

On reaching the deck of the "Pyrmont," the scene which presented itself was such as I think I shall never forget. The three rescued ladies were on the poop; and ladies you could see they were, in spite of their scanty and disheveled garments. The dress of one of them consisted of a common striped man's shirt, a water-proof cloak made into a skirt, and a pair of coarse canvas slippers, while on her finger glittered a magnificent diamond ring. The other ladies were no better dressed, and none of them had any covering for the head. Their faces bore distinct traces of the sufferings they had undergone. Their eyes were sunken, their cheeks pale, and every now and then a sort of spasmodic twitch seemed to pass over their features. One of them could just stand, but could not walk; the others were comparatively helpless. A gentleman was lying close by the ladies, still suffering grievously in his hands and feet from the effects of his long exposure in the open boat, while one side of his body was completely paralyzed. One poor little boy could not move, and the doctor said he must lose one or two of his toes through mortification.

One of the ladies was the wife of the passenger gentleman who had first come on board of our ship. She was a young lady, newly married, who had just set out on her wedding trip. What a terrible beginning of married life! I found she had suffered more than the others through her devotion to her husband. He was, at one time, constantly employed in baling the boat, and would often have given way but for her. She insisted on his taking half her allowance of water, so that he had three table-spoonfuls daily instead of two, whereas she had only one!

While in the boat the women and children were forced to sit huddled up at one end of it, covered with a blanket, the seas constantly breaking over them and soaking through every thing. They had to sit upright, and in very cramped postures, for fear of capsizing the boat; and the little sleep they got could only be snatched sitting. Yet they bore their privations with great courage and patience, and while the men were complaining and swearing, the women and children never uttered a complaint.

I had a long talk with the ladies, whom I found very resigned and most grateful for their deliverance. I presented my books, which were thankfully received; and the newly-married lady, forgetful of her miseries, talked pleasantly and intelligently about current topics and home news. It did seem strange for me to be sitting on the deck of the "Pyrmont," in the middle of the Atlantic, talking with these shipwrecked ladies about the last new novel!

At last we took our leave, laden with thanks, and returned on board our ship. It was now growing dusk. We had done all that we could for the help of the poor sufferers on board the "Pyrmont," and, a light breeze springing up, all sail was set, and we resumed our voyage south.

Two of the gold-diggers, who had been second-class passengers by the "Blue Jacket," came on board our ship with the object of returning with us to Melbourne, and it is from their recital that I have collated the above account of the disaster.

CHAPTER V.

IN THE SOUTH ATLANTIC.

Preparing for Rough Weather.—The "George Thompson" Clipper.—A Race at Sea.—Scene from "Pickwick" acted.—Fishing for Albatross.—Dissection and Division of the Bird.—Whales.—Strong Gale.—Smash in the Cabin.—Shipping a Green Sea.—The Sea-birds in our Wake.—The Crozet Islands.

11th April.—We are now past the pleasantest part of our voyage, and expect to encounter much rougher seas. Every thing is accordingly prepared for heavy weather. The best and newest sails are bent; the old and worn ones are sent below. We may have to encounter storms or even cyclones in the Southern Ocean, and our captain is now ready for any wind that may blow. For some days we have had a very heavy swell coming up from the south, as if there were strong winds blowing in that quarter. We have, indeed, already had a taste of dirty weather to-day—hard rain, with a stiffish breeze; but as the ship is still going with the wind and sea, we do not as yet feel much inconvenience.

A few days since we spoke a vessel that we had been gradually coming up to for some time, and she proved to be the "George Thompson," a splendid Aberdeen-built clipper, one of the fastest ships out of London. No sooner was this known than it became a matter of great interest as to whether we could overhaul the clipper. Our ship, because of the height and strength of her spars, enables us to carry much more sail, and we are probably equal to the other ship in lighter breezes; but she, being clipper-built and so much sharper, has the advantage of us in heavier winds. The captain was overjoyed at having gained upon the other vessel thus far, for she left London five days before we sailed from Plymouth. As we gradually drew nearer, the breeze freshened, and there became quite an exciting contest between the ships. We gained upon our rival, caught up to her, and gradually forged ahead, and at sundown the "George Thompson" was about six miles astern. Before we caught up to her she signaled to us, by way of chaff, "Signal us at Lloyds!" and when we had passed her, we signaled back, "We wish you a good voyage!"

The wind having freshened during the night, the "George Thompson" was seen gradually creeping up to us with all her sail set. The wind was on our beam, and the "George Thompson's" dark green hull seemed to us sometimes almost buried in the sea, and we only saw her slanting deck as she heeled over from the freshening breeze. What a cloud of canvas she carried! The spray flew up and over her decks as she plunged right through the water.

The day advanced; she continued to gain, and toward evening she passed on our weather side. The captain, of course, was savage; but the race was not lost yet. On the following day, with a lighter wind, we again overhauled our rival, and at night left her four or five miles behind. Next day she was not to be seen. We had thus far completely outstripped the noted clipper.*

* It may, however, be added, that, though we did not again sight the "George Thompson" during our voyage, she arrived at Melbourne about forty-eight hours before our ship.

We again begin to reconsider the question of giving a popular entertainment on board. The ordinary recreations of quoit-playing and such like have become unpopular, and a little variety is wanted. A reading from "Pickwick" is suggested; but can not we contrive to *act* a few of the scenes! We determine to get up three of the most attractive: 1st. The surprise of Mrs. Bardell in Pickwick's arms; 2d. The notice of action from Dodson and Fogg; and, 3d. The Trial scene. A great deal of time is, of course, occupied in getting up the scenes, and in the rehearsals, which occasion a good deal of amusement. A London gentleman promises to make a capital Sam Weller; our clergyman a very good Buzfuz; and our worthy young doctor the great Pickwick himself.

At length all is ready, and the affair comes off in the main hatch, where there is plenty of room. The theatre is rigged out with flags, and looks quite gay. The passengers of all classes assemble, and make a goodly company. The whole thing went off very well—indeed, much better than was expected—though I do not think the third-class passengers quite appreciated the wit of the piece. Strange to say, the greatest success of the evening was the one least expected—the character of Mrs. Cluppins. One of the middies, who took the part, was splendid, and evoked roars of laughter.

Our success has made us ambitious, and we think of getting up another piece—a burlesque, entitled "Sir Dagobert and the Dragon," from one of my Beeton's "Annuals." There is not much in it; but, *faute de mieux*, it may do very well. But to revert to less "towny" and much more interesting matters passing on board.

We were in about the latitude of the Cape of Good

Hope when we saw our first albatross; but as we proceeded south we were attended by increasing numbers of those birds, as well as of Mother Carey's chickens, the storm-birds of the South Seas. The albatross is a splendid bird, white on the breast and the inside of the wings, the rest of the body being deep brown and black.

One of the most popular amusements is "fishing" for an albatross, which is done in the following manner: A long and stout line is let out, with a strong hook at the end baited with a piece of meat, buoyed up with corks. This is allowed to trail on the water at the stern of the ship. One or other of the sea-birds wheeling about, seeing the floating object in the water, come up, eye it askance, and perhaps at length clumsily flop down beside it. The line is at once let out, so that the bait may not drag after the ship. If this be done cleverly, and there be length enough of line to let out quickly, the bird probably makes a snatch at the meat, and the hook catches hold of his curved bill. Directly he grabs at the pork, and it is felt that the albatross is hooked, the letting out of the line is at once stopped, and it is hauled in with all speed. The great thing is to pull quickly, so as to prevent the bird getting the opportunity of spreading his wings, and making a heavy struggle as he comes along on the surface of the water. It is a good heavy pull for two men to get up an albatross if the ship is going at any speed. The poor fellow, when hauled on deck, is no longer the royal bird that he seemed when circling above our heads with his great wings spread out only a few minutes ago. Here he is quite helpless, and tries to waddle about like a great goose; the first thing he often does being to void all the contents of his stomach, as if he were sea-sick.

The first albatross we caught was not a very large one, being only about ten feet from tip to tip of the wings, whereas the larger birds measure from twelve to thirteen feet. The bird, when caught, was held firmly down, and dispatched by the doctor with the aid of prussic acid. He was then cut up, and his skin, for the sake of the feathers and plumage, divided among us. The head and neck fell to my share, and, after cleaning and dressing it, I hung my treasure by a string out of my cabin window; but, when I next went to look at it, lo! the string had been cut, and my albatross's head and neck were gone.

All day the saloon and various cabins smelt very fishy by reason of the operations connected with the dissecting and cleaning of the several parts of the albatross. One was making a pipe-stem out of one of the long wing-bones. Another was making a tobacco-pouch out of the large feet of the bird. The doctor's cabin was like a butcher's shop in these bird-catching times. Part of his floor would be occupied by the bloody skin of the great bird, stretched out upon boards, with the doctor on his knees beside it working away with his dissecting scissors and pincers, getting the large pieces of fat off the skin. Esculapius seemed quite to relish the operation; while, on the other hand, the clergyman, who occupied the same cabin, held his handkerchief to his nose, and regarded the débris of flesh and feathers on the floor with horror and dismay.

Other birds, of a kind we had not before seen, shortly made their appearance, flying round the ship. There is, for instance, the whale-bird, perfectly black on the top of the wings and body, and white underneath. It is in size between a Mother Carey and a Molly-hawk, which latter is very nearly as big as an albatross. Ice-birds and Cape pigeons also fly about us in numbers; the latter are about the size of ordinary pigeons, black mottled with white on the back, and gray on the breast.

A still more interesting sight was that of a great grampus, which rose close to the ship, exposing his body as he leaped through a wave. Shortly after, a few more were seen at a greater distance, as if playing about and gamboling for our amusement.

17th April.—The weather is growing sensibly colder. Instead of broiling under cover, in the thinnest of garments, we now revert to our winter clothing for comfort. Toward night the wind rose, and gradually increased until it blew a heavy gale, so strong that all the sails had to be taken in—all but the foresail and the main topsail closely reefed. Luckily for us, the wind was nearly aft, so that we did not feel its effects nearly so much as if it had been on our beam. To-night we rounded the Cape, twenty-four days from the Line, and forty-five from Plymouth.

On the following day the wind was still blowing hard. When I went on deck in the morning I found that the mainsail had been split up the middle and carried away with a loud bang to sea. The ship was now under mizzen topsail, close-reefed main topsail, and fore topsail and foresail, no new mainsail having been bent. The sea was a splendid sight. Waves, like low mountains, came rolling after us, breaking along each side of the ship. I was a personal sufferer by the gale. I had scarcely got on deck when the wind whisked off my Scotch cap with the silver thistle in it, and blew it away to sea. Then, in going down to my cabin, I found my books, boxes, and furniture lurching about; and, to wind up with, during the evening I was rolled over while sitting on one of the cuddy chairs, and broke it. Truly a day full of small misfortunes for me!

In the night I was awakened up by the noise and the violent rolling of the ship. The mizzen mast strained and creaked; chairs had broken loose in the saloon; crockery was knocking about and smashing up in the steward's pantry. In the cabin adjoining, the water-can and bath were rambling up and down; and in the midst of all the hubbub the Major could be heard shouting, "Two to one on the water-can!" "They were just taking the fences," he said. There were few but had some mishap in their cabins. One had a hunt after a box that had broken loose; another was lamenting the necessity of getting up after his wash-hand basin and placing his legs in peril outside his bunk. Before breakfast I went on deck to look at the scene. It was still blowing a gale. We were under topsails and mainsail, with a close-reefed topsail on the mizzen mast. The sight from the poop was splendid. At one moment we were high up on the top of a wave, looking into a deep valley behind us; at another we were down in the trough of the sea, with an enormous wall of water coming after us. The pure light green waves were crested with foam, which curled over and over, and never stopped rolling. The deck lay over at a dreadful slant to a landsman's eye; indeed, notwithstanding holding on to every thing I could catch, I fell four times during the morning.

With difficulty I reached the saloon, where the passengers had assembled for breakfast. Scarcely had we taken our seats when an enormous sea struck the ship, landed on the poop, dashed in the saloon skylight, and flooded the table with water. This was a bad event for those who had not had their breakfast. As I was mounting the cuddy stairs, I met the captain coming down thoroughly soaked. He had been knocked down, and had to hold on by a chain to prevent himself being washed about the deck. The officer of the watch afterward told me that he had seen his head bobbing up and down amid the water, of which there were tons on the poop.

This was what they call "shipping a green sea"—so called because so much water is thrown upon the deck that it ceases to have the frothy appearance of smaller seas when shipped, but looks a mass of solid green water. Our skipper afterward told us at dinner that the captain of the "Essex" had not long ago been thrown by such a sea on to one of the hen-coops that run round the poop, breaking through the iron bars, and that he had been so bruised that he had not yet entirely recovered from his injuries. Such is the tremendous force of water in violent motion at sea.*

When I went on deck again the wind had somewhat abated, but the sea was still very heavy. While on the poop, one enormous wave came rolling on after us, seeming as if it must ingulf the ship. But the stern rose gradually and gracefully as the huge wave came on, and it rolled along, bubbling over the sides of the main deck, and leaving it about two feet deep in water. As

---

* Mr. G. Stevenson registered a force of three tons per square foot at Skerryvore during a gale in the Atlantic, when the waves were supposed to be twenty feet high.

the day wore on the wind gradually went down, and it seemed as if we were to have another spell of fine weather.

The next morning the sun shone clear; the wind had nearly died away, although a heavy swell still crossed our quarter. Thousands of sea-birds flew about us, and clusters were to be seen off our stern as far as the eye could reach. They seemed, though on a much larger scale, to be hanging upon our track, just as a flock of crows hang over the track of a plow in the field, and doubtless for the same reason—to pick up the food thrown up by the mighty keel of our ship. Most of them were ice-birds, blue petrels, and whale-birds, with a large admixture of albatrosses and Mother Carey's chickens. One of the passengers caught and killed one of the last-named birds, at which the captain was rather displeased, the sailors having a superstition about these birds that it is unlucky to kill them. An ice-bird was caught, and a very pretty bird it is, almost pure white, with delicate blue feet and beak. Another caught a Cape pigeon, and I caught a stink-pot, a large bird measuring about eight feet from wing to wing. The bird was very plucky when got on deck, and tried to peck at us; but we soon had him down. As his plumage was of no use, we fastened a small tin plate to his leg, with "Yorkshire" scratched on it, and let him go. But it was some

time before he rose from his waddling on the deck, spread his wings, and sailed into the air.

Some of the passengers carry on shooting at the numerous birds from the stern of the ship; but it is cruel sport. It may be fun to us, but it is death to the birds. And not always death. Poor things! It is a pitiful sight to see one of them, pricked or winged, floating away with its wounds upon it until quite out of sight. Such sport seems cruel, if it be not cowardly.

23d April.—We are now in latitude 45° 16′ south, and the captain tells us that during the night we may probably sight the Crozet Islands. It seems that these islands are inaccurately marked on the charts, some of even the best authorities putting them from one and a half to two degrees out both in latitude and longitude, as the captain showed us by a late edition of a standard work on navigation. Once he came pretty well south on purpose to sight them; but when he reached the precise latitude in which, according to his authority, they were situated, they were not to be seen.

At eight P.M. the man on the lookout gave the cry of "Land ho!" "Where away?" "On the lee beam." I strained my eyes in the direction indicated, but could make out nothing like land. I could see absolutely nothing but water all round. Two hours passed before I could discern any thing which could give one the idea of land—three small, misty, cloud-looking objects, lying far off to the south, which were said to be the islands. In about an hour more we were within about five miles of Les Apôtres, part of the group, having passed Cochon in the distance. Cochon is so called because of the number of wild pigs on the island. The largest, Possession Island, gave refuge to the shipwrecked crew of a whaler for about two years, when they were at length picked off by a passing ship. The Crozets are of volcanic origin, and some of them present a curious, conical, and sometimes fantastic appearance, more particularly Les Apôtres. The greater number of them are quite barren, the only vegetation of the others consisting of a few low stunted bushes.

CHAPTER VI.

NEARING AUSTRALIA—THE LANDING.

Acting on Board.—The Cyclone.—Clearing the Ship for Port.—Contrary Winds.—Australia in Sight.—Cape Otway.—Port Phillip Heads.—Pilot taken on Board.—Inside the Heads.—Williamstown.—Sandridge.—The Landing.

MORE theatricals! "Sir Dagobert and the Dragon" is played, and comes off very well. The extemporized dresses and "properties" are the most amusing of all. The company next proceed to get up "Aladdin and the Wonderful Scamp" to pass the time, which hangs heavy on our hands. We now begin to long for the termination of our voyage. We have sailed about 10,000 miles, but have still about 3000 more before us.

30th April.—To-day we have made the longest run since we left Plymouth, not less than 290 miles in twenty-four hours. We have before made 270, but then the sea was smooth, and the wind fair. Now the wind is blowing hard on our beam, with a heavy sea running. About 3 P.M. we sighted a barque steering at right angles to our course. In a short time we came up with her, and found that she was the Dutch barque "Vrede," ninety-eight days from Amsterdam, and bound for Batavia. She crossed so close to our stern that one might almost have pitched a biscuit on board.

During the night the sea rose, the wind blowing strong across our beam, and the ship pitched and rolled as she is said never to have done since she was built. There was not much sleep for us that night. The wind increased to a strong gale, until at length it blew quite a hurricane. It was scarcely possible to stand on deck. The wind felt as if it blew solid. The ship was driving furiously along under close-reefed topsails. Looking over the side, one could only see the black waves, crested with foam, scudding past.

It appears that we are now in a cyclone—not in the worst part of it, but in the inner edge of the outside circle. Skillful navigators know by experience how to make their way out of these furious ocean winds, and our captain was equal to the emergency. In about seven hours we were quite clear of it, though the wind blew fresh, and the ship rolled heavily, the sea continuing for some time in a state of great agitation.

For some days the wind keeps favorable, and our ship springs forward as if she knew her port, and was eager to reach it. A few more days and we may be in sight of Australia. We begin almost to count the hours. In anticipation of our arrival, the usual testimonial to the captain is set on foot, all being alike ready to bear testimony to his courtesy and seamanship. On deck, the men begin to holystone the planks, polish up the brass-work, and make every thing shipshape for port. The middies are at work here on the poop, each "with a sharp knife and a clear conscience," cutting away pieces of tarry rope. New ratlines are being fastened up across the shrouds. The standing rigging is re-tarred and shines black. The deck is fresh scraped as well as the mizzen mast, and the white paint-pot has been used freely.

9th May.—We are now in Australian waters, sailing

along under the lee of Cape Leeuwin, though the land is not yet in sight. Australian birds are flying about our ship, unlike any we have yet seen. We beat up against the wind, which is blowing off the land, our yards slewed right round. It is provoking to be so near the end of our voyage, and blown back when almost in sight of port.

14th May.—After four days of contrary wind, it changed again, and we are now right for Melbourne. Our last theatrical performance came off with great *éclat*. The captain gave his parting supper after the performance; and the *menu* was remarkable, considering that we had been out eighty-one days from Gravesend. There were ducks, fowls, tongues, hams, with lobster-salads, oyster pattés, jellies, blanc-manges, and dessert. Surely the art of preserving fresh meat and comestibles must have nearly reached perfection. To wind up, songs were sung, toasts proposed, and the captain's testimonial was presented amid great enthusiasm.

18th May.—We sighted the Australian land to-day about thirteen miles off Cape Otway. The excitement on board was very great; and no wonder, after so long a voyage. Some were going home there to rejoin their families, relatives, and friends. Others were going there for pleasure or for health. Perhaps the greater number regarded it as the land of their choice—a sort of promised land—where they were to make for themselves a home, and hoped to carve out for themselves a road to competency, if not to fortune.

We gradually neared the land until we were only about five miles distant from it. The clouds lay low on the sandy shore, the dark green scrub here and there reaching down almost to the water's edge. The coast is finely undulating, hilly in some places, and well wooded. Again we beat off the land to round Cape Otway, whose light we see. Early next morning we signal the lighthouse, and the news of our approaching arrival will be forthwith telegraphed to Melbourne. The wind, however, dies away when we are only about thirty miles from Port Phillip Heads, and there we lie idly becalmed the whole afternoon, the ship gently rolling in the light blue water, the sails flapping against the masts, or occasionally drawing half full, with a fitful puff of wind. Our only occupation was to watch the shore, and with the help of the telescope we could make out little wooden huts half hidden in the trees, amid patches of cultivated land. As the red sun set over the dark green hills, there sprang up the welcome evening breeze, which again filled our canvas, and the wavelets licked the ship's sides as she yielded to the wind, and at last sped us on to Port Phillip.

At midnight we are in sight of the light at the entrance of the Bay. Then we are taken in tow by a tug up to the Heads, where we wait until sunrise for our pilot to come on board. The Heads are low necks of sandy hillocks, one within another, that guard the entrance to the extensive bay of Port Phillip. On one side is Point Lonsdale, and on the other Point Nepean.

21st May.—Our pilot comes on board early, and takes our ship in charge. He is a curious-looking object, more like a Jew bailiff than any thing else I can think of, and very unlike an English "salt." But the man seems to know his work, and away we go, tugged by our steamer.

A little inside the Heads we are boarded by the quarantine officer, who inquires as to the health of the ship, which is satisfactory, and we proceed up the Bay. Shortly after, we pass, on the west, Queenscliffe, a pretty village built on a bit of abrupt headland, the houses of which dot the greensward. The village church is a pleasant object in the landscape. We curiously spy the land as we pass. By the help of the telescope we can see signs of life on shore. We observe, among other things, an early tradesman's cart, drawn by a fast-trotting pony, driving along the road. More dwellings appear amid a pretty, well cultivated, rolling landscape.

At length we lose sight of the shore, proceeding up the Bay toward Melbourne, which is nearly some thirty miles distant, and still below the horizon. Sailing on, the tops of trees rise up; then low banks of sand, flat tracts of bush, and, slightly elevated above them, occasional tracts of clear yellow space. Gradually rising up in the west, distant hills come in sight; and toward the north an undulating region is descried stretching round the Bay inland.

We now near the northern shore, and begin to perceive houses, and ships, and spires. The port of Williamstown comes in sight, full of shipping, as appears by the crowd of masts. Outside of it is Her Majesty's ship "Nelson" lying at anchor. On the right is the village or suburb of St. Kilda, and still farther round is Brighton. Sandridge, the landing-place of Melbourne, lies right ahead of us, and over the masts of shipping we are pointed to a mass of houses in the distance, tipped with spires and towers, and are told, "There is the city of Melbourne!"

At 5 P.M. we were alongside the large wooden railway pier of Sandridge, and soon many of our fellow-passengers were in the arms of their friends and relatives. Others, of whom I was one, had none to welcome us; but, like the rest, I took my ticket for Melbourne, only some three miles distant, and in the course of another quarter of an hour I found myself safely landed in the great city of the Antipodes.

CHAPTER VII.

MELBOURNE.

First Impressions of Melbourne.—Survey of the City.—The Streets.—Collins Street.—The Traffic.—Newness and Youngness of Melbourne.—Absence of Beggars.—Melbourne an English City.—The Chinese Quarter.—The Public Library.—Pentridge Prison.—The Yarra River.—St. Kilda.—Social Experiences in Melbourne.—A Marriage Ball.—Melbourne Ladies.—Visit to a Serious Family.

I ARRIVE in Melbourne toward evening, and, on stepping out of the railway train, find myself amid a glare of gas-lamps. Outside the station the streets are all lit up, the shops are brilliant with light, and well-dressed people are moving briskly about.

What is this large building in Bourke Street, with the

crowd standing about? It is the Royal Theatre. A large stone-faced hall inside the portico, surrounded by bars brilliantly lit, is filled with young men in groups lounging about, talking and laughing. At the farther end of the vestibule are the entrances to the different parts of the house.

Farther up the same street I come upon a large market-place, in a blaze of light, where crowds of people are moving about, buying vegetables, fruit, meat, and such like. At the farther end of the street the din and bustle are less, and I see a large structure standing in an open space, looking black against the starlit sky. I afterward find that it is the Parliament House.

Such is my first introduction to Melbourne. It is evidently a place stirring with life. After strolling through some of the larger streets, and every where observing the same indications of wealth, and traffic, and population, I took the train for Sandridge, and slept a good sound sleep in my bunk on board the "Yorkshire" for the last time.

Next morning I returned to Melbourne in the broad daylight, when I was able to take a more deliberate survey of the city. I was struck by the width and regularity of some of the larger streets, and by the admirable manner in which they are paved and kept. The whole town seems to have been laid out on a systematic plan, which some might think even too regular and uniform. But the undulating nature of the ground on which the city is built serves to correct this defect, if defect it be.

The streets are mostly laid out at right angles; broad streets one way, and alternate broad and narrow streets crossing them. Collins and Bourke Streets are perhaps the finest. The view from the high ground at one end of Collins Street, looking down the hollow of the road, and right away up the hill on the other side, is very striking. This grand street, of great width, is probably not less than a mile long. On either side are the principal bank buildings, tall and handsome. Just a little way up the hill, on the farther side, is a magnificent white palace-like structure, with a richly ornamented façade and tower. This is the new Town Hall. Higher up is a fine church spire, and beyond it a red brick tower, pricked out with yellow, standing in bold relief against the clear blue sky. You can just see Bourke and Wills' monument there, in the centre of the roadway; and at the very end of the perspective, the handsome gray front of the Treasury bounds the view.

Among the peculiarities of the Melbourne streets are the deep, broad stone gutters on either side of the roadway, evidently intended for the passage of a very large quantity of water in the rainy season. They are so broad as to render it necessary to throw little wooden bridges over them at the street-crossings. I was told that these open bridges are considered by no means promotive of the health of the inhabitants, which one can readily believe; and it is probable that before long they will be covered up.

Walk over Collins and Bourke Street at nine or ten in the morning, and you meet the business men of Melbourne on their way from the railway station to their offices in town; for the great number of them, as in London, live in the suburbs. The shops are all open, every thing looking bright and clean. Pass along the same streets in the afternoon, and you will find gayly-dressed ladies flocking the pathways. The shops are bustling with customers. There are many private carriages to be seen, with two-wheeled cars, on which the passengers sit back to back, these (with the omnibuses) being the public conveyances of Melbourne. Collins Street may be regarded as the favorite promenade, more particularly between three and four in the afternoon, when shopping is merely the excuse of its numerous fashionable frequenters.

One thing struck me especially—the very few old or gray-haired people one meets with in the streets of Melbourne. They are mostly young people; and there are comparatively few who have got beyond the middle stage of life. And no wonder. For how young a city Melbourne is! Forty years since there was not a house in the place.

Where the Melbourne University now stands, a few miserable Australian blacks would meet and hold a corroboree; but, except it might be a refugee bushranger from Sydney, there was not a white man in all Victoria. The first settler, John Batman,* arrived in the harbor of Port Phillip as recently as the year 1835, since which time the colony has been planted, the city of Melbourne has been built, and Victoria covered with farms, mines, towns, and people. When Sir Thomas Mitchell first visited the colony in 1836, though comprehending an area of more than a hundred thousand square miles, it did not contain 200 white people. In 1845 the popula-

---

* Mr. Batman died in September, 1869, at the age of 77, and his funeral was one of the largest ever seen in Melbourne. This "father of Melbourne" kept the first store, and published the first newspaper in the settlement.

tion had grown to 32,000; Melbourne had been founded, and was beginning to grow rapidly; now it contains a population of about 200,000 souls, and is already the greatest city in the southern hemisphere.

No wonder, therefore, that the population of Melbourne should be young. It consists, for the most part, of immigrants from Great Britain and other countries—of men and women in the prime of life—pushing, enterprising, energetic people. Nor is the stream of immigration likely to stop soon. The land in the interior is not one tenth part occupied, and "the cry is still they come." Indeed, many think the immigrants do not come quickly enough. Every ship brings a fresh batch; and the "new chums" may be readily known, as they assemble in knots at the corners of the streets, by their ruddy color, their gaping curiosity, and their home looks.

Another thing that strikes me in Melbourne is this—that I have not seen a beggar in the place. There is work for every body who will work, so there is no excuse for begging. A great many young fellows who come out here, no doubt, do not meet with the fortune they think they deserve. They expected that a few good letters of introduction were all that was necessary to enable them to succeed. But they are soon undeceived. They must strip to work if they would do any good. Mere clerks, who can write and add up figures, are of no use; the colony is overstocked with them. But if they are handy, ready to work, and willing to turn their hand to any thing, they need never be without the means of honest living.

In many respects Melbourne is very like home. It looks like a slice of England transplanted here, only every thing looks fresher and newer. Go into Fitzroy or Carlton Gardens in the morning, and you will see almost the self-same nurses and children that you see in the Parks in London. At dusk you see the same sort of courting couples mooning about, not knowing what next to say. In the streets you see a corps of rifle volunteers marching along, just as at home, on Saturday afternoons. Down at Sandridge you see the cheap-trip steamer, decked with flags, taking a boat-load of excursionists down the bay to some Australian Margate or Ramsgate. On the wooden pier, the same steam-cranes are at work, loading and unloading trucks.

One thing, however, there is at Melbourne that you can not see in any town in England, and that is the Chinese Quarter. There the streets are narrower and dirtier than any where else, and you see the yellow-faced folks standing jabbering at their doors—a very novel sight. The Chinamen, notwithstanding the poll-tax originally imposed on them of £10 a head, have come into Victoria in large and increasing numbers, and before long they threaten to become a great power in the colony. They are a very hard-working, but, it must be confessed, a very low class, dirty people.

Though many of the Chinamen give up their native dress and adopt the European costume, more particularly the billycock hat, there is one part of their belongings that they do not part with even in the last extremity, and that is their tail. They may hide it away in their billycock or in the collar of their coat, but, depend upon it, the tail is there. My friend, the doctor of the "Yorkshire," being a hunter after natural curiosities, had, among other things, a great ambition to possess himself of a Chinaman's tail. One day, walking up Collins Street, I met my enthusiastic friend. He recognized me, and waved something about frantically that he had in his hand. "I've got it! I've got it!" he exclaimed, in a highly-excited manner. "What have you got?" I asked, wondering. "Come in here," said he, "and I'll show it you." We turned into a bar, when he carefully undid his parcel, and exposed to view a long black thing. "What *is* it?" I asked. "A Chinaman's pigtail, of course," said he, triumphantly; "and a very rare curiosity it is, I can assure you."

Among the public institutes of Melbourne, one of the finest is the Public Library, already containing, I was told, about 80,000 volumes. It is really a Library for the People, and a noble one too. So far as I can learn, there is nothing yet in England that can be compared with it.* Working men come here, and read at their leisure scientific books, historical books, or whatever they may desire. They may come in their working dress, signing their names on entering, the only condition required of them being quietness and good behavior. About five hundred readers use the library daily.

Nor must I forget the Victorian collection of pictures, in the same building as the Public Library. The galleries are good, and contain many attractive paintings. Among them I noticed Goodall's "Rachel at the Well," Cope's "Pilgrim Fathers" (a replica), and some excellent specimens of Chevalier, a rising colonial artist.

* The public library was inaugurated under Mr. La Trobe's government in 1853, when £4000 was voted for books and an edifice. The sum was doubled in the following year, and greatly increased in succeeding years. In 1863, £40,000 of public money had been expended on the building, and £30,000 on the library.

The Post-office is another splendid building, one of the most commodious institutions of the kind in the world. There the arrival of each mail from England is announced by the hoisting of a large red flag, with the letter A (arrival).

In evidence of the advanced "civilization" of Melbourne, let me also describe a visit which I paid to its jail. But it is more than a jail, for it is the great penal establishment of the colony. The prison at Pentridge is about eight miles from Melbourne. Accompanied by a friend, I was driven thither in a covered car along a very dusty but well-kept road. Alighting at the castle-like entrance to the principal court-yard, we passed through a small doorway, behind which was a strong iron-bar gate, always kept locked, and watched by a warder. The gate was unlocked, and we shortly found ourselves in the great prison area, in the presence of sundry men in gray prison uniform with heavy irons on. Passing across the large clean yard, we make for a gate in the high granite wall at its farther side. A key is let down to us by the warder, who is keeping armed watch in his sentry-box on the top of the wall. We use it, let ourselves in, lock the door, and the key is hauled up again.

We enter the female prison, where we are shown the cells, each with its small table and neatly-folded mattress. On the table is a Bible and Prayer-book, and sometimes a third book for amusement or instruction. In some of the cells, where the inmates are learning to read and write, there is a spelling primer and a copy-book for pothooks. The female prisoners are not in their cells, but we shortly after find them assembled in a large room above, seated and at work. They all rose at our entrance, and I had a good look at their faces. There was not a single decent, honest face among them. They were mostly heavy, square-jawed, hard-looking women. Judging by their faces, vice and ugliness would seem to be pretty nearly akin.

We were next taken to the centre of the prison, from which we looked down upon the narrow, high-walled yards, in which the prisoners condemned to solitary confinement take their exercise. These yards all radiate from a small tower, in which a warder is stationed, carefully watching the proceedings below.

We shortly saw the prisoners of Department A coming in from their exercise in the yard. Each wore a white mask on his face with eye-holes in it; and no prisoner must approach another nearer than five yards, at risk of severe punishment. The procession was a very dismal one. In the half-light of the prison they marched silently on one by one, with their faces hidden, each touching his cap as he passed.

Department B came next. The men here do not work in their separate cells like the others, but go out to work in gangs, guarded by armed warders. The door of each cell throughout the prison has a small hole in it, through which the warders, who move about the galleries in list shoes, can peep in, and, unknown to the prisoner, see what he is about.

Both male and female prisons have Black Holes attached to them for the solitary confinement of the refractory. Dreadful places they look: small cells about ten feet by four, into which not a particle of light is admitted. Three thick doors, one within another, render it impossible for the prisoner inside to make himself heard without.

Next comes Department C, in which the men finish their time. Here many sleep in one room, always under strict watch, being employed during the day at their respective trades, or going out in gangs to work in the fields connected with the establishment. Connected with this department is a considerable factory, with spinning machines, weaving-frames, and dye-vats; the whole of the clothes and vats used in the jail being made by the prisoners, as well as the blankets supplied by the government to the natives. Adjoining are blacksmiths' shops, where manacles are forged; shoemakers' shops; tailors' shops; a bookbinder's shop, where the jail books are bound; and shops for various other crafts.

The prison library is very well furnished with books. Dickens's and Trollope's works are there, and I saw a well-read copy of "Self-Help," though it was doubtless through a very different sort of self-help that most of the prisoners who perused it had got there.

Last of all, we saw the men searched on coming in from their work in the fields or in the different workshops. They all stood in a line while the warder passed his hands down their bodies and legs, and looked into their hats. Then he turned to a basin of water standing by, and carefully washed his hands.

There were about 700 prisoners of both sexes in the jail when we visited it. I was told that the walls of the prison inclose an area of 132 acres, so that there is abundance of space for all kinds of work. On the whole, it was a very interesting, but, at the same time, a sad sight.

I think very little of the River Yarra Yarra, on which Melbourne is situated. It is a muddy, gray-colored stream, very unpicturesque. It has, however, one great advantage over most other Australian rivers, as indicated by its name, which in the native language means the "ever-flowing;" many of the creeks and rivers in Australia being dry in summer. I hired a boat for the purpose of a row up the Yarra. A little above the city its banks are pretty and ornamental, especially where it passes the Botanic Gardens, which are beautifully laid out, and well stocked with India-rubber plants, gum-trees, and magnificent specimens of the Southern fauna. Higher up, the river—though its banks continue green—becomes more monotonous, and we soon dropped back to Melbourne with the stream.

It is the sea-side of Melbourne that is by far the most interesting—Williamstown, with its shipping; but more especially the pretty suburbs, rapidly growing into towns, along the shores of the Bay of Port Phillip, such as St. Kilda, Elsternwick, Brighton, and Cheltenham. You see how they preserve the old country names. St. Kilda is the nearest to Melbourne, being only about three miles distant by rail, and it is the favorite resort of the Melbourne people. Indeed, many of the first-class business men reside there, just as Londoners do at Blackheath and Forest Hill. The esplanade along the beach is a fine promenade, and the bathing along shore is exceedingly good. There are large inclosures for the bathers, surrounded by wooden piles; above the inclosure, raised high on platforms, are commodious dressing-rooms, where, instead of being cooped up in an uncomfortable bathing machine, you may have a lounge outside in the bright sunshine while you dress. The water is a clear blue, and there is a sandy bottom sloping down from the shore into any depth—a glorious opportunity for swimmers!

I must now tell you something of my social experiences in Melbourne. Thanks to friends at home, I had been plentifully supplied with letters of introduction to people in the colony. When I spoke of these to old colonials in the "Yorkshire," I was told that they were "no good"—no better than so many "tickets for soup," if worth even that. I was, therefore, quite prepared for a cool reception, but nevertheless took the opportunity of delivering my letters shortly after landing.

So far from being received with coldness, I was received with the greatest kindness wherever I went. People who had never seen me before, and who knew nothing of me or my family, gave me a welcome that was genuine, frank, and hearty in the extreme. My letters, I found, were far more than "tickets for soup." They introduced me to pleasant companions and kind friends, who entertained me hospitably, enabled me to pass my time pleasantly, and gave me much practical good advice. Indeed, so far as my experience goes, the hospitality of Victoria ought to become proverbial.

One of the first visits I made was to a recent schoolfellow of mine at Geneva. I found him at work in a bank, and astonished him very much by the suddenness of my appearance. He was most kind to me during my stay in Melbourne, as well as his family, to whom I owed a succession of kindnesses which I can never forget.

I shall always retain a pleasant recollection of a marriage festivity to which I was invited within a week after my arrival. A ball was given in the evening, at which about 300 persons were present—the *élite* of Melbourne society. It was held in a large marquee, with a splendid floor, and ample space for dancing. Every thing was ordered very much the same as at home. The dresses of the ladies seemed more costly; the music was probably not so good, though very fair, and the supper rather better. I fancy there was no " contract Champagne" at that ball.

One thing I must remark about the ladies—they seemed to me somehow a little different in appearance. Indeed, when I first landed, I fancied I saw a slightly worn look, a want of freshness, in the people generally. They told me there that it is the effect of the dry Australian climate and the long summer heat, native-born Australians having a tendency to grow thin and lathy. Not that there was any want of beauty about the Melbourne girls, or that they were not up to the mark in personal appearance. On the contrary, there was quite a bevy of belles, some of them extremely pretty girls, most tastefully dressed, and I thought the twelve bridemaids, in white silk trimmed with blue, looked charming.

I spent a very pleasant evening with this gay company, and had my fill of dancing after my long privation at sea. When I began to step out the room seemed to be in motion. I had got so accustomed to the roll of the ship that I still felt unsteady, and when I put my foot down it went farther than I expected before it touched the floor. But I soon got quit of my sea-legs, which I had so much difficulty in finding.

Before concluding my few Melbourne experiences, I will mention another of a very different character from the above. I was invited to spend the following Saturday and Sunday with a gentleman and his family. I was punctual to my appointment, and was driven by my carman up to the door of a new house in a very pretty situation. I was shown into the drawing-room, where I waited some time for the mistress of the house to make her appearance. She was a matronly person, with a bland smile on her countenance. Her dress was of a uniform gray, with trimmings of the same color. We tried conversation, but somehow it failed. I fear my remarks were more meaningless than usual on such occasions. Certainly the lady and I did not hit it at all. She asked me if I had heard such and such a Scotch minister, or had read somebody's sermons which she named. Alas! I had not so much as heard of their names. Judging by her looks, she must have thought me an ignoramus. For a mortal hour we sat together, almost in silence, her eyes occasionally directed full upon me. We were for the moment relieved by the entrance of a young lady, one of the daughters of the house, who was introduced to me. But, alas! we got on no better than before. The young lady sat with downcast eyes, intent upon her knitting, though I saw that her eyes were black, and that she was pretty.

Then the master of the house came home, and we had dinner in a quiet, sober fashion. In the evening the lady and I made a few farther efforts at conversation. I was looking at the books on the drawing-room table, when she all at once brightened up, and asked, "Have you ever heard of Robbie Burns?" I answered (I fear rather chaffingly) that "I had once heard there was such a person." "Have you, though?" said the lady, relapsing into crochet. The gentleman went off to sleep, and the young lady continued absorbed in her knitting. A little later in the evening the hostess made a farther effort. "Have you ever tasted whisky toddy?" To which I answered, "Yes, once or twice," at which she seemed astonished. But the whisky toddy, which might have put a little spirit into the evening, did not make its appearance. The subject of the recent marriage festivity having come up, the lady was amazed to find I had been there, and that I was fond of dancing! I fear this sent me down a great many more pegs in her estimation. In fact, my evening was a total failure, and I was glad to get to bed —though it was an immense expanse of bed, big enough for a dozen people.

To make a long story short, next morning I went with the family to "the kirk," heard an awfully long sermon, during which I nipped my fingers to keep myself awake; and as soon as I could I made my escape back to my lodgings, very well pleased to get away, but feeling that I must have left a very unfavorable impression upon the minds of my worthy entertainers.

CHAPTER VIII.

UP-COUNTRY.

Obtain a Situation in an Up-country Bank.—Journey by Rail.—Castlemaine.—Farther Journey by Coach.—Maryborough.—First Sight of the Bush.—The Bush Tracks.—Evening Prospect over the Country.—Arrival at my Destination.

I HAD now been in Melbourne some weeks, and the question arose, What next? I found the living rather expensive, and that it was making a heavy drain upon my funds. I had the option of a passage home, or of staying in the colony if I could find some employment wherewith to occupy myself profitably in the mean while. But I could not remain much longer idle, merely going about visiting and enjoying myself.

I took an opportunity of consulting the eminent physician, Dr. Halford, who pronounced my lungs sound, but recommended me, because of the sudden changes of temperature to which Melbourne is liable, either to return home immediately, in order to establish the benefit I had derived from the voyage, or, if I remained, to proceed up-country, north of the Dividing Range, where the temperature is more equable.

I accordingly determined to make the attempt to obtain some settled employment in the colony that might enable me to remain in it a little longer. I found that there were many fellows, older and more experienced than myself, who had been knocking about Melbourne for some time, unable to find berths. It is quite natural that the young men of the colony, desirous of entering merchants' houses, banks, or insurance offices, should have the preference over new comers, and hence those young men who come here, expecting to drop into clerks' offices, soon find themselves *de trop*, and that they are a drug in the market.

The prospect of obtaining such employment in my own case did not, therefore, look very bright; yet I could but try and fail, as others had done. In the last event there was the passage home, of which I could avail myself. Well, I tried, and tried again, and at last succeeded, thanks to the friendly gentlemen in Melbourne who so kindly interested themselves in my behalf. In my case luck must have helped me, for I am sure I did not owe my success to any special knowledge. But happy I was when, after a great deal of running about, it was at length communicated to me that there was a vacancy in an up-country branch of one of the principal colonial banking companies which was open to my acceptance.

I took the position at once, and made my arrangements for starting to enter upon the duties of the office forthwith. I of course knew nothing of the country in which the branch bank was situated, excepting that it was in what is called a digging township—that is, a township in which digging for gold is the principal branch of industry. When I told my companions what occupation I had before me, and where I was going, they tried to frighten me. They pictured to me a remote place, with a few huts standing on a gravelly hill, surrounded by holes and pools of mud. "A wretched life you will lead up there," they said; " depend upon it, you

MAP OF THE GOLD-MINING DISTRICT, VICTORIA.

will never be able to bear it, and we shall see you back in Melbourne within a month, disgusted with up-country life." "Well, we shall see," I said: "I am resolved to give it a fair trial, and, in the worst event, I can go home by the next Money Wigram."

After the lapse of two days from the date of my appointment, I was at the Spencer-Street Station of the Victoria Railway, and booked for Castlemaine, a station about eighty miles from Melbourne. Two of my fellow-passengers by the "Yorkshire" were there to see me off, wishing me all manner of kind things. Another parting, and I was off up-country. What would it be like? What sort of people were they among whom I was to live? What were to be my next experiences?

We sped rapidly over the flat, lowly undulating, and comparatively monotonous country north of Melbourne until we reached the Dividing Range, a mountainous chain covered with dark green scrub, separating Bourke from Dalhousie County, where the scenery became more varied and interesting.

In the railway carriage with me was a boy of about twelve or fourteen, who at once detected in me a "new chum," as recent arrivals in the colony are called. We entered into conversation, when I found he was going to Castlemaine, where he lived. He described it as a large up-country town, second only to Ballarat and Melbourne. But I was soon about to see the place with my own eyes, for we were already approaching it; and before long I was set down at the Castlemaine Station, from whence I was to proceed to my destination by coach.

The town of Castlemaine by no means came up to the description of my traveling companion. Perhaps I had expected too much, and was disappointed. The place is built on the site of what was once a very great rush, called Forest Creek. Gold was found in considerable abundance, and attracted a vast population into the neighborhood. But other and richer fields having been discovered, the rush went elsewhere, leaving behind it the deposit of houses now known as Castlemaine.* It contains but few streets, and those not very good ones. The houses are mostly small and low; the greater number are only one-storied erections. Every thing was quiet, with very little traffic going on, and the streets had a most dead-alive look.

The outskirts of the town presented a novel appearance. Small heaps of gravelly soil, of a light red color, lying close to each other, covered the ground in all directions almost as far as the eye could reach. The whole country seemed to have been turned over, dug about, and abandoned; though I still observed here and there pools of red muddy water, and a few men digging, searching for gold among the old workings.

I put up at one of the hotels, to wait there until the coach started at midnight. The place was very dull, the streets were very dull, and every body seemed to have gone to bed. At length the hours passed and the coach drew up. It was an odd-looking vehicle, drawn by four horses. The body was simply hung on by straps innocent of springs. There were no windows to the carriage, but only leather aprons in their place. This looked rather like rough traveling.

Away we went at last, at a good pace, over a tolera-

* Before railways were introduced, the town was a great dépôt for goods going up-country to the different diggings.

bly good road. Soon, however, we began to jolt and pitch about, the carriage rolling and rocking from side to side. There was only one passenger besides myself, a solitary female, who sat opposite to me. I held on tight to the wood-work of the coach, but; notwithstanding all my efforts, I got pitched into the lady's lap more than once. She seemed to take it all very coolly, however, as if it were a mere matter of course.

After changing horses twice, and after a good deal more jolting, the road became better and smoother; and then I observed, from the signs outside, that we were approaching a considerable place. I was told that it was Maryborough, and shortly after the coach pulled up at the door of a hotel, and I alighted. It was now between four and five in the morning, so I turned into bed and had a sound sleep.

I was wakened up by a young gentleman, who introduced himself to me as one of my future "camarades" in the bank, to whom my arrival had been telegraphed. After making a good breakfast, I stepped on to the veranda in front of the hotel, and the high street of Maryborough lay before me. It seemed a nice, tidy town. The streets were white and clean; the shops, now open, were some of brick, and others of wood. The hotel in which I had slept was a two-storied brick building. Two banks were in the main street, one of them a good building. Every thing looked spic-and-span new, very unlike our old-fashioned English country towns.

The township to which I was destined being distant about six miles from Maryborough, I was driven thither in the evening, full of wonderment and curiosity as to the place to which I was bound. As we got outside

Maryborough into the open country, its appearance struck me very much. It was the first time I had been among the gum-trees, which grow so freely in all the southern parts of Australia.

For a short distance out of the town the road was a made one, passing through some old workings, shown by the big holes and heaps of gravel that lay about. Farther on it became a mere hardened track, through among trees and bushes, each driver choosing his own track. As soon as one becomes the worse for wear, and the ruts in it are worn too deep, a new one is selected. Some of these old ruts have a very ugly look. Occasionally we pass a cottage with a garden, but no village is in sight. The brown trees have a forlorn look; the pointed leaves seem hardly to cover them. The bushes, too, that grow by the road-side, seem straggling and scraggy; but then I must remember that it is winter time in Australia.

At length we reach the top of a hill, from which there is a fine view of the country beyond. I have a vivid recollection of my first glimpse of a landscape which afterward became so familiar to me. The dark green trees stretched down into the valley and clothed the undulating ground which lay toward the right. Then, on the greener and flatter-looking country in front, there seemed to extend a sort of whitish line—something that I could not quite make out. At first I thought it must be a town in the distance, with its large white houses. In the blue of the evening I could not then discern that what I took to be houses were simply heaps of pipe-clay. Farther off, and beyond all, was a background of brown hills, fading away in the distance. Though it was winter time, the air was bright and clear, and the blue sky was speckled with fleecy clouds.

But we soon lose sight of the distant scene as we rattle along through the dust down hill. We reach another piece of made road, indicating our approach to a town, and very shortly we arrive at a small township close by a creek. We pass a shed in which stampers are at work, driven by steam—it is a quartz mill; then a blacksmith's shop; then a hotel, and other houses. I supposed this was to be my location; but no! The driver turns sharp off the high road down toward the creek. It is a narrow stream of dirty-colored water, trickling along between two high banks. We drive down the steep on one side and up the other with a tremendous pull, the buggy leaning heavily to one side. On again, over a crab-holey plain, taking care to avoid the stumps of trees and bad ground. Now we are in among the piles of dirt which mark abandoned diggings.

Another short bit of made road, and we are in the township. It is still sufficiently light to enable me to read "Council Chambers" over the door of a white-painted, shed-like wooden erection of one story. Then up the street, past the shops with their large canvas signs, until at length we pull up alongside a wooden one-storied house, roofed with iron, and a large wooden veranda projecting over the pathway in front. The sign-board over the door tells me this is the Bank. I have reached my destination, and am safely landed in the town of Majorca.

CHAPTER IX.

MAJORCA.

Majorca founded in a Rush.—Description of a Rush.—Diggers camping out.—Gold-mining at Majorca.—Majorca High Street.—The People.—The Inns.—The Churches.—The Bank.—The Chinamen.—Australia the Paradise of Working-men.—" Shouting" for Drinks.—Absence of Beggars.—No Coppers up-country.

In my school-days Majorca was associated in my mind with " Minorca and Ivica," and I little thought to encounter a place of that name in Australia. It seems that the town was originally so called because of its vicinity to a rocky point called Gibraltar, where gold had been found some time before. Like many other towns up-country, the founding of Majorca was the result of a rush.

In the early days of gold-digging, when men were flocking into the colony to hunt for treasure, so soon as the news got abroad of a great nugget being found by some lucky adventurers, or of some rich gold-bearing strata being struck, there was a sudden rush from all quarters to the favored spot. Such a rush occurred at Majorca in the year 1863.

Let me try to describe the scene in those early days of the township as it has been related to me by those who witnessed it. Fancy from fourteen to fifteen thousand diggers suddenly drawn together in one locality, and camped out in the bush within a radius of a mile and a half.

A great rush is a scene of much bustle and excitement. Long lines of white tents overtop the heaps of pipe-clay, which grow higher from day to day. The men are hard at work on these hills of "mullock," plying the windlasses by which the stuff is brought up from below, or puddling and washing off "the dirt." Up come the buckets from the shafts, down which the diggers are working, and the dirty yellow water is poured down hill, to find its way to the creek as it best may. Unmade roads, or rather tracks, run in and out among the claims, knee-deep in mud, the ground being kept in a state of constant sloppiness by the perpetual washing for the gold. Perhaps there is a fight going on over the boundary-pegs of a claim which have been squashed by a heavy dray passing along, laden with stores from Castlemaine.

The miners are attended by all manner of straggling followers, like the sutlers following a camp. The life is a very rough one: hard work and hard beds, heavy eating and heavy drinking. The diggers mostly live in tents, for they are at first too much engrossed by their search for gold to run up huts; but many of them sleep in the open air or under the shelter of the trees. A pilot-coat or a pea-jacket is protection enough for those who do not enjoy the luxury of a tent; but the dryness and geniality of the climate are such that injury is very rarely experienced from the night exposure. There are very few women at the first opening of new diggings, the life is too rough and rude; and some of those who do come rock the cradle—but not the household one—with the men. The diggers, however genteel the life they may have led before, soon acquire a dirty, rough, unshaven look. Their coarse clothes are all of a color, being that of the clay and gravel in which they work, and the mud with which they become covered when digging.

There is a crowd of men at an open bar drinking. Bar, indeed! It is but a plank supported on two barrels, and across this improvised counter the brandy bottle and glasses are eagerly plied. A couple of old boxes in front serve for seats, while a piece of canvas, rigged on two poles, shades off the fierce sun. Many a large fortune has been made at a rude bar of this sort; for too many of the diggers, though they work like horses, spend like asses. Here, again, in the long main street of tents, where the shafts are often uncomfortably close to the road, the tradesmen are doing a roaring business. Stalwart men with stout appetites are laying in their stores of grocery, buying pounds of flour, sugar, and butter—meat and bread in great quantities. The digger thrusts his parcels indiscriminately into the breast of his dirty jumper, a thick shirt; and away he goes, stuffed with groceries, and perhaps a leg of mutton over his shoulder. In the evening some four thousand camp-fires in the valleys, along the gulleys, and up the sides of the hills, cast a lurid light over a scene which, once witnessed, can never be forgotten.

There were, of course, the usual rowdies at Majorca as at other rushes. But very soon a rough discipline was set up and held them in check; then a local government was formed, and eventually order was established. Although the neighboring towns look down on "little Majorca"—say it is the last place made—and tell of the riotous doings at its first settlement, Majorca is quoted by Brough Smyth, whose book on the Goldfields is the best authority on the subject, as having been a comparatively orderly place, even in the earliest days of the rush. He says, "Shortly after the workings were opened it presented a scene of busy industry, where there was more of order, decency, and good behavior than could probably be found in any mining locality in England, or on the Continent of Europe."*

The contrast, however, must be very great between the Majorca of to-day and the Majorca of seven years since, when it was a great gold-diggers' camp. It had its first burst, like all other celebrated places in the gold-fields. As the shallower and richer ground became worked out, the diggers moved off to some new diggings, and the first glories of the Majorca rush gradually passed away. Still, the place continued prosperous. The mining was carried down into deeper strata. But after a few years the yield fell off, and the engines were gradually withdrawn. Some few claims are doing well in

---

* The following is from Mr. Brough Smyth's book:

"I need only now speak of Majorca. Here a prospecting shaft was bottomed in the beginning of March, 1863, in the middle of a very extensive plain, known as M'Cullum's Creek Plain. The depth of the shaft was 85 feet, through thick clay, gravel, and cement. The wash-dirt was white gravel, intermixed with heavy boulders, on a soft pipe-clay bottom, its thickness being from 2 to 3 feet. It averaged in some places 3 oz. to the load. Finally a rush set in, and before three months had elapsed there were more then 15,000 miners on the ground. The sinking became deeper as the work went on, and was so wet that whims had to be erected; and at one time, in 1865, over 170 might have been seen at work, both night and day. Subsequently steam machinery was procured, and now no less than ten engines, varying from 15- to 20-horse power, are constantly employed in pumping, winding, and puddling. The lead in its lower part is 160 feet in depth, and is evidently extending toward the Carisbrooke, Moolart, and Charlotte Plains, where so much is expected by all scientific men."—*Mr. E. O'Farrell, formerly Chairman of the Mining Board of the Maryborough District.*—*Brough Smyth*, p. 98, 99.

new offshoots of the lead, and the miners are vigorously following it up. Two engine companies are pushing ahead and hoping for better things. Over at the other side of the creek, in among the ranges, there is still plenty of fair yielding quartz, which is being got out of mother earth, and the miners consider that they have very fair prospects before them.*

Indeed, Majorca has subsided into a comparatively quiet country place, containing about eight hundred inhabitants. It is supported in a great measure by the adjoining farming population; and I observed, during my stay at the place, that the more prudent of the miners, when they had saved a few hundred pounds—and some saved much more—usually retired from active digging and took to farming. The town consists, for the most part, of one long street, situated on a rising ground. There are not many buildings of importance in it. The houses are mostly of wood, one-storied, and roofed with corrugated iron. There is only one brick shop-front in the street, which so overtops the others that malicious, perhaps envious neighbors, say it is sure to topple down some day on to the footway. The shops are of the usual description, grocers, bakers, butchers, and drapers; and the most frequent style of shop is a store containing every thing from a pickaxe and tin dish (for gold washing) to Perry Davis's patent Pain-killer. We have, of course, our inns—the Imperial, where the manager of

---

* Since my return home, letters from Majorca inform me that things have recently taken a turn for the better. Several of the alluvial mining companies are getting gold in increased quantities. New shafts have been bottomed on rich ground, and the remittances of gold are gradually on the increase.

the bank and myself lived; **the Harp** of Erin, the Irish rendezvous, as its name imports, even its barroom being papered with green; **the** German Hotel, where the Verein is held, and over which the German tri-color flag floats on fête-days; and **there is also a** Swiss **restaurant, the** Guillaume Tell, with the Swiss flag and **cap of liberty painted on its white front.**

I must also mention the churches, standing off the main street, which are the most prominent buildings in Majorca. The largest is the Wesleyan Chapel, a substantial brick building, near which still stands the old wooden shanty first erected and used in the time of the rush. Then there is the Church of England, a neat though plain edifice, **well fitted and arranged.** The Presbyterians worship in a battered-looking wooden erection; and the Roman Catholics have a shed-like place, which in week-days is used as a school.

Our inns and our churches will give you some idea of the population of Majorca. I should say the most of it— the substance—is English. The Irish are hard workers, but generally spendthrift, though there are some excellent exceptions. The Irish hold together in religion, politics, and drink. The Scotch are not so numerous as the Irish, but somehow they have a knack of getting on. They are not clannish like the Irish. Each hangs by his own hook. Then there are the Germans, who are pretty numerous, a very respectable body of men, with a sprinkling of Italians and Swiss. The Germans keep up their old country fashions, hold their Verein, meet and make speeches, sing songs, smoke pipes, and drink thin wine. Lager-beer has not reached them yet.

The building in Majorca in which I am, of course,

most of all interested, is that in which I officiate as "Accountant," the only other officer in the bank being the "Manager." You will thus observe that there are only officers in our establishment—all rank and no file. Let me give you an idea of our building. Its walls are wooden, with canvas inside, and its roof is of corrugated iron. The office fronts the main street, and is fitted with a plain counter facing the door, at one end of which are the gold-weighing scales, and at the other the ledger-desk. Two rooms are attached to the office, in which we sleep—one behind, the other at the side. There is a pretty little garden in the rear, a veranda covered with a thickly growing Australian creeper (the Dolichos) sheltering us as we sit out there occasionally, enjoying the quiet cool of the evenings, reading or talking.

You will thus observe that our establishment is by no means of a stately order.* Indeed, the place is not weather-proof. When the wind blows the canvas inside the boards flaps about, and in my queer little sleeping-room, when the rain falls it runs down the sides of the canvas walls, and leaves large stains upon the gay paper. But I contrived to make the little place look tolerably comfortable; hung it round with photographs reminding me of relations and friends at home, and at length I came quite to enjoy my little retreat.

A look up and down the main street of Majorca is not particularly lively at any time. Some of the shopkeepers are in front of their stores, standing about under the verandas which cover the pathway, and lazily enjoying a

* Since I left Majorca a neat and substantial brick building has been erected for the purposes of the Bank, in lieu of the former wooden structure.

pipe. At the upper end of the town the blacksmith is busily at work shoeing some farmer's horses in front of the blazing smithy fire. Five or six diggers come slouching along, just from their work, in their mud-bespattered trowsers and their shirt sleeves, a pick or spade over their shoulders, and a tin "billy" in their hands. But for the occasional rattle of a cart or buggy down the street, the town would be lapped in quiet.

Here comes a John Chinaman with his big basket of vegetables. And let me tell you that the Chinamen, who live in the neighborhood of the town, form no unimportant part of our community. But for them, where should we be for our cabbages, cauliflowers, and early potatoes? They are the most indefatigable and successful of gardeners. Every morning three or four of them are seen coming into the town from their large gardens near the creek, each with a pole across his shoulders, and a heavily laden basket hanging from each end. What tremendous loads they contrive to carry in this way! Try to lift one of their baskets, and you will find you can hardly raise it from the ground. Then you see the "Johns" moving along from house to house, selling their stuffs. It takes a very clever woman to get the better of one of the Chinamen in a bargain. I found, by watching closely, that those got best off who chose what they wanted out of the basket, paid what they thought a fair price, and stuck to their purchase. John would at last agree, but go away grumbling.

Of course there is not much in the way of what is called "society" at this place. Like all the new towns in Australia, it consists for the most part of a settlement of working people. Australia may, however, be regarded as the paradise of working-men when they choose to avail themselves of the advantages which it offers. Here there is always plenty of profitable work for the industrious. Even Chinamen get rich. The better sort of working families live far more comfortably than our clerking or business young men do at home. The respectable workman belongs to the Mechanics' Institute, where there is a very good circulating library; he dresses well on Sundays, and goes to church; hires a horse, and takes a pleasure ride into the bush on holidays; puts money in the bank, and when he has accumulated a fund, builds a house for himself, or buys a lot of land and takes to farming. Any steady working-man can do all this here, and without any difficulty.

Where the digger or mechanic does not thrive and save money, the fault is entirely due to his own improvidence. Living is cheap. Clothes are dear; but the workman does not need to wear expensive clothes; and food is reasonable. Good mutton sells at 3*d*. a pound, and bread at 6*d*. the four-pound loaf. Thanks to the Chinamen also, vegetables are moderate in price. Every one may, therefore, save money if he has the mind to do so. But many spendthrifts seem to feel it a sort of necessity to throw away their money as soon as they have earned it. Of course, the chief source of waste here, as at home, is drink. There is constant "shouting" for drinks—that is, giving drinks all round to any acquaintances who may be present; and as one shouts, so another follows with his shout, and thus a great deal of drink is swallowed. Yet I must say that, though there may be more drinking here than in England, there is much less drunkenness. I have very seldom seen a man really drunk during my stay in Majorca. Perhaps the pure dry atmosphere may have something to do with it. But often, also, when there is a shout, the call of many may be only for lemonade, or some simple beverage of that sort. It must also be stated, as a plea for men resorting so much as they do to public houses, that there are few other places where they can meet and exchange talk with each other.

That every body may thrive here who will is evident from the utter absence of beggars in Australia. I have not seen one regular practitioner. An occasional "tramp" may be encountered hard up, and in search of work. He may ask for assistance. He can have a glass of beer at a bar, with a crust of bread, by asking for it. And he goes on his way, most likely getting the employment of which he is in search at the next township. The only beggars I ever encountered at Majorca are genteel ones—the people who come round with lists, asking for subscriptions in aid of bazars for the building of churches and the like. Nor did I find much of that horrid "tipping" which is such a nuisance in England. You may "shout" a liquor if you choose, but "tipping" would be considered an insult.

There is an almost entire absence of coppers up-country; the lowest change is a threepenny bit, and you can not well spend any thing under a sixpence. I never had any copper in my pocket except only a lucky farthing. Many asked me for it, to keep as a curiosity, saying they had never seen one since they left home. But I would not part with my farthing

CHAPTER X.

MY NEIGHBORHOOD AND NEIGHBORS.

"Dining out."—Diggers' Sunday Dinner.—The old Workings.—The Chinamen's Gardens.—Chinamen's Interiors.—The Cemetery.—The High Plains.—The Bush.—A Ride through the Bush.—The Savoyard Wood-cutter.—Visit to a Squatter.

There is no difficulty in making friends in Victoria. New chums from home are always made welcome. They are invited out, and hospitably entertained by people of all classes. But for the many kind friends I made in Majorca and its neighborhood I should doubtless have spent a very dull time there. As it was, the eighteen months I lived up-country passed pleasantly and happily.

The very first Sunday I spent in Majorca I "dined out." I had no letters of introduction, and therefore did not owe my dinner to influence, but to mere free-and-easy hospitality. Nor did the party with which I dined belong to the first circles, where letters of introduction are of any use; for they were only a party of diggers. I will explain how it happened.

After church my manager invited me to a short walk in the neighborhood. We went in the direction of M'Cullum's Creek, about a mile distant. This was the village at the creek which I passed on the evening of my first drive from Maryborough. Crossing the creek, we went up into the range of high ground beyond, and from the top of the hill we had a fine view of the surrounding country. Majorca lay below, glistening amid its hillocks of pipe-clay. The atmosphere was clear, and the sky blue and cloudless. Though the town was two miles distant, I could read some of the names on the large canvas sign-boards over the hotel doors; and with the help of an opera-glass I easily distinguished the windows of a house six miles off. The day was fine and warm, though it was midwinter in June; for it must be borne in mind that the seasons are reversed in this southern hemisphere.

Descending the farther side of the hill, we dropped into a gully where we shortly came upon a little collection of huts roofed with shingle. The residents were outside, some amusing themselves with a cricket-ball, while others were superintending the cooking of their dinners at open fires outside the huts. One of the men having recognized my companion, a conversation took place, which was followed by an invitation to join them at dinner. As we were getting rather peckish after our walk, we readily accepted their proffered hospitality. The mates took turn and turn about at the cooking, and when dinner was pronounced to be ready we went into the hut.

The place was partitioned off into two rooms, one of which was a sleeping apartment, and the other the dining-room. It was papered with a gay-colored paper, and photographs of friends were stuck up against the wall. We were asked to be seated. To accommodate the strangers, an empty box and a billet of wood were introduced from the outside. I could not say the table was laid, for it was guiltless of a table-cloth; indeed, all the appointments were rather rough. When we were seated, one of the mates, who acted as waiter, brought in the smoking dishes from the fire outside, and set them before us. The dinner consisted of roast beef and cauliflower, and a capital dinner it was, for our appetites were keen, and hunger is the best of sauces. We were told that on Sundays the men usually had pudding; but "Bill," who was the cook that week, was pronounced to be "no hand at a plum duff." We contrived, however, to do very well without it.

I afterward found that the men were very steady fellows—three of them English and one a German. They worked at an adjoining claim; and often afterward I saw them at our bank, selling the gold, or depositing their savings.

After dinner we had a ramble through the bush with our hosts, and then, toward dusk, we wended our way back to the township. Such was my first experience of diggers' hospitality in Australia, and it was by no means the last.

Another afternoon we made an excursion to the Chinamen's gardens, which lie up the creek, under the rocky point of Gibraltar, about a mile and a half distant from the township. We went through the lead—that is, the course which the gold takes underground, and which can be traced by the old workings. Where the gold lies from five to seven feet beneath the surface, the whole ground is turned over to get at it; but where the gold-bearing stratum lies from fifty to two hundred feet deep, and shafts have to be sunk, the remains of the old workings present a very different appearance. Then mounds of white clay and gravel, from twenty to forty feet high, lie close together, sometimes not more than fifteen feet apart. Climb up to the top of one of these mounds, and you can see down the deserted shaft which formerly led to the working ground below. Look round; see the immense quantity of heaps, and the extent of ground they cover, almost as far as the eye can reach up the lead, and imagine the busy scene which the place must have presented in the earlier days of the rush, when each of these shafts was fitted with its windlass, and each mound was covered with toiling men. In one place a couple of engine-sheds still remain, a gaunt erection supporting the water-tanks; the poppet-heads towering above all, still fitted with the wheels that helped to bring the gold to the surface. How deserted and desolate the place looks! An abandoned rush must be as melancholy a sight to a miner as a deserted city to a townsman. But all is not dead yet. Not far off you can see jets of white steam coming up from behind the high white mounds on the new lead, showing that miners are still actually at work in the neighborhood; nor are they working without hope.

Passing through the abandoned claims, we shortly found ourselves on the brow of the hill overlooking the Chinamen's gardens, of which we had come in search, and, dipping into the valley, we were soon in front of them. They are wonderfully neat and well kept. The oblong beds are raised some ten inches above the level of the walks, and the light and loamy earth is kept in first-rate condition. The Chinamen are far less particular about their huts, which are both poor and frail. Some of them are merely of canvas, propped up by gum-tree branches, to protect them from the wind and weather. But John has more substantial dwellings than these, for here, I observe, is a neat little cluster of huts, one in the centre being a well-constructed weather-board, with a real four-paned glass window in it.

Crossing the ditch surrounding the gardens upon a tottering plank, and opening the little gate, we went in. The Chinamen were, as usual, busily at work. Some were hoeing the light soil, and others, squatted on their haunches, were weeding. They looked up and wished us "Good evening" as we passed along. Near the creek, which bounded one end of the ground, a John was hauling up water from the well; I took a turn at the windlass, and must confess that I found the work very hard.

The young vegetables are reared with the greatest care, and each plant is sedulously watched and attended to. Here is a John down on his haunches, with a pot of white mixture and a home-manufactured brush, painting over the tender leaves of some young cabbages to save them from blight. He has to go through some hundreds of them in this way. Making our way into one of the larger huts, we stroll into the open door, and ask a more important-looking man if he has any watermelon. We get a splendid one for "fourpin," and have a delicious "*gouter*." Our host—a little, dry, withered-up fellow, dressed in a soiled blue cotton jacket, and wide trowsers which flap about his ankles—collects the rind for his fowls. The hard-beaten ground is the only flooring of the hut, and the roof is simply of bark.

In one of the corners of the cabin was a most peculiar-looking affair, very like a Punch and Judy show. On the proscenium, as it were, large Chinese letters were painted. Inside was an image or idol (the joss), carved in wood, with gorgeous gilded paper stuck all round him.

A small crowd of diminutive Chinamen knelt before him, doing homage. On the ledge before the little stage was a glass of *porter* for the idol to drink, and some rice and fruit to satisfy his appetite. Numerous Chinese candles, like our wax tapers, were put up all round inside, and the show, when lit up, must have looked very curious.

The Chinamen are always pleased at any notice taken of their houses, so we penetrated a little farther into the dwelling. In one little room we found a young fellow reading a Chinese book with English words opposite the characters. It seemed a sort of primer or word-book. My friend having asked the Chinaman to give us some music on an instrument hanging above him, which looked something like our banjo, he proceeded to give us some Celestial melodies. The tunes were not bad, being in quick time, not unlike an Irish jig, but the chords were most strange. He next played a tune on the Chinese fiddle, very thin and squeaky. The fiddle consists of a long, straight piece of wood, with a cross-piece fixed on to the end of it. Two strings stretch from the tip of the cross-piece to the end of the long piece. The instrument is rested on the knee, and the gut of the bow, which is between the two strings, is drawn first across one and then the other. An invisible vocalist in the adjoining cabin gave us a song to the accompaniment of the violin. I should imagine that it was a sentimental song, as it sounded very doleful; it must surely have been the tune that the old cow died of!

We were now in the bedroom, which was a most quaint affair. You must not imagine that the Chinamen sleep on beds at all—at least the Chinamen here do not. A wooden stretcher, covered with fine straw matting, is sufficient for their purpose. The room was lit by a small window; the walls were decorated with a picture or two from the "Illustrated London News," placed side by side with Chinese likenesses of charming small-footed ladies, gaudily dressed in blues and yellows.

In another adjoining hut we found a Chinaman whom we knew—a man who comes to the bank occasionally to sell us gold. He was cooking his supper, squatting over the fire, with an old frying-pan containing something that looked very like dried worms frizzling in fat. "Welly good" he told us it was; and very good he seemed to be making it, as he added slice after slice of cucumber to the mixture. John showed us the little worm-like things before they were put in the pan, and told us they came "all the way Canton." He offered us, by way of refreshment, his very last drop of liquor from a bottle that was labeled "Burnett's fine Old Tom," which he kept, I suppose, for his private consumption. John's mates shortly after came into their meal, when we retired—I with a cucumber in my pocket, which he gave me as a present, and a very good one it was. I often afterward went over to see the Chinamen, they were so quaint and funny in their ways.

I observe that in the cemetery the Chinamen have a separate piece of burying-ground apportioned to them. There their bodies are interred, but only to be dug up again, inclosed in boxes, and returned to China for final burial; the prejudice said to prevail among them being that if their bones do not rest in China their bodies can not enter Paradise. Not only are they careful that their bodies, but even that bits of their bodies, should be returned to their native land. There was a Chinaman in Majorca, whom I knew well, that had his finger taken off by an accident. Shortly after he left the township; but, three months after, he one day made his appearance at our bank. I asked him where he had been, and why he had come back to Majorca. "Oh!" said he, holding up his hand, "me come look after my finger." "Where is it?" I asked. "Oh! me put em in the ground in bush—me know." And I have no doubt he recovered his member, and went away happy.

My greatest pleasure while at Majorca was in riding or walking through the bush—that is, the country as Nature made it and left it—still uncleared and unoccupied except by occasional flocks of sheep, the property of the neighboring squatters. North of Majorca lies a fine tract of country which we call the high plains, for we have to cross a creek and climb a high hill before we get on to them. Then for an invigorating gallop over the green turf, the breeze freshening as we pace along. These plains are really wonderful. They look like a large natural amphitheatre, being level for about fifteen miles in every direction, and encircled all round by high hills. There is very little timber on the plains.

The bush covers the ranges of hills between Majorca and these plains or lower grounds, amid which the creeks run. Here, in some places, the trees grow pretty thickly; in others, the country is open and naturally clear. There is, however, always enough timber about to confuse the traveler unless he knows the track.

Shortly after my settling in Majorca, having heard that one of my fellow-passengers by the "Yorkshire" was staying with a squatter about fourteen miles off, I determined to pay him a visit. I thought I knew the track tolerably well; but on my way through the bush I got confused, and came to the conclusion that I had lost my way. When travelers get lost, they usually "*coo-ee*" at the top of their voice, and the prolonged note, rising at the end, is heard at a great distance in the silence of the bush. I *coo-ied* as loud as I could, and listened; but there was no response. I rode on again, and at length I thought I heard a sort of hammering noise in the distance. I proceeded toward it, and found the noise occasioned by a man chopping wood. Glad to find I was not yet lost, I went up to him to ask my way. To my surprise, he could not speak a word of English. I tried him in German, I tried him in French. No! What was he, then? I found, by his *patois*, a few words of which I contrived to make out, that he was a Savoyard, who had only very recently arrived in the colony. By dint of signs as much as words, I eventually made out the direction in which I was to go in order again to find the track that I had missed, and I took leave of my Savoyard with thanks.

I succeeded in recovering the track, and eventually reached the squatter's house in which my friend resided. It was a large stone building, erected in the modern style of villa architecture. Beside it stood the original squatter's dwelling. What a contrast they presented! the one a tall, handsome house; the other a little, one-storied, shingle-roofed hut, with queer little doors and windows. My friend, as he came out and welcomed me, asked me to guess what he had been just doing. He had been helping to put in the new stove in the kitchen, for the larger house is scarcely yet finished. He told me what a good time he was having: horses to ride, doing whatever he liked, and enjoying a perfect Liberty Hall.

The host himself shortly made his appearance, and gave me a cordial welcome. After dinner we walked round and took a view of the place. Quite a little community, I found, lived about, for our host is a large squatter, farmer, and miller, all the people being supplied with rations from the station store. There is even a station church provided by the owner, and a clergyman comes over from Maryborough every Sunday afternoon to hold the service and preach to the people. After a very pleasant stroll along the banks of the pretty creek which runs near the house, I mounted my nag, and rode slowly home in the cool of the evening.

CHAPTER XI.

AUSTRALIAN WINTER—THE FLOODS.

The Victorian Climate.—The Bush in Winter.—The Eucalyptus, or Australian Gum-tree.—Ball at Clunes.—Fire in the main Street.—The Buggy saved.—Down-pour of Rain.—Going Home by Water.—The Floods out.—Clunes submerged.—Calamity at Ballarat.—Damage done by the Flood.—The Chinamen's Gardens washed away.

I WAS particularly charmed with the climate of Victoria. It is really a pleasure to breathe the air, it is so pure, dry, and exhilarating. Even when the temperature is at its highest, the evenings are delightfully cool. There is none of that steamy, clammy, moist heat during the day, which is sometimes so difficult to bear in the English summer; and as for the spring of Australia, it is simply perfection.

It was midwinter when I arrived in Majorca—that is, about the end of June, corresponding with our English December. Although a wood fire was very pleasant, especially in the evenings, it was usually warm at midday. The sky was of a bright, clear blue, and sometimes the sun shone with considerable power. No one would think of going out with a greatcoat in winter excepting for a long drive through the bush or at night. In fact, the season can scarcely be termed winter; it is rather like a prolonged autumn, extending from May to August. Snow never falls—at least I never saw any during the two winters I spent in the colony; and although there were occasional slight frosts at night in the month of August, I never observed the ice thicker than a wafer. I once saw a heavy shower of hail, as it might fall in England in summer, but it melted off the ground directly.

In proof of the mildness of the climate, it may further be mentioned that the Australian vegetation continues during the winter months. The trees remain clothed in their usual garb, though the leaves are of a somewhat browner hue than in the succeeding seasons.

The leaves of the universal gum-tree, or Eucalyptus of Australia, are pointed, each leaf seeming to grow separately, and they are so disposed as to give the least possible shade. Instead of presenting one surface to the sky and the other to the earth, as is the case with the trees of Europe, they are often arranged vertically, so that both sides are equally exposed to the light. Thus the gum-tree has a pointed and sort of angular appearance, the leaves being thrust out in all directions and at every angle. The blue gum and some others have the peculiarity of throwing off their bark in white-gray longitudinal strips or ribbons, which, hanging down the branches, give them a singularly ragged look, more particularly in winter. From this description, it will be gathered that the gum-tree is not a very picturesque tree; nevertheless, I have seen some in the far bush which were finely proportioned, tall, and might even be called handsome.

The fine winter weather continues for months, the days being dry and fine, with clear blue sky overhead, until about the end of August, when rain begins to fall pretty freely. During the first winter I spent at Majorca, very little rain fell during two months, and the country was getting parched, cracked, and brown. Then everybody prayed for rain, for the sake of the flocks and herds, and the growing crops. At last the rain came, and it came with a vengeance.

It so happened that about the middle of October I was invited to accompany a friend to a ball given at Clunes, a township about fifteen miles distant, and we decided to accept the invitation. As there had been no rain to speak of for months, the tracks through the bush were dry and hard. We set off in the afternoon in a one-horse buggy, and got down to Clunes safely before it was dark.

Clunes is a rather important place, the centre of a considerable gold-mining district. Like most new up-country towns, it consists of one long street, and this one long street is situated in a deep hollow, close to a creek. The creek was now all but dry, like the other creeks or rivers in the neighborhood.

The ball was given in a large square building belonging to the Rechabites, situated in the upper part of the town. The dancing began about half past nine, and was going on very briskly, when there was a sudden cry of "fire." All rushed to the door; and, sure enough, there was a great fire raging down the street, about a quarter of a mile off. A column of flame shot up behind the houses, illuminating the whole town. The gentlemen of the place hastened away to look after their property, and the dance seemed on the point of breaking up. I had no property to save, and I remained. But the news came from time to time that the fire was spreading; and here, where nearly every house was of wood, the progress of a fire, unless checked, is necessarily very rapid. Fears now began to be entertained for the safety of the town.

The fire was said to be raging in the main street, quite close to the principal inn. Then suddenly I remembered that I too had something to look after. There was the horse and buggy, for which my friend and I were responsible, as well as our changes of clothes. I ran down the street, elbowing my way through the crowd, and reached close to where the firemen were hard at work plying their engines. Only two small wooden houses intervened between the fire and the inn. I hastened into the stable, but found my companion had been there before me. He had got out the horse and buggy, and our property was safe. Eight houses had been burnt down along one side of the street before the fire was got under.

After this excitement, nothing remained but to go back and finish the dance. Our local paper at Majorca —for you must know we have "an organ"—gave us a hard hit, comparing us to Nero, who fiddled while Rome was burning, whereas *we* danced while Clunes was burning. But we did not resume the dance till the fire was extinguished. However, every thing must come to an end, and so did the dance at about five o'clock in the morning.

Shortly after the fire the rain had begun to fall, and it was now coming down steadily. We had nothing for it but to drive back the fifteen miles to Majorca, as we had to be at business by 10 o'clock. We put on our heaviest things, and set off just as the first streaks of daylight appeared. As we drove down the street, we passed the smouldering remains of the fire. Where, the night before, I had been talking to a chemist across his counter, there was nothing but ashes; every thing had been burnt to the ground. Farther on were the charred timbers and smoking ruins of the house at which the fire had been stayed.

The rain came down heavier and heavier. It seemed to fall solid, in masses, soaking through rugs, top-coats, and water-proofs, that we had before deemed impervious. However, habit is every thing, and when once we got thoroughly soaked, we became comparatively indifferent to the rain, which never ceased falling. We were soon in the bush, where there was scarcely a track to guide us. But we hastened on, knowing that every moment increased the risk of our missing the way or being hindered by the flood. We splashed along through the mud and water. As we drove through a gully, we observed that what had before been a dry track was now changed into a torrent. Now hold the mare well in! We are in the water, and it rushes against her legs as if striving to pull her down. But she takes willingly to the collar again, and with one more good pull lands us safely on the other side, out of reach of the ugly, yellow, foaming torrent.

By the gray light of the morning we saw the water pouring down the sides of the high ground as we passed. It was clear that we must make haste if we would reach Majorca before the waters rose. We knew that at one part of the road we should have to drive near the bank of the creek, which was sure to be flooded very soon. Our object, accordingly, was to push on so as to pass this most perilous part of our journey.

On we drove, crossing dips in the track where foaming streams were now rushing along, while they roared down the gullies on either side. It was fortunate that my companion knew the road so well, as, in trying to avoid the deeper places, we might have run some risk from the abandoned shafts which lay in our way. At last we got safely across the water, alongside the swollen creek, now raging in fury; and glad I was when, rising the last hill, and looking down from the summit, I saw the low-roofed houses of Majorca before me.

I found that we had been more fortunate than a party that left Clunes a little later, who had the greatest difficulty in reaching home by reason of the flood. At some places the gentlemen had to get out of the carriages into the water up to their middle, and sound the depth of the holes in advance, before allowing the horses to proceed, and hours passed before they succeeded in reaching their destination.

During the course of the day we learned by telegraph —for telegraphs are well established all over the colony —that the main street of Clunes had become turned into a river. The water was seven feet deep in the very hotel where we had dressed for the ball! All the back bedrooms, stables, and outbuildings had been washed away, and carried down the creek, and thousands of pounds' worth of damage had been done in the lower parts of the town.

A few days later, when the rain had ceased and the flood had subsided, I went down to Deep Creek to see something of the damage that had been done. On either side, a wide stretch of ground was covered by a thick deposit of sludge, from one to four feet deep. This was the débris or crushings which the rain had washed down from the large mining claims above; and as it was barren stuff, mere crushed quartz, it ruined for the time every bit of land it covered. The scene which the track along the creek presented was most pitiable. Fences had been carried away, crops beaten down, and huge logs lay about, with here and there bits of furniture, houses, and farm-gear.

I find the floods have extended over the greater part of the colony. Incalculable damage has been done, and several lives have been lost. The most painful incident of all occurred at Ballarat, where the miners were at work on one of the claims, when a swollen dam burst its banks and suddenly flooded the workings. Those who were working on the top of the shaft fled; but down below, ten of the miners were at work at a high level, in drives many feet above the bottom of the claim. The water soon filling up the drives through which they had passed from the main shaft, the men were unable to get out. They remained there, cooped up in their narrow, dark workings, without food, or drink, or light, for three days, until at last the water was got under by the steam-pumps, and they were reached. Two had died of sheer privation, and the rest were got out more dead than alive.

The poor Chinamen's gardens down by the creek under Gibraltar had also suffered severely by the flood. M'Cullum's Creek, in ordinary seasons, is only a tiny stream, consisting of water-holes communicating with each other by a brook; but during a flood it becomes converted into a raging torrent, and you can hear its roar a mile off. Within about five hours the water in it had risen not less than twenty feet! This will give you an idea of the tremendous force and rapidity of the rainfall in this country. Of course the damage done was great, in M'Cullum's as in Deep Creek. A heavy timber bridge had been carried quite away, not a trace of it remaining. Many miners' huts in the low ground had been washed away, while others, situated in more sheltered places, out of the rush of the torrent, had been quite submerged, the occupants saving themselves by hasty flight in the early morning, some of them having been only wakened up by the water coming into their beds.

One eccentric character, a Scotchman, who determined to stick to his domicile, took refuge on his parlor table as the water was rising. Then, as it got still higher, he placed a chair upon the table, and stood up on it, the water continuing to rise, over his legs, then up and up; yet still he stuck to his chair. His only regret, he afterward said, was that he could not get at his whisky bottle, which he discerned upon a high shelf temptingly opposite him, but beyond his reach. The water at last began to fall; he waded up to his neck for the bottle; and soon the water was out of the house, for its fall is almost as sudden as its rise.

I was sorry for the poor Chinamen, whom I found, two days later, still wandering about amid the ruins of their gardens. Their loamy beds had been quite washed away, and their fences and some of their huts carried clean down the creek. One of them told me he had lost £30 in notes, which he had concealed in his cabin, but the flood had risen so quickly that he had been unable to save it. I picked up a considerable-sized stone that had been washed on to the Chinamen's ground: it was a piece of lava, thrown from one of the volcanic hills which bound the plain—how many thousands of years ago! These volcanic stones are so light and porous that they swim like corks, and they abound in many parts of this neighborhood.

CHAPTER XII.

SPRING, SUMMER, AND HARVEST.

Spring Vegetation.—The Bush in Spring.—Garden Flowers.—An Evening Walk.—Australian Moonlight.—The Hot North Wind.—The Plague of Flies.—Bush Fires.—Summer at Christmas.—Australian Fruits.—Ascent of Mount Greenock.—Australian Wine.—Harvest.—A Squatter's Farm.—Harvest-Home Celebration.—Aurora Australis.—Autumn Rains.

AFTER a heavy rainfall the ground becomes well soaked with water, and vegetation proceeds with great rapidity. Although there may be an occasional fall of rain at intervals, there is no recurrence of the flood. The days are bright and clear, the air dry, and the weather most enjoyable. It is difficult to determine when one season begins and another ends here; but I should say that spring begins in September. The evenings are then warm enough to enable us to dispense with fires, while at midday it is sometimes positively hot.

Generally speaking, spring-time is the most delightful season in Australia. The beautiful young vegetation of the year is then in full progress; the orchards are covered with blossom; the fresh, bright green of the grass makes a glorious carpet in the bush, when the trees put off their faded foliage of the previous year, and assume their bright spring livery. In some places the bush is carpeted with flowers—violet flowers of the pea and vetch species. There is also a beautiful plant, with flowers of vivid scarlet, that runs along the ground; and in some places the sarsaparillas, with their violet flowers, hang in festoons from the gum-tree branches. And when the wattle-bushes (a variety of the acacia tribe) are covered over with their yellow bloom, loading the air with their peculiarly sweet perfume, and the wild flowers are out in their glory, a walk or a ride through the bush is one of the most enjoyable of pleasures.

I must also mention that all kinds of garden flowers, such as we have at home, come to perfection in our gardens here, such as anemones, ranunculuses, ixias, and gladiolas. All the early spring flowers—violets, lilacs, primroses, hyacinths, and tulips — bloom most freely. Roses also flower splendidly in spring, and even through the summer, when not placed in too exposed situations. At Maryborough our doctor had a grand selection of the best roses—Lord Raglan, John Hopper, Marshal Neil, La Reine Hortense, and such like—which, by careful training and good watering, grew green, thick, and strongly, and gave out a good bloom nearly all the summer through.

By the beginning of November full summer seems already upon us, it is so hot at midday. Only toward the evening, when the sun goes down—as it does almost suddenly, with very little twilight—it feels a little chilly, and even cold. By the middle of the month, however, it has grown very warm indeed, and we begin to have a touch of the hot wind from the north. I shall not soon forget my first experience of walking in the face of that wind. It was like encountering a blast from the mouth of a furnace; it made my cheeks quite tingle, and it was so dry that I felt as if the skin would peel off.

On the 16th of November I found the thermometer was 98° in the shade. Try and remember if you ever had a day in England when it was so hot, and how intolerable it must have been! Here, however, the moisture is absent, and we are able to bear the heat without much inconvenience, though the fine white dust sometimes blows in at the open door, covering ledger, cash-book, and every thing. On the 12th of December I wrote home, "The weather is frightfully hot; the ledger almost scorches my hands as I turn over the leaves." Then again, on the 23d, I wrote that "the heat has risen to 105°, and even 110°, in the shade; yet, in consequence of the dryness and purity of the atmosphere, I bear it easily, and even go out to walk."

My favorite walk in the bush, in early summer, is toward the summit of a range of hills on the south of the township. I set out a little before sunset, when the heat of the day is well over, and the evening begins to feel deliciously cool. All is quiet; there is nothing to be heard but the occasional note of the piping crow, and the chatter of a passing flock of parroquets. As I ascend the hill, passing an abandoned quartz mine, even these sounds are absent, and perfect stillness prevails. From the summit an immense prospect lies before me. Six miles away to the south, across the plain, lies the town of Talbot; and beyond it the forest seems to extend to the foot of the Pyrenees, standing up blue in the distance some forty miles away. The clouds hang over the mountain summits, and slowly the monarch of day descends seemingly into a dark rift, leaving a track of golden light behind him. The greeny-blue sky above shines and glows for a few minutes longer, and then all is suffused in a soft and mournful gray. The change is almost sudden. The day is over, and night has already come on. Darkness follows daylight so suddenly that in nights when there is no moon, and it is cloudy, one has to hasten homeward, so as not to miss the track, or run the risk of getting benighted in the bush.

But, when the moon is up, the nights in Australia are as brilliant as the days. The air is cool, the sky cloudless, and walking in the bush is then most delightful. The trees are gaunt and weird-like, the branches standing in bold relief against the bright moonlight. Yet all is so changed, the distant landscape is so soft and lovely, that one can scarcely believe that it is the same scene we have so often looked upon in broad daylight. It is no exaggeration to say that the Australian moonlight is so bright that one may easily read a book by it of moderately-sized type.

But Australian summer weather has also its *desagrémens*. The worst of these is the hot north wind, of which I have already described my foretaste; though old colonists tell me that these have become much less intolerable, and occur much seldomer since the interior of the country has been settled and comparatively cultivated. But the hot winds are still bad to bear, as I can testify. They blow from the parched lands of Central Australia, and bring with them clouds of dust and insects. I should think they must resemble the African simoom. The Melbourne people call these burning blasts the "brickfielders." The parching wind makes one hot and feverish, and to fly to the bar for cooling drinks; but there even the glasses are hot to the touch. Your skin becomes so dry and crisp that you feel as if it would crackle off.

The temperature rises to 120°—a pretty tidy degree of heat! There is nothing for it but to fly within doors, shut up every cranny to keep out the hot dust, and remain in darkness.

While the hot wind lasts the air is of a heavy copper color. Every thing looks yellow and withered. The sun appears through the dust dull red, and no bigger than the moon, just as it does on a foggy morning in London. Perhaps, after an hour or two of this choking heat, the hot wind, with its cloud of dust, passes away southward, and we have a deliciously cool evening, which we enjoy all the more contrasted with the afternoon's discomfort. The longest time I have known the hot wind to last was two days, but it is usually over in a few hours. The colonials say that these winds are even of use by blowing the insect tribes out to sea, and that but for them the crops would, in summer time, be completely eaten away.

Another source of discomfort is the flies in summer. They abound every where. They fill the rooms, and as you pass along the streets they rise in clouds. The ceilings are sometimes black with them, and no food can be left exposed for an instant without the certainty of its being covered with them. There is one disgusting yellow-bodied blow-fly, which drops his maggots with extraordinary fecundity. The flies are also a nuisance in the bush, where veils are usually worn when driving to prevent their annoyance; and in the swamps there are vigorous and tormenting musquitoes, as I have elsewhere described.

After the parching heat of summer, and especially after the excessive dryness occasioned by the hot winds, the whole face of the country becomes, as it were, combustible, and bush-fires have at such times burst forth apparently spontaneously, and spread with great rapidity. The "Black Thursday" of the colony, some fifteen years since, when fire covered many hundreds of miles, is still remembered with horror; but, as settlement and cultivation have extended, these sudden outbreaks of fire have become comparatively rare.

When Christmas arrives, summer is at its height. It finds us perhaps gasping with heat, sitting in our shirt-sleeves for coolness, and longing for the cool evening. Yet there are few who do not contrive to have their Christmas roast and plum-pudding, as at home. As strawberries are then in their prime and in great abundance, many hold strawberry picnics on Christmas Day, while sober church-goers enjoy them at home.

The abundance of fruits of all kinds affords one of the best proofs of the geniality of the climate. First come strawberries, followed by abundance of plums, peaches, and apricots, and afterward by pears and apples in plenty. Our manager's garden at Maryborough is a sight worth seeing in summer time. Having a plentiful supply of water, he is able to bring his fruit to great perfection. The plum and peach trees seemed almost overburdened with their delicious loads. Through the centre of the garden is a cool green alley, shaded with a vine-covered trellis. The bunches of fast-ripening grapes are hanging on all sides, and promise an abundant crop.

Some of my pleasantest associations are connected with the January afternoons spent in the orchards about Majorca. One day a party of us drove out in search of a good fruit-garden. We went over the hill to the south, and down the long valley on the Talbot road, raising clouds of white dust as we went; then up another hill, from the summit of which, down by the banks of the creek, and almost close to the foot of Mount Greenock, we discovered the garden of which we had come in search. We descended and entered the garden, still covered with greenery, notwithstanding the tremendous heat, and there found the fruit in perfection.

Mount Greenock is one of the many volcanic hills which abound in this neighborhood. It is almost a perfect cone, some eight or nine hundred feet high. "What a splendid prospect from the summit!" said one of my companions. "Well, let us go up; there will probably be a fine breeze on the top." "Too hot by far," was the answer. "Not at all," said I; "the thing is to be done." "Well," said my friend, "you may go if you like, but if you do, and are back in three quarters of an hour, I'll undertake to shout fruits and drinks for the remainder of the afternoon."

A noble offer! So I immediately stripped, took one look at the steep hill above, the withered grass upon it almost glittering in the sun, and started. I was soon across the nearly dry creek, and, beginning the ascent, went on pretty steadily until I was within about two hundred feet of the summit, when the great heat began to tell upon me. I stopped, looked down the steep hill up which I had come, saw what a little way farther comparatively I had to go, and clambered upward again. It was still a long and fatiguing pull, mostly over loose lava-stones; but at last I reached the top, panting and out of breath. After such a tremendous pull as that, I do not think any one will venture to say that my lungs can be unsound.

I looked round at the magnificent view. It was, indeed, well worth climbing the hill to see. I first turned my eyes northward toward Majorca. There it was, with its white streak of pipe-clay above it. Beyond, in the distance, lay Carisbrooke, with the bald hill standing out in bold relief behind it. Nearer at hand are the mining works of several companies, with their engine-sheds surrounded by huge piles of refuse. Turning my eyes southward, I saw Talbot, about a mile off, looking quite an important place, with its numerous red-brick buildings and clusters of comfortable-looking houses. On the west, toward Maryborough, lay a wide extent of bush, clad in its never-varying dark green verdure. The sky was clear, blue, and cloudless; and though the sun was in all his strength, the light breeze that played round the top of the mount made the air pleasant and exhilarating to breathe.

I shortly turned my steps down hill, tacking and zigzagging in the descent because of the steepness. I was soon at the foot of the mount, across the brook, and seated in the garden, enjoying the fresh fruit, with an occasional draught of colonial wine.

Apropos of wine and grapes. It is anticipated by those who have had the longest experience of the climate and soil of Victoria, that it is not unlikely before long to become one of the principal wine-growing countries in the world. The vine grows luxuriantly, and the fruit reaches perfection in all parts of the colony, but more particularly in the fine district situated along the River Murray. Most of the farmers up-country make their own wines for home use. It is a rough, wholesome sort of claret. But when the Germans, who are well accustomed to the culture of the vine, give the subject their attention, a much finer quality is produced. There are already several vineyard associations at work, who expect before long to export largely to England, though at present the greater part of the wine grown is consumed in the colony.* A friend of mine at Melbourne has planted an extensive vineyard at Sunbury, some thirty miles north of the city, cultivated by Swiss vignerons; and, though I am no judge of wine, the Burgundy which I tasted at his table was very grateful to my inexperienced palate, and I was told that it was of very superior quality.*

After summer comes harvest, when the farmer gathers in the produce of his year's industry, takes stock, and counts his gains. Harvest is well over by the end of February. When I rode out to Perry's Farm on the second day of March, I found the fields already cleared, and the grain housed. All the extra hands had gone. Only a week before, the fields had been busy with reapers, binders, and machine-men, for whom enormous meat pies had to be cooked and great joints of meat roasted; for laboring men in Australia are accustomed to consume much larger quantities of flesh meat than at home.

The scene is now perfectly quiet. The cows are coming in to be milked, and a very fine lot they are—fifteen or more. The great stacks of straw are shining in the

* The kinds of wine principally produced in the colony are Burgundy, Claret, white wine of the Sauterne kind, and a very excellent sort of still Champagne. There are now regular autumn wine-sales at Melbourne and Geelong, at which large quantities are sold, and good prices realized. The total quantity produced in 1870 was 629,219 gallons.

red sunlight, for the sun is getting low, though it is still warm. We go up to the farm-house, having hung our horses' reins over the rail, and saunter in through the back door. Here no handing in of cards is required, for we know we are sure of being made welcome; and in Australia hospitality is boundless. We taste the grapes, which are just ripe, and wash them down with a glass of home-brewed mead. But beware of that mead! Though it looks very innocent, it is really very strong and heady.

The farmer then took us into his barn, and proudly pointed with his heavy whip to the golden grain piled up on the floor; then over his stable, to look at his horses. There we found our own nags, which had been taken in for a feed. Bringing them out, and mounting again, we rode on a little farther to another farm situated on a hillside a little higher up the valley.

The farm-house here is a little gem of a dwelling, situated in a nice shady place, in the midst of a luxurious garden. Here, too, we dismounted and entered the house, for we knew the host—a most genial fellow, whose honest English face it was always a pleasure to see, it was so full of kindness and good humor. We took a stroll round the garden while the sun was setting, and then turned in for a cup of good tea, which "missus" had got ready for us.

One of our entertainer's greatest delights was in talking about "old times"—though they were only a year or two old after all—yet "new chums" were always ready to sit listening to his tales open-mouthed. He had been a digger, like most of the farmers hereabout, and he told us how he was the first to find the gold at the great rush at Maryborough; how he saw the gold glistening in the gravel one day that he was out in the bush; how, for weeks, he lived quietly, but digging and gathering gold early and late, until, having made his little golden harvest, enough to buy and stock a farm, he went and gave information to the commissioner as to the find, and then what a 'rush of thousands of diggers there was to the ground! how streets sprang up, stores were opened, hotels were built, and at last Maryborough became the great place that it is—the thriving centre of a large mining as well as agricultural district.

In such old diggers' talk two hours had passed almost before we were aware, and then we rose to go. The horses were brought out, and we mounted and rode cautiously home, for it was now quite dark. It was a fine mild night, and we had plenty of time, so we talked and laughed our way through the bush, our voices the only sounds to be heard, except it might be the noise of a bird rising on the wing, startled from its perch by our merry laughter, or the clatter of our horses' hoofs on the hard ground as we trotted along.

Another day I drove out with one of the neighboring farmers to his place on the other side of the Deep Creek. At this late season the brush is dried up and melancholy looking—very different from what it is in the lovely spring-time. Now the bush seems dead-alive, fast putting on its winter garb, while withered stalks of grass cover the plains. We pass the neighborhood of a large squatter's station, the only one about here, the run being very large, extending for a great distance over the plains. It consists of not less than 60,000 acres of purchased land and 60,000 acres of government land, on which the squatter exercises the usual rights of pasturage.

Crossing the creek by a wooden bridge, we were shortly at my friend's farm. We heard the buzzing noise of the threshing machine in the adjoining fields. There was the engine busily at work, just as at home. Steam penetrates every where—across the seas, over the mountains, and into the bush. We soon came up to the engine where the men were at work. It was pretty severe under a hot sun, amid clouds of dust and bits of chaff flying about from the thresher. Many of the men wore spectacles to protect their eyes from the glare of the sun's heat.

The engine was just about to stop, to allow the men to have their midday spell of rest, and they were soon at their meal of meat and cold tea. The farmer came upon some of the men smoking quite unconcernedly beside the great piles of straw, and wroth he was at their carelessness, as well he might be, for, had a fire burst out, it would have destroyed straw, wheat, engine, and all. The wheat seemed of excellent quality, and the farmer was quite pleased with his crop, which is not always the case with farmers.

We afterward went over the farm buildings, which are neat and substantial. A large stone barn has at one end of it a kitchen attached, where the men's victuals are cooked during harvest time, and close at hand is a comfortable stone cottage for the accommodation of the manager and his family.

After going over the farm I had a refreshing bathe in the creek at a convenient place, though I have heard that it is not unusual for bathers who get into a muddy water-hole to be startled by a sudden sting, and, when they emerge from the water, to find half a dozen hungry leeches hanging on to their skin; for leeches are plentiful in Australia, and even form an article of considerable export to England.

We afterward went out to Perry's harvest dance and supper, with which the gathering in of the crops is usually celebrated, as at home. The wheat had by this time all been sold and cleared out of the barn, and it was now rigged up as a ballroom. We had a good long spell of dancing, to the music of a violin and a bush piano. Perhaps you don't know what a bush piano is? It consists of a number of strings arranged on a board, tightened up and tuned, upon which the player beats with a padded hammer, bringing out sounds by no means unmusical. At all events, the bush piano served to eke out the music of our solitary violin.

After the dance there was the usual bounteous supper, with plenty to eat and drink for all; and then our horses were brought out, and we rode homeward. It was the end of harvest, just the time of the year when, though the days were still warm, the nights were beginning to be cool and sharp, as they are about the beginning of October in England. One night there was a most splendid aurora, one of the finest, it is said, that had been seen, even in Australia. A huge rose-colored curtain seemed to be let down across half the sky, striped with bright golden color, shaded off with a deeper yellow. Beneath the red curtain, close to the horizon, was a small semicircle of bright greenish-yellow, just as if the sun were about to rise; and bright gleams of light shot up from it far into the sky, making the rose-colored clouds glow again. The brilliancy extended upward almost to the zenith, the stars glimmering through the darker or less bright part of the sky. Though I have mentioned "clouds," there was not a cloud to be seen; the clouds I name were really masses of brilliant light, obscuring the deep blue beyond. I feel the utter powerlessness of words to describe the magnificence of the scene.

The weather-wise people predicted a change of weather, and, sure enough, a change shortly followed. We had had no rain for weeks, but early on the second morning after the appearance of the aurora I was awakened by the noise of heavy rain falling upon our slight iron roof. I found a tremendous storm raging, and the rain falling in masses. Our large iron tank was completely filled in half an hour, and, overflowing, it ran in upon our bank floor and nearly flooded us out. We had an exciting time of it baling out the water as fast as it ran in, for somehow the drain running underneath our boarded house had got stopped. At last the rainfall ceased and the water was got rid of, leaving every thing in a state of damp — damp stools and chairs, damp sheets, damp clothes, damp books, damp paper, damp every thing.

CHAPTER XIII.

BUSH ANIMALS—BIRDS—SNAKES.

The 'Possum. — A Night's Sport in the Bush. — Musquitoes. — Wattle Birds. — The Piping Crow.—"Miners."—Parroquet Hunting. — The Southern Cross.—Snakes.—Marsupial Animals.

A FAVORITE sport in Australia is 'possum-shooting. The Australian opossum is a marsupial quadruped, living in trees, and feeding on insects, eggs, and fruits. Its body is about twenty-five inches in length, besides which it has a long prehensile tail, with which it clings to the branches of the trees in which it lives. Its skin is covered with thick fur, of a uniform smoky-black color, tinged with chestnut, and it is very much sought after because of its warmth and beauty.

The proper time for 'possum-shooting is at night, when the moon is nearly at her full, and one can see about almost as well as in the daytime. Even Venus is so bright that, on a night when the moon was absent, I have seen her give light enough to drive by.

A well-trained dog is almost indispensable for scenting the 'possums and tracking them to their tree, beneath which he stands and gives tongue. When the dog stands and barks, you may be sure there is the "'possum up a gum-tree." I never had the good fortune to be accompanied by a well-trained dog, but only by young ones new to the sport.

We had, therefore, to find and sight our own game.

This is done by looking carefully along each branch, with the tree between you and the bright moonlight; and if there be a 'possum there, you will see a little black, furry-like ball motionless in the fork of a limb. On the first night that I went out 'possum-shooting with a party of friends, we trudged a good way into the bush, and searched the trees for a long time in vain.

At length the old colonial who accompanied us, coming up to a large tree, said, "Ah! here is a likely place;" and we began carefully to spy the branches. "There he is," said the colonial, pointing to a limb where he said the 'possum was. At first I could make out nothing, but at last I spied the little round ball. He fired, and the animal fell to the ground dead.

A little farther on we searched again and found another. Now it was my turn. I took steady aim at the black object between me and the moon, and fired. Looking through the smoke, I saw Joey hanging on to the branch by his tail, and in half a minute more he dropped to the ground. I found that this was one of the ring-tailed species, the top of the tail being bare for about two inches, and formed like a white ring. 'Possums of this sort use their tails for climbing, like the spider-monkey of Africa. I found I could carry my ring-tailer hanging on to my finger even after he was quite dead.

The next 'possum fell wounded from the tree and took to his heels, with the little dogs after him, and they settled him after a short fight. Sometimes the 'possum, after being hit, will cling a long time to the tree by his tail, with his body hanging down. Then the best and lightest climber goes up to shake him down, and he soon drops among the dogs, which are all excitement, and ready to fall upon him. Occasionally he will give them a good run, and then the object is to prevent him getting up another tree.

Proceeding on our search, we found ourselves on some low swampy ground, where there were said to be abundance of 'possums; but I had no sooner entered the swamp than I was covered with musquitoes of the most ravenous character. They rose from the ground in thousands, and fastened on my "new chum" skin, from which the odor of the lime-juice had not yet departed,* and in a few minutes I was literally in torment, and in full retreat out of the swamp. Not even the prospect of a full bag of 'possums would tempt me again in that direction.

In all, we got seven 'possums, which is considered a very small bag. There is a practised sportsman in the town who goes out with a well-trained dog, accompanied by a horse and cart, and he is disappointed if he does not bring home quite a cart-load of fur.

When we had got done with our sport and resolved on wending our way homeward, I had not the faintest idea where we were, or of the direction in which we were to proceed. Of course, near the town there are plenty of tracks, but here there were none; and there is such a complete sameness in the bush that I wondered that even my experienced friend should be able to guide us back. But he had no difficulty in finding the way, and we were soon tramping steadily along under the

---

* It is said in the colony that the musquitoes scent out each "new chum," or fresh importation, by the lime-juice he has taken on board ship; and that, being partial to fresh blood, they attack the "new chums" in preference to the seasoned inhabitants.

bright moonlight, the straggling gum-trees looking more gaunt and unshapely than usual, the dry twigs crackling under our feet; and we reached the township long after midnight.

On another occasion I accompanied the Maryborough doctor into the bush to shoot wattle birds for a pie; but we did not succeed in getting a pieful. I have an idea that the gray-colored dress of a young lady who accompanied us frightened the birds away. There were plenty of birds about, but very few of the sort we wanted—a bird as large as a pigeon, plump and tender to eat. The doctor drove us in and out among the trees, and had once nearly turned us all perforce out of the buggy, having got his wheels locked in the stump of a tree.

The speckled honeysuckers, yellow and black, chirped and gabbled up among the trees. The leather-heads, with their bare necks and ruffle of white feathers, almost like so many vultures in miniature, gave out their loud and sudden croak, then lazily flapped their wings and flew away to the next tree. Suddenly there is heard the single cry of the bell-bird, just like the ringing of a glass bell, while far off in the bush you could hear the note of the Australian magpie or piping crow, not unlike that of a silver flute, clear, soft, and musical. The piping crow is, indeed, a clever bird, imitating with wonderful accuracy the cries of other birds, and when tamed it is exceedingly amusing, readily learning to whistle tunes, which it does extremely well.

Another day I went out shooting with the Presbyterian minister, an enthusiastic taxidermist, now occupied in making a very nice collection of Australian birds. We had a gay time of it in the bush that day. There were plenty of gray and black mina-birds, or "miners" as they are called here, chattering away in the trees in groups of four or five. They are a species of grakle, and are lively and intelligent birds, some of them possessing a power of imitating human speech equal to any of the parrot tribe. They are very peculiar looking, gray in the body, with a black dab on the head, and a large bright yellow wattle just behind the eye. We pass the "miners" unmolested, for the minister tells me they are "no good" if you want eating, while as specimens they are too common.

Then there are the tiny gray wrens sitting about in scores—so small that an English wren looks monstrous beside them. Across the sunlight, and away over a hollow, there flies a flock of green and yellow parroquets, screaming as they fly. The brilliant colors of their wings flash and glitter as they come from under the shadow of the trees. Now we stalk a solitary piping crow from tree to tree; but no sooner do you get near enough to take a pot shot at him than he pipes his note and is off. The only way of getting at him is to proceed cautiously from bush to bush; but even then, so shy a bird is he that it is very difficult to bag him.

There is a flock of great white sulphur-crested cockatoos clustered up in a high tree. Can we get a shot? They seem to anticipate our design, for on the moment they rise and wheel overhead with elevated crests, uttering their shrill, hoarse cries. These are the fellows that occasion our farmers so much trouble by eating the freshly-sown grain.

Then look! on that branch are twenty or thirty lovely little swift parroquets, with green and dark blue wings tipped with yellow. They are climbing in and out of the scant leafage, under and over the limbs of the tree, hanging on by their claws, and they only rise if they see us near enough to take a shot at them, when they take to wing screaming, and fly away in a flock.

One, when I had gone out parrot-potting with another young fellow almost as green as myself, we had very nearly got bushed. We had been following up a flock of Blue Mountain parrots—handsome birds—of which we wanted specimens for our collection. After some slight success, we turned our way homeward. The sun was just setting. Marking its position in the heavens, we took what we thought was the right direction. There were no tracks to guide us—no landmarks—nothing but bush. After walking for some time, and looking again at the light of the sky where the sun had gone down, we found that we had made a circuit upon our track, and were walking exactly in the opposite direction to our township. We hastily retraced our steps, for we knew that it would soon be dark, as the twilight is so short in Australia. Fortunately for us, it was a very clear night, and as the stars came brightly out we saw before us the Southern Cross high up on our left, which guided us on our way. Had it been a cloudy night, most probably we should have had to spend it in the bush; but, thanks to the Southern Cross and good legs, we at length, though late, reached our township in safety.

There are sometimes snakes met with in the bush, though I saw but few of them, and these are always ready to get out of your way. The largest fellow I saw was drawn out from under the flooring of a weather-boarded hut on the hill-side above Majorca. I was coming down early one morning from the school-house, when I stopped at the hut to speak with the occupant. It is a very tidy little place, divided into two rooms—parlor and bedroom. The parlor was pasted all over with cheap prints, reminding one of home, mostly taken from "Punch" and the "Illustrated London News." Photographs of old friends were also hung over the mantel-shelf. The floor was neat and clean; the little pot was simmering over the little fire, and all was getting ready for breakfast. A very pleasant picture of a thriving emigrant's home.

As I was standing outside, about to take my leave, casting my eyes on the ground, I saw beneath the bench close to the door a long, brownish-gray thing lying quite still. I at once saw that it was a snake, and snatched up a billet of wood to make a blow at him; but my friend, who had more experience in such matters, held me back. "Just wait a moment," said he, "and let me get hold of him." Quick as thought, he stooped down, seized firm hold of the snake by the tail, and, whirling him rapidly round his head three or four times, he dashed him against the boards of the hut and let him drop, crushing the reptile's head with his boot-heel. The snake was four feet six inches in length, and said to be of a very poisonous sort.

Snakes are much more common in the less cleared parts of the colony, and fatal snake-bites are not infrequent. The most successful method of treatment is that invented by Dr. Halford, of Melbourne, which consists in injecting a solution of ammonia into a vein dissected out and opened for the purpose. This is said at once and almost completely to destroy the effects of the poison.

Since my return home I observe that Dr. Halford has been publicly rewarded for his discovery.

Kangaroo hunting is one of the great sports of Victoria, but it was not my fortune to see a hunt of this sort. There are now very few, if any, kangaroo in this immediate neighborhood.* Yet there is no lack of marsupial animals of the same character: the opossum is one of these. There is also a small kind of kangaroo, called the wallaby, which, though I have not hunted, I have eaten; and wallaby stew is by no means a bad dish: the flesh tastes very much like venison. Indeed, the marsupial animals of Australia are of almost endless variety, ranging from a very tiny animal, no bigger than our field-mouse, to the great old-man kangaroo, which measures between seven and eight feet from the nose to the tip of the tail. The peculiarity of all this class of animals, from the smallest to the largest, is the marsupium, or pouch, in which the females carry their immature young until they are old enough to shift for themselves. The kangaroo is almost confined to Australia, though several species are also to be met with in the neighboring islands.

* There is a Hunt Club at Avoca that hunts kangaroo. The animals abound north of the Murray River, and some parts of the unsettled country in Gipps Land still swarm with them.

CHAPTER XIV.

GOLD-BUYING AND GOLD-MINING.

How the Gold is found.—Gold-washing.—Quartz-crushing.—Buying Gold from Chinamen.—Alluvial Companies.—Broken-down Men.—Ups and Downs in Gold-mining.—Visit to a Gold Mine.—Gold-seeking.—Diggers' Tales of lucky Finds.

I MUST now be excused if I talk a little "shop." Though my descriptions hitherto have for the most part related to up-country life, seasons, amusements, and such like, my principal concern, while living in Majorca, was with bank business and gold-buying. The ordinary business of a banking office is tolerably well known, but the business of gold-buying is a comparatively new feature, peculiar to the gold-producing districts, and is, therefore, worthy of a short description.

The gold is found and brought to us in various forms. The Majorca gold is generally alluvial, consisting of coarse gold-dust and small nuggets washed out from the gravel. There are also some quartz reef mining companies, whose gold is bought in what we call a retorted state. Let me explain. The quartz containing the gold is stamped and broken up by heavy iron hammers falling upon it; and a stream of water constantly running down into the box in which the stampers work, the soluble dirt is washed away, while the particles of quartz and gold are carried forward over boards, in which, at intervals, are small ripples containing quicksilver. The quicksilver clings to the gold and forms an amalgam with it. This is collected, taken out, and squeezed in bags of chamois leather, by which the greater part of the quicksilver is pressed out and saved for a repetition of the process. The residue is placed in a retort and is exposed to heat, by which the remainder of the quicksilver is driven off by evaporation, leaving the gold in a solid lump. There are, however, various other processes by which the gold is separated from the quartz.

Sometimes the gold is offered for sale in a very imperfectly separated state, and then considerable judgment is required in deciding as to its value. In alluvial gold there is always a certain proportion of chips of iron, which have flown from the picks used in striking and turning up the gravel. These pieces of iron are carefully extracted by means of a magnet. The larger bits of gold, if there be any, are then taken out and put to one side. The remainder is put into a shallow tin dish, which is shaken with a peculiar turn of the wrist, and all the sand and dirt thus turned to the point of the dish. This is blown off; then up goes the gold again, and you blow and blow until all the sand is blown off. If there remain any gold with quartz still adhering to it, the particles are put into a big iron mortar and well beaten, and the process above described is repeated. The gold is then ready for weighing and buying, and there is usually no difficulty in settling the price with English diggers, the price varying according to the assay of the gold.*

---

* The ordinary price of good gold is £3 19s. 6d. the ounce. In the early days of gold-digging the gold was never cleaned, but bought right off at a low price, £2 15s. or £2 17s. 6d. an ounce, the bankers thus often realizing immense profits.

Our great difficulty is with the Chinamen, who are very close-fisted fellows. They mostly work at sludge, which Englishmen have already washed; and they are found hanging on to the tailings of old workings, washing the refuse in order to extract the gold that had been missed. Old tailings are often thus washed several times over, and never without finding gold to a greater or less amount. When a party of Chinamen think they can do better elsewhere, they may be seen moving off, carrying their whole mining apparatus on their backs, consisting of tubs, blankets, tin scoops, and a small washing-cradle.

The Chinamen get their gold in a very rude way, though it seems to answer their purpose. They put the stuff to be washed on to their cradle, and by scooping water over it and keeping the cradle going they gradually rinse it away, the fluid running over two or three ledges of blankets, and leaving the fine gold remaining behind adhering to the wool. After the process has been continued sufficiently long, the gold-dust is collected from the blankets, and is retorted by the Chinamen themselves, and then they bring it for sale. The retorting has usually been badly done, and there remains a good deal of quicksilver and nitric acid adhering to the gold. The only way of dealing with it is to put the whole into a crucible, then make it red hot, and keep the gold at the melting-point for five or ten minutes.

As we have got no furnace of our own on the premises, I have frequently to march up the street to the blacksmith's shop to put John Chinaman's gold to the test. If John is allowed to go by himself, he merely waits till the gold gets warm, takes it out again, and brings it back, saying, "All light; welly good, welly good gole; no gammon." But you should see John when I go up to the blacksmith's myself, put the crucible into the hottest part of the fire, and begin to blow the bellows! When the gold begins to glow with heat, and he knows the weight is diminishing by the quicksilver and dirt that are flying off, he cries, "Welly hot! too muchee fire; me losem too muchee money!" But the thing must be done, and John must take the choice of his dirty gold or the regular price for it when cleaned. I have known it lose, by this process of purifying, as much as from five to six pennyweights in the ounce.

Sometimes he will bring only a few shillings' worth, and, when the money is tendered for it, he will turn it over in his hand, like a London cabman when his regular fare is given him. One man, who almost invariably brought only a very small quantity, would begin his conversation with "No more money now—no more chow-chow (dinner)—no more opium!" Sometimes matters come to a climax, and he tells us that we "too much lie and cheatem," on which we send him out at the door.

The lower orders of Chinamen are almost invariably suspicious that Englishmen cheat them, although some of them are very decent fellows, and, indeed, kind and even polite. Several times I have asked them how they were going to spend the money for which they had sold their gold—say five shillings, and they would answer, ingenuously enough, "Two shillings for opium, three shillings for chow-chow," leaving no margin for sundries.

We buy from the Chinamen as little as three shillings' worth of gold, and from the mining companies up to any amount. Some of the latter bring in hundreds of pounds' worth of gold at a time. The quartz companies bring theirs in large yellow lumps, of over 200 ounces, fresh from the retort; and the alluvial companies generally deposit theirs in leather bags containing their washings until the end of the week or fortnight, when they sell the accumulated product.

There is, of course, a good deal of excitement and anxiety about gold-digging. When men get into good gold-yielding ground, by steady work they contrive to make fair earnings, and sometimes a good deal of money; but they have usually to work pretty hard for it. Of course the most successful men are working miners, men who understand the business; for gold-mining is a business, like any other. The amateur men, who come in search of lucky finds and sudden fortunes, rarely do any good. Nearly all the young fellows, sons of gentlemen, who could do no good at home and came out here during the "rushes," are still in no better position than they were at starting. A few of them may have done well; but the greater number are bullock-drivers in the country, cab-drivers in Melbourne, shepherds in the bush, or, still worse, loafers hanging about the drinking-bars.

I know many men, of good family and education, still working as common miners in this neighborhood. Although their life is a rough one, they themselves think it is better than a struggling clerk's life at home; and perhaps they are right. I know one young man, formerly a medical student in England, digging for weekly wages, hired by a company of miners at £2 10s. a week; but he is not saving money. He came out with two cousins, one of whom broke away and pursued his profession; he is now the head of a military hospital in India. The other cousin remained in the colony, and is now a hanger-on about up-country stations. There is also the son of a baronet here, who came out in the time of the gold fever. He has never advanced a step, but is wood-cutting and rail-splitting in the bush like a poor Savoyard. Still the traces of his education can be seen through the "jumper" shirt and moleskin trowsers, in spite of rough ways and hard work.

There are many ups and downs in gold-mining. Sometimes men will work long and perseveringly, and earn little more than their food; but, buoyed up by hope, they determine to go on again, and at last, perhaps, they succeed. One day two men came into the bank with £120 worth of gold, the proceeds of four days' mining on a new claim. They had been working for a long time without finding any thing worth their while, and at last they struck gold. The £120 had to be divided among six men, and out of it they had to pay toward the cost of sinking their shaft and maintaining their three horses which worked the "whip" for drawing up the water and dirt out of the mine. When they brought in their gold in a little tin billy, the men did not seem at all elated by their good fortune. They are so accustomed to a sudden turn of luck—good or ill, as the case may be—that the good fortune on this occasion seemed to be taken as a matter of course.

One day the manager and I went out to see a reef where some men had struck gold. It lay across the bare-looking ranges at the north of the township, in a pretty part of the bush, rather more wooded than usual. The reef did not look a place for so much gold to come out of. There were a couple of shafts, small windlasses above them, and two or three heaps of dirty-looking brown quartz and refuse. I believe the reef is very narrow—only from eight inches to a foot in width; the quartz yielding from eight to twelve ounces of gold per ton. Thus ten tons crushed would give a value of about £400. Though this may seem a good yield, it is small compared with richer quartz. I have heard of one mine which gave 200 ounces, or £800, to the ton of quartz crushed, but this was unusually rich.

At some of the larger claims the works are carried on upon a large scale with the aid of complete machinery. Let me describe one of the mines, close to Majorca, down which I went one day to inspect the operations. It is called the Lowe Kong Meng mine, and was formerly worked by Chinamen, but had to be abandoned because of the great quantity of water encountered, as well as the accidents which constantly happened to the machinery. The claim was then taken up by an English company of tributors, who pay a percentage of the proceeds of the mine to the proprietor, the large Chinese merchant, Mr. Lowe Kong Meng, who resides in Melbourne.

In some of the shallower workings the men go down the shaft with their feet in a noose at the end of the rope, or, in some small and narrow shafts, by holding on to the sides with their knees and feet; but in large workings, such as this (which is about 150 feet deep), we descend in a bucket, as in ordinary mines. What a speed we go down at! We seem to shoot down into darkness. There—bump! we are at the bottom. But I can see nothing; I only hear the drip, drip, and splashing of water.

In a few minutes my eyes get accustomed to the darkness; then I see the dim light of a candle held by some one not far off. "Come up here," says the guide; and we shortly find ourselves in a somewhat open space, more light than the actual bottom of the shaft. We are each supplied with a dip tallow candle, by means of which we see where we are. The two drives branch off from this space: the main is 6 feet 3 inches in height, broad, and splendidly timbered with stout wood all the way along. The Chinamen did this work.

Water is running every where. We try to walk upon the rails on which the trucks run, to keep our feet dry. But it is of no use, as there is more water in our way to get through. Every now and then we slipped off the rail and down into the water. As we got into the narrower and lower drives I was continually coming to grief, my head bumping against the dirty top, my hat coming off, or my candle getting extinguished.

We were taken first up to the place where the water had broken in so heavily upon the Chinamen, and in which direction the mine could not be worked. Strong supports of wood held up the gravel, through which the water poured in, running down the drives to the well underneath the shaft. What a labyrinth all these different passages seemed to me! yet I suppose this claim is a small one compared with many others in the gold-mining districts.

Then we were shown a monkey—not the animal, but a small upright shaft leading into a drive above, where the wash-dirt was being got out. Should the course of the wash-dirt, in which the gold is, go downward below the level of the well or the drives for draining the mine, the shaft must then be sunk deeper down. The monkey was rather difficult for me to scramble up. However, by holding on, and using the niches at the sides, I managed to mount, as usual with the loss of my light.

Along the drive we went, waiting in a corner until a truck of dirt passed by, and its contents were shot down the monkey into the tram waiting for it below. Now we creep up from the drive into a narrower space, where we crawl along upon our hands and knees. We shortly came upon four men getting out the wash-dirt, using their picks while squatting or lying down, and in all sorts of uncomfortable positions. The perspiration was streaming down the men's faces as they worked, for the heat was very great.

We did not stay long in that hot place, and I did *not* take a pick and happen to strike upon a nugget, as it is said the Duke of Edinburg did, though I saw a small dish of the dirt washed when we reached the top, and it yielded a speck or two. We saw "the color," as the expression is. I felt quite relieved at last to find myself at the top of the shaft, and in the coolness and freshness of the open air. Here the dirt raised from the mine is put into the iron puddling machine, and worked round and round with water. The water carries off the mud, the large stones are picked out, and the gold in the bottom of the machine is cradled off. Such was my little experience in mine prospecting.

I must also tell of my still smaller experience in gold-seeking. One morning a little boy brought in a nugget for sale which he had picked up from a heap of dirt while he was strolling down the lead outside the town. After a heavy, washing fall of rain, it is not unusual for small bits of gold to be exposed to sight, and old diggers often take a ramble among the mullock after rain to make a search among the heaps. A piece of gold was once brought to us for sale, weighing about two ounces, that had been thus washed up by a heavy shower of rain. Inspired by the success of the little boy, I went out in the afternoon in a pair of thick boots, and with a pair of sharp eyes to search for treasure! It had been raining hard for several days, and it was a good time for making an inspection of the old washed-out dirt-heaps. After a long search I found only one speck of gold, of the value of about 4d. This I was showing with pride to a young lady friend, who, being playfully inclined, gave my hand a shake, and my microscopical speck was gone, the first and last fruits of my gold-seeking.

Some of the tales told by the old diggers of their luck in the early days of gold-finding are very interesting. One of these I can relate almost in the very words of the man himself to whom the incident occurred, and it was only an ordinary digger's tale.

"My mates and I," he said, "were camped in a gully with some forty or fifty other miners. It was a little quiet place, a long way from any township. We had been working some shallow ground; but as the wash-dirt, when reached, only yielded about three quarters of a pennyweight (about 3s.) to the dish, we got sick of it, left our claim, and went to take up another not far off. About a day or two after we had settled upon our new ground, an old acquaintance of mine looked in upon us by chance. He was hard up—very hard up—and wanted to know whether we could give him any thing to do. 'Well, there is our old place up there,' said I; 'it is not much good, but you can find enough to keep body and soul together.' So he went up to our old place, and kept himself in tucker. A few days after he had been at work, he found that the farther down he dug in one direction the more gold the soil yielded. At one end of the ground a reef cropped up, shelving inward very much. He quickly saw that against the reef, toward which the gold-yielding gravel lay, the ground sloping downward toward the bottom must be still richer. He got excited, threw aside the gravel with his shovel to come at the real treasure he expected to find. Down he went till he reached the slope of the reef, where the gravel lay up against it. There, in the corner of the ground, right in the angle of the juncture, as it were, lay the rich glistening gold, all in pure particles, mixed with earth and pebbles. He filled his tin dish with the precious mixture, bore it aloft, and brought it down to our tent, where, aided by the mates, he washed off the dirt, and obtained as the product of his various washings about 1000 ounces of pure gold! The diggers who were camped about in the gully being a rough lot, we were afraid to let them know any thing of the prize that had been found. So, without saying any thing, two of us, late one night, set out with the lucky man and his fortune to the nearest township, where he sold his gold and set out immediately for England, where, I believe, he is now. He left us the remainder of his dirt, which he did not think any thing of compared with what he had got, and three of us obtained from it the value of £600, or £200 a man."

The same digger at another time related to us how and when he had found his first nugget. He declared that it was all through a dream. "I dreamt," he said,

" that I sunk a shaft down by the side of a pretty creek, just under a gum-tree, and close to the water; that I worked down about 10 feet there, put in a drive, and, while I was working, chanced to look up, and there, sticking in the pipe-clay, was a piece of gold as big as my fist. Such was my dream. It took complete possession of me. I could think of nothing else. Some weeks after, I selected just such a site for a shaft as that I had dreamt of, under a gum-tree, close by a creek; and there, new chum-like, I put in the drive at the wrong depth. But one day, when I had got quite sick at fruitlessly working in the hole, on accidentally looking up, sure enough, there was my nugget sticking up in the pipe-clay, just as I had dreamt of it. I took out the gold, sat with it in my hand, and thought the thing over, but couldn't make it out at all."

CHAPTER XV.

ROUGH LIFE AT THE DIGGINGS—"STOP THIEF!"

Gold-rushing.—Diggers' Camp at Havelock.—Murder of Lopez.—Pursuit and Capture of the Murderer.—The Thieves hunted from the Camp.—Death of the Murderer.—The Police.—Attempted Robbery of the Collingwood Bank.—Another supposed Robbery.—"Stop Thief!"—Smart Use of the Telegraph.

IN the times of the early rushes to the goldfields there was, as might be expected, a good deal of disorder and lawlessness. When the rumor of a new goldfield went abroad, its richness was, as usual, exaggerated in proportion to the distance it traveled, and men of all classes rushed from far and near to the new diggings. Melbourne was half emptied of its laboring population; sailors deserted their ships; shepherds left their flocks, and stockmen their cattle; and, worst of all, there also came pouring into Victoria the looser part of the convict population of the adjoining colonies. These all flocked to the last discovered field, which was invariably reputed the richest that had yet been discovered.

Money was rapidly made by some where gold was found in any abundance; but when the soil proved comparatively poor, the crowd soon dispersed in search of other diggings. A population so suddenly drawn together by the fierce love of gain, and containing so large an admixture of the desperado element, could scarcely be expected to be very orderly, yet it is astonishing how soon, after the first rush was over, the camp would settle down into a state of comparative order and peaceableness; for it was always the interest of the majority to put down plundering and disorder. Their first concern was for the security of their lives, and their next for the security of the gold they were able to scrape together.

When the lawless men about a camp were numerous, and robberies became frequent, the diggers would suddenly extemporize a police, rout out the thieves, and drive them perforce from the camp. I may illustrate this early state of things by what occurred at Havelock, a place about seven miles from Majorca. The gully there was "rushed" about nine years since, when some twenty thousand diggers were drawn together, with even more than the usual proportion of grog-shanty keepers, loafers, thieves, and low men and women of every description. In fact, the very scum of the roving population of the colony seems to have accumulated in the camp, and crime upon crime was committed, until at length an affair occurred, more dreadful and outrageous than any thing that had preceded it, which thoroughly roused the digger population, and a rising took place, which ended in their hunting the whole of the thieves and scoundrels into the bush.

The affair has been related to me by three of the persons who were themselves actors in it, and it is briefly as follows: At the corner of one of the main thoroughfares of the camp, composed of canvas tents and wooden stores, there stood an extemporized restaurant, kept by a Spaniard named Lopez. A few yards from his place was a store occupied by a Mr. S——, now a storekeeper in Majorca, and a customer at our bank. Opposite to S——'s store stood a tent, the occupants of which were known to be among the most lawless ruffians in the camp. S—— had seen the men more than once watching his store, and he had formed the conviction that they meant at some convenient opportunity to rob him, so he never slept without a loaded revolver under his pillow. One night in particular he was very anxious. The men stood about at the front of his store near closing-time, suspiciously eying his premises, as he thought. So he put a bold face on, came to the door near where they were standing, discharged his pistol in the air—a regular custom in the diggings at night—reloaded, entered his store, and bolted himself in. He went to bed at about ten o'clock, and lay awake listening, for he could not sleep. It was not very long before he heard some person's steps close by his hut, and a muttering of smothered voices. The steps passed on; and then, after the lapse of about ten minutes, he heard a shot — a scream — and hurried footsteps running close past his hut. He lay in bed, determined not to go out, as he feared that this was only a *ruse* on the part of the thieves to induce him to open his door. But soon he heard shouts outside as of persons in pursuit of some one, and, jumping out of bed, he ran out half dressed and joined in the chase.

Now this is what had happened during the ten minutes that he had lain in bed listening. The thieves had stolen past his store, as he had heard them, and gone forward to the restaurant kept by the Spaniard. They looked into the bar, and through the chinks of the wood they saw Lopez counting over the money he had taken during the day. The bar was closed, but the men knocked at the door for admission. Lopez asked what they wanted;

the reply was that they wished for admission to have a drink. After some demur, Lopez at last opened the door, and the men entered. Nobblers were ordered, and while Lopez was reaching for a bottle, one of the thieves, named Brooke, made a grab at the money lying in the open drawer. The landlord saw his hand, and instantly snatching up a large Spanish knife which lay behind the counter, he made a lunge at Brooke, and so fiercely did he strike that the knife ripped up the man's abdomen. With a yell of rage, Brooke drew his revolver, instantly shot Lopez through the head, and he fell dead without a groan.

Meanwhile the other thieves had fled; and now Brooke himself, holding his wound together with his hand, ran out of the house, through the street of tents, across the lead, and into the bush. But the hue and cry had been raised; the diggers bundled out of their tents, and before the murderer had reached the cover of the bush already a dozen men were on his track. It was full moon, and they could see him clearly, holding on his way, avoiding the crab-holes, and running at a good speed notwithstanding his fearful wound. Among the foremost of the pursuers were a trooper, and an active little fellow who is now living in Majorca. They got nearer and nearer to Brooke, who turned from time to time to watch their advance. The trooper was gaining upon him fast; but when within about fifteen yards of him, Brooke turned, took aim with his revolver, and deliberately fired. The aim was too true: the trooper fell dead, shot right through the heart. Brooke turned to fly immediately he had fired his shot, but the root of a tree behind him tripped him up, and the little man who followed close behind the trooper was upon him in an instant, with his knee upon his body holding him down. Brooke managed to turn himself half round, presented his revolver at his captor, and fired. The cap snapped on the nipple! My friend says he will never forget the look the wretch gave him when his pistol missed fire. A few minutes—long, long minutes—passed, and at length help arrived, and the murderer was secured. The number shortly increased to a crowd of angry diggers. At first they wished to hang Brooke at once upon the nearest tree; but moderate counsels prevailed, and at last they agreed to take him into Havelock and send for a doctor.

When the crowd got back to Havelock their fury broke out. They determined to level the thieves' tents and the grog-shanties that had harbored them. What a wild scene it must have been! Two or three thousand men pulling down huts and tents, smashing crockery and furniture, ripping up beds, and leveling the roosts of infamy to the ground. When Dr. Laidman, the doctor sent for from Maryborough, arrived to attend the dying man, he saw a cloud of "white things" in the air, and could not make out what they were. They turned out to be the feathers of the numerous feather-beds which the diggers had torn to pieces that were flying about. The diggers' blood was fairly up, and they were determined to make "a clean job of it" before they had done. And not only did they thoroughly root out and destroy all the thieves' dens and low grog-shops and places of ill fame, but they literally hunted the owners and occupants of them right out into the bush.

I must now tell you of the murderer's end. He was taken to the rude theatre of the place, and laid down upon the stage, with his two victims beside him—the dead Lopez on one side, and the dead trooper on the other. When the doctor arrived he examined Brooke, and told him he would try to keep him alive, so that justice might be done. And the doctor did his best. But the Spaniard's wound had been terrible and deadly. Brooke died in about half an hour from the time of the doctor's arrival. The murderer remained impenitent to the last, and opened his mouth only once to utter an oath. Such was the horrible ending of this diggers' tragedy.

Cases such as this are, however, of rare occurrence. So soon as a digging becomes established, a regular police is employed to insure order, and local self-government soon follows. We had often occasion to ride over to Maryborough, taking with us gold; but, though we were well known in the place, and our errand might be surmised, we were never molested, nor, indeed, entertained the slightest apprehension of danger. It is true that in the bank we usually had a loaded revolver lying in the drawer, ready at hand in case it should be needed, but we had never occasion to use it.

Some years ago, however, an actual attempt was openly made to rob a bank in Collingwood, a suburb of Melbourne, which was very gallantly resisted. The bank stood in a well-frequented part of the town, where people were constantly passing to and fro. One day two men entered it during office hours. One of them deliberately bolted the door, and the other marched up to the counter and presented a pistol at the head of the accountant who stood behind it. Nothing daunted, the young man at once vaulted over the counter, calling loudly to the manager for help, and collared the ruffian, whose pistol went off as he went down. The manager rushed out from his room and tackled the other fellow. Both the robbers were strong, powerful men, but they fought without the courage of honesty. The struggle was long and desperate, until at last assistance came, and both were secured. A presentation of plate was made to the two officials who had so courageously done their duty, and they are still in the service of the same bank.

In direct contrast to this case, I may mention a rather mysterious circumstance which occurred at an up-country bank, situated in a quartz-mining district. I must first explain that the bank building is situated in a street, with houses on both sides, and that any noise in it would readily be heard by the neighbors. One young fellow only was in charge of the place. The manager of a neighboring branch called weekly for the surplus cash and the gold bought during the week. The youth in charge suddenly reported one day that he had been "stuck up," as the colonial phrase is for being robbed. He said that one night, as he was going into the bank, where he slept—in fact, just as he was putting the key into the lock—a man came up to him, and, clapping a pistol to his head, demanded the key of the safe. He gave it him, showed him where the gold and notes were kept, and, in fact, enabled the robber to make up a decent "swag." The man, whoever he was, got away with all the money. The bank thought it their duty to proceed against the clerk himself for appropriating the money; but the proof was insufficient, and the verdict brought in was "Not guilty."

We were one day somewhat alarmed at Majorca by a

letter received from our manager at Maryborough, informing us that a great many bad characters were known to be abroad and at work, and cautioning us to be particularly upon our guard. We were directed to discharge our fire-arms frequently and keep them in good order, so that in case of need they should not miss fire. We were also to give due notice when we required notes from Maryborough, so that the messenger appointed to bring them over should be accompanied by a complete escort, *i. e.*, a mounted trooper. All this was very alarming, and we prepared for events accordingly.

A few nights after, as we were sitting under the manse veranda, we heard a loud cry of "Stop thief!" The robbers, then, were already in the township! We jumped up at once, looked round the corner of the house, and saw two men running off as fast as they could, followed at some distance by another man shouting frantically "Stop thief!" We immediately started in pursuit of the supposed thieves. We soon came up with the man who had been robbed, and whom we found swearing in a most dreadful way. This we were very much astonished at, as we recognized in him one of the most pious Wesleyans in the township. But we soon shot ahead of him, and gradually came up with the thieves, whom we at first supposed to be Chinamen. As we were close upon them they suddenly stopped, turned round, and burst out laughing! Surely there must be some mistake. We recognized in the "thieves" the son of the old gentleman whom we had just passed, with one of his companions, who had pretended to steal his fowls, as Chinamen are apt to do, whereas they had really carried off nothing at all. In short, we, as well as our respected Wesleyan friend, felt ourselves completely "sold."

The only attempt at dishonesty practiced upon our branch which I can recollect while at Majorca was one of fraud, and not of force. We had just been placed in telegraphic communication with the other towns in the colony. The opening of the telegraph was celebrated, as usual, by the Town Council "shouting" Champagne. Some time before, a working-man, who had some money deposited with us, called in a fluster to say his receipts had been stolen. This was noted. Now came a telegram from Ballarat, saying that a receipt of our branch had been presented for payment, and asking if it was correct. We answered sharp, ordering the man to be detained. He was accordingly taken into custody, handed over to the police, and remanded to Newstead, where the receipt had been stolen. Newstead is a long way from Majorca, but our manager drove over with a pair of horses to give his evidence. It turned out that our customer's coat, containing the receipt, had been stolen while he was at his work. The thief was identified as having been seen hanging about the place, and the result was that he was committed, tried, and duly convicted. So you see that we are pretty smart out here, and not a long way behind the old country after all.

CHAPTER XVI.

PLACES ABOUT.

Visit to Ballarat.—The Journey by Coach.—Ballarat founded on Gold.—Description of the Town.—Ballarat "Corner."—The speculative Cobbler.—Fire Brigades.—Return Journey.—Crab-holes.—The Talbot Ball.—The Talbot Fête.—The Avoca Races.—Sunrise in the Bush.

ONE of the most interesting visits to places that I made while staying at Majorca was to Ballarat, the mining capital of the colony, sometimes called here the Victorian Manchester. The time of my visit was not the most propitious, for it was shortly after a heavy fall of rain, which had left the roads in a very bad state. But I will describe my journey.

Three of us hired a one-horse buggy to take us on to Clunes, which lay in our way. The load was rather too much for the horse, but we took turn and turn about at walking, and made it as light for the animal as possible. At Clunes I parted with my companions, who determined to take the buggy on to Ballarat. I thought it preferable to wait for the afternoon coach; and, after being hospitably entertained at dinner by the manager of our branch bank at Clunes, I took my place in the coach for Ballarat.

We had not gone more than about a mile when the metaled road ended and the Slough of Despond began— the road so called, though it was little more than a deep mud-track, winding up a steepish ascent. All the passengers got out and walked up the hill. In the distance we saw a buggy in difficulties. I had already apprehended the fate of my mates who had gone on before me, and avoided sharing it by taking my place in the coach. But we were in little better straits ourselves. When we got up to the buggy, we found it fairly stuck in the mud in one of the worst parts of the road, with a trace broken. I got under the rails of the paddock in which the coach passengers were walking—for it was impossible to walk in the road—and crossed over to where my former mates were stuck. They were out in the deep mud, almost knee-deep, trying to mend the broken trace. Altogether they looked in a very sorry plight.

At the top of the hill we again mounted the coach, and got on very well for about three miles, until we came to another very bad piece of road. Here we diverged from it altogether, and proceeded into an adjoining field, so as to drive alongside the road, and join it a little farther on. The ground looked to me very soft, and so it was; for we had not gone far when the coach gave a plunge, and the wheels sank axle-deep in a crab-hole. All hands had now to set to work to help the coach out of the mud, while the driver urged his horses with cries and cracks of his long whip. But it was of no use. The two wheelers were fairly exhausted, and their struggling only sent them deeper into the mud. The horses were then unharnessed, and the three strongest were yoked in a line, so as to give the foremost of them a better foothold. But it was still of no use. It was not until the mud round the wheels had been all dug out, and the passengers lifted the hind wheels and the coach bodily up, that the horses were at last able to extricate the vehicle.

By this time we were all in a sad state of dirt and wet, for the rain had begun to fall quite steadily.

Shortly after, we reached the halfway house and changed horses. We now rattled along at a pretty good pace. But every now and then the driver would shout "Look out inside!" and there would be a sudden roll, followed by a jerk and pitch combined, and you would be thrown over upon your opposite neighbor, or he upon you. At last, after a rather uncomfortable journey, we reached the outskirts of a large town, and in a few minutes more we found ourselves safely jolted into Ballarat.

I am not at all up in the statistics of the colony, and can not tell the population or the number of inhabited houses in Ballarat.* But it is an immense place, second in importance in the colony only to Melbourne. Big though it be, like most of these up-country towns, Ballarat originated in a rush. It was only in September, 1851, that a blacksmith at Buningong, named Hiscocks, who had long been searching for gold, traced a mountain torrent back into the hills toward the north, and came upon the rich lode which soon became known as the "Ballarat Diggings." When the rumor of the discovery got abroad, there was a great rush of people to the place, accompanied by the usual disorders; but they gradually settled down, and Ballarat was founded. The whole soil of the place was found to contain more or less gold. It was gathered in the ranges, on the flats, in the water-courses, and especially in the small veins of blue clay, lying almost above the so-called "pipe-clay." The gold was, to all appearance, quite pure, and was found in

---

* The population in 1857 was 4971; in 1861, 21,104. It is now nearly 50,000.

rolled or water-course irregular lumps of various sizes, from a quarter or half an ounce in weight, sometimes incorporated with round pebbles of quartz, which appeared to have formed the original matrix.

The digging was at first for the most part alluvial, but when skilled miners arrived from England operations were begun on a much larger scale, until now it is conducted upon a regular system, by means of costly machinery and highly organized labor. To give an idea of the extensive character of the operations, I may mention that one company, the Band of Hope, has erected machinery of the value of £70,000. The main shaft, from which the various workings branch out, is 420 feet deep; and 350 men are employed in and about the mine. It may also be mentioned that, the deeper the workings have gone, the richer has been the yield of gold. This one company has, in a comparatively short time, raised gold worth over half a million sterling; the quantity produced by the Ballarat mines, since the discovery of gold in September, 1851, to the end of 1866, having been worth about one hundred and thirty millions sterling.

The morning after my arrival in Ballarat I proceeded to survey the town. I was certainly surprised at the fine streets, the large buildings, and the number of people walking along the broad pathways. Perhaps my surprise was magnified by the circumstance that nearly fifteen months had passed since I had been in a large town, and, after Majorca, Ballarat seemed to me like a capital. After wandering about the streets for half an hour, I looked into the court-house, where an uninteresting case of drunkenness was being heard. I next went into the adjoining large building, which I found to be the Public Library. The commodious reading-room was amply supplied with books, magazines, and newspapers, and here I amused myself for an hour in reading a new book. Over the mantel-piece of the large room hangs an oil painting of Prince Alfred, representing him and his "mates" after the visit they had made to one of the Ballarat mines. This provision of excellent reading-rooms—free and open to all—seems to me an admirable feature of the Victorian towns. They are the best sort of supplement to the common day-schools, and furnish a salutary refuge for all sober-minded men from the temptations of the grog-shops. But, besides the Public Library, there is also the Mechanics' Institute in Sturt Street; a fine building, provided also with a large library, and all the latest English newspapers, free to strangers.

The features of the town that most struck me in the course of the day were these. First, Sturt Street; a fine, broad street, at least three chains wide. On each side are large, handsome shops, and along the middle of the road runs a broad strip of garden, with large trees and well-kept beds of flowers. Sturt Street is on an incline; and at the top of it runs Ledyard Street, at right angles, also a fine broad street. It contains the principal banks, of which I counted nine, all handsome stone buildings—the London Chartered, built on a foundation of bluestone, being perhaps the finest of them in an architectural point of view. Close to it is the famous "Corner." What the Bourse is in Paris, Wall Street in New York, and the Exchange in London, that is the "Corner" at Ballarat. Under the veranda of the Unicorn Hotel, and close to the Exchange Buildings, there is a continual swarm of speculators, managers of companies, and mining men, standing about in groups, very like so many circles of betting-men on a race-course. Here all the mining swindles originate. Specimens of gold-bearing quartz are shown, shares are bought and sold, new schemes are ventilated, and old ones revived. Many fortunes have been lost and won on that bit of pavement.

One man is reckoned as good as another in Ballarat. Even the cad of a baker's boy has the chance of making "a pile," while the swell broker, who dabbles in mines and reefs, may be beggared in a few days. As one of the many instances of men growing suddenly rich by speculation here, I may mention the following. A short time since, a cobbler at Ballarat had a present made to him of twenty scrip in a company that was looking so bad that the shares had become unsalable. The cobbler knew nothing of the mine, but he held the scrip. Not only so, but he bought more at a shilling or two apiece, and he went on accumulating them, until at the end of the year he had scraped together some two or three hundred. At length he heard that gold had been struck. He went to a bank, deposited his scrip certificates, and raised upon them all the money he could borrow. He bought more shares. They trebled in value. He held on. They trebled again. At last, when the gold was being got almost by the bucket, and a great mania for the shares had set in, the cobbler sold out at £250 a share, and found himself a rich man. The mine was, I think, the Sir William Don, one of the most successful in Ballarat, now yielding a dividend of about £2 per share per month, or a return of about 500 per cent. on the paid-up capital.

But to return to my description of Ballarat. The town lies in a valley between two slopes, spreading up on both sides and over the summits. Each summit is surmounted by a lofty tower, built by the Eastern and Western Fire Brigades. These towers command a view of the whole place, and are continually occupied by watchmen, who immediately give the alarm on the outbreak of fire. The people here say that the Ballarat Fire Brigade is the smartest in the southern hemisphere, though the engines are all manned by volunteers; and a fire must be a serious matter in Ballarat, where so many of the buildings—stores as well as dwellings—are built entirely of wood. Many of the streets are even paved with wood.

In the afternoon I ascended the western hill, from which I obtained a fine bird's-eye view of the town. The large, broad streets, at right angles to each other, looked well laid out, neat, and clean looking. What seemed strangest of all was the lazy puffing of the engines over the claims, throwing out their white jets of steam. But for the width of the streets and the cleanness of the place, one might also have taken Ballarat for a manufacturing town in Yorkshire, though they have no flower-gardens along the middle of their streets!

In the evening I went to the Opera—for Ballarat has an Opera! The piece was "Faust," and was performed by Lyster and Smith's company from Melbourne. The performers did their best, but I can not say they are very strong in opera yet at the Antipodes.

After thoroughly doing Ballarat I set out on my return to Majorca. There was the same jolting as before, but this time the coach did not stick in the mud. On reaching Clunes, I resolved to walk straight to Majorca across the plain, instead of going the roundabout way by the road. But the straightest route is not always the shortest, as my experience on this occasion proved. I had scarcely got fairly into the plain before I found myself in the midst of a succession of crab-holes. These are irregular depressions, about a yard or so apart, formed by the washing up of the soil by eddies during floods, and now the holes were all full of water. It was a difficult and tedious process to work one's way through among them, for they seemed to dovetail into one another, and often I had to make a considerable détour to get round the worst of them. This crab-holey ground continued for about four miles, after which I struck into the bush, making for the ranges, and keeping Mount Greenock and Mount Glasgow before me as landmarks. Not being a good bushman, I suspect I went several miles out of my way. However, by dint of steady walking, I continued to do the sixteen miles in about four hours; but if I have ever occasion to walk from Clunes again, I will take care to take the roundabout road, and not to make the journey *en zigzag* round crab-holes and through the bush.

Among the other places about here that I have visited were Talbot, about seven miles distant, and Avoca, about twenty. One of the occasions of my going to Talbot was to attend a ball given there, and another to attend a great fête for the benefit of the Amherst Hospital. Talbot gives its name to the county, though by no means the largest town in it. The town is very neat and tidy, and contains some good stone and brick buildings. It consists of one principal street, with several little offshoots.

The ball was very like a ball at home, though a little more mixed. The young ladies were some of them very pretty and nicely dressed—some in dresses "direct from London"—while a few of the elder ladies were gorgeous, but incongruous. One old lady, in a juvenile dress, wore an enormous gold brooch, large enough to contain the portraits of several families. I was astonished to learn the great distances that some of the ladies and gentlemen had come to be present at the ball. Some had driven through the bush twenty and even thirty miles; but distance is thought nothing of here, especially when there is a chance of "meeting company." The ball was given in the Odd Fellows' Hall, a large square room. One end of it was partitioned off as a supper-room, and on the partition was sewn up in large letters this couplet from "Childe Harold:"

"No sleep till morn, when Youth and Pleasure meet,
 To chase the glowing hours with flying feet."

And, to speak the truth, the young ladies, as well as the young gentlemen present, did ample justice to the text. The dancing continued until daybreak, and we drove back to Majorca as the sun was rising; but remember it was summer time, in November, when the sun rises very early.

One little event arose out of this ball which may serve to illustrate the comparative freeness of up-country manners. A nice young lady with whom I danced asked me if I would not like to be very great friends with her. "Oh yes, certainly." And great friends we became at once. Perhaps she took pity on the stranger boy so far from home. She asked if I was fond of riding. "Very fond." "Then I will come over to Majorca, and call upon you, and we shall have a ride in the bush together." And I was to be sure and have some sweets ready for her, as she was very fond of them. I took this to be merely a little ballroom chaff; but judge my surprise when, next afternoon, the young lady rode up to the bank door and called on me to fulfill my promise—which I did, lollipops and all.

A great event in Talbot is the Annual Fête, held on the Prince of Wales's birthday, which is observed as a public holiday in Victoria. The fête this year was held in aid of the funds of Amherst Hospital, a valuable local institution. At this affair the whole population of the neighborhood turned out. It began at midday with a grand procession through the town. Let me endeavor to give you an idea of the pageant. First came the well-mounted Clunes Lancers, in their light blue and white uniforms, 150 strong, blue and white pennons fluttering from their long lances. Then came lines of members of Friendly Societies, in gay scarves, accompanied by banners. Then a good band of music. The Talbot 42d Sectional Lancers next turn the corner of the street, gorgeous in scarlet and white. Then comes something comic—a Welsh lady and gentleman riding a pony bare-backed. These are followed by an Irish couple, also mounted. Then comes a Highlandman, in a vehicle such as the Highlands never saw, discoursing music from his bagpipes. A large open boat follows, mounted on a car; it is filled with sailor-boys in blue and white. This boat is a model of the "Cerberus," the turret-ship that Mr. Reed is building in England for the defense of Port Phillip. A genuine old salt, with long white hair, plays the part of admiral. In cocked hat, blue admiral's coat, and white ducks, he waves his sword frantically, and gives the word of command to repel boarders; all the while two little cannons in the model are being constantly fired, reloaded, and fired again. This noisy exhibition having passed, a trophy representing the Australian chase appears. A huntsman, dressed in green, blowing his horn, stands amid some bushes holding a handsome leash of hounds; dead kangaroos and other Australian animals lie around him. Then follow more lancers. After this comes a huge car, two stories high, with all sorts of odd characters in it: a clown, with his "Here we are again!" playing pranks on two sedate-looking Chinamen; a little fairy boy or girl flirting with a magician; dragons snapping; strange birds screeching; three bears, one playing a violin, but the tune it plays is drowned by the hubbub of noise and bands. A lady, of the time of Elizabeth, gorgeous in ruffles, follows on horseback. Then knights in armor, one of them with a stuffed 'possum snarling on the top of his helmet. Another band. Then the solemn brethren of the Order of Druids, in white gowns, bald heads, and gray beards. A company of sweeps comes next, attended by an active Jack-in-the-Green. Now an Indian doctor appears, smoking a long pipe in his chariot, drawn by a Brahmin bull. Another band, and then the rear is brought up by more cavalry. There were seven bands—good ones too —in the procession, which took fully twenty minutes to pass the hotel, on the balcony of which I stood. I have seen the London Lord Mayor's Show, but must confess the Talbot procession beats it hollow.

After the procession we all adjourned to the racecourse, where the collection for the hospital was to be made. The admission was eighteen pence; a good sum for working-people to give, yet every body was there. There was an amateur Richardson's show, a magician's tent, Cheap Johns, merry-go-rounds, and all sorts of amusements to be had by paying for them; and, above all, there was the bazar, presided over by the ladies of Talbot, who succeeded in selling a large quantity of useless things at the usual exorbitant prices. There was also a large dancing platform roofed with canvas, which was very well frequented. Most popular of all, perhaps, were the refreshment bars, where the publicans gave the liquor free, but charged the usual prices for the good of the hospital fund; and the teetotallers, not to be outdone, managed a very comfortable tea-room. In short, all the usual expedients for raising money were cleverly resorted to, and the result was that between £1400 and £1500 was added to the funds of the hospital, about £500 of which was taken at the ladies' bazar. Altogether there were not less than 5000 people on the ground, though I believe the newspapers gave a considerably higher number.

The Avoca races were not very different from races in England. Every town hereabouts has its races, even Majorca. The Carisbrooke race-course, about four miles from our town, is considered second to none in the colony. Avoca, however, is a bigger place, and the races there draw a much larger crowd. We drove the twenty miles thither by road and bush-track. The ground was perfectly dry, for there had been no rain for some time; and as the wind was in our faces, it drove the clouds of dust behind us. I found the town itself large and well built. What particularly struck me was the enormous width of the main street—at least three chains wide. The houses on either side of the road were so remote from each other that they might have belonged to different townships. I was told that the reason of this great width of street was, that the government had reserved this broad space of ground, the main street of Avoca forming part of the road to Adelaide, which may at some future time become a great and crowded highway. One of the finest buildings in the town is a handsome hotel, built of stone and brick, provided with a ballroom, billiard-rooms, and such like. It is altogether the finest up-country place of the kind that I have seen. Here we put up, and join the crowd of loungers under the veranda—young swells got up in high summer costume—cut-away coats, white hats, and blue net veils, just as at Epsom on the Derby Day. There are also others, heavy-looking colonials, who have come out evidently to make a day of it, and are already freely imbibing cold brandy and water. Traps and cars are passing up and down the street in quest of passengers for the race-course, about two miles from the town.

There we find the same sort of entertainments provided for the public as on like occasions at home. The course is about a mile and a half in extent, with the ground well cleared. There is the saddling paddock, in which the "knowing ones" take great interest; and there are the usual booths for the sale of refreshments, and especially of drink. In front of the grand stand, the betting-men from Melbourne are pointed out to me: a sharp, rough-looking set they are, dressed in Tweed suits and flash ties, wearing diamond rings. One of them, a blear-eyed, tall, strong man, with bushy brown whiskers, bawling out his "two to one" on such and such a horse—an ugly-looking customer—was described to me as "the *second* biggest blackguard in Victoria; give him a wide berth." Another of the betting-men was pointed out to me as having been a guard on the Southeastern Railway some ten years ago. I need not describe the races: they were like most others. There were flat races and hurdle races. Six horses ran for the District Plate. Four of them came in to the winning-post running neck and neck. The race was won by only a head.

My friend remained on the course until it was too late to return to Majorca that night. As the moon did not rise until toward morning, we were under the necessity of waiting until then, otherwise we might get benighted in the bush. We tried to find a bed in the hotel, but in vain. All the beds and sofas in Avoca were occupied. Even the billiard-tables were engaged for the night.

We set out on our return journey to Majorca just as the moon was rising. She was only in her second quarter, and did not yet give light enough to enable us to see the road very clearly, so that we went very cautiously at first. While my companion drove, I snatched the opportunity for a sleep. I nodded and dozed from time to time, wakening up suddenly to find a large bright star blinking before my eyes. The star sank lower and lower toward the horizon. The green-gold rays of the morning sun rose up to meet it. The star hovered between the pale growing light below and the dark blue sky above. Then it melted away in the glow of sunrise. The half moon still cast our shadow on the dusty track. But not for long. The zone of yellow light in the east grows rapidly larger and brighter. The brilliant edge of the god of day tips the horizon; a burst of light follows; and now the morning sun, day's harbinger, "comes dancing up the east." The summits of the trees far away in the silent bush are bathed in gold. The nearer trees, that looked so weird-like in the moon's half light, are now decked in green. The chill of the night has departed. It is already broad day. By the time we reach Amherst, eight miles from Majorca, we are glad to shade ourselves from the blazing sun. In an hour more we reach our destination, and after breakfast and a bath are ready to begin the day's duties.

CHAPTER XVII.

CONCLUSION OF MAJORCAN LIFE.

Victorian Life English.—Arrival of the Home Mail.—News of the Franco-German War.—The German Settlers in Majorca.—The single Frenchman.—Majorcan Public Teas.—The Church.—The Ranters.—The Teetotalers.—The Common School.—The Roman Catholics.—Common School Fête and Entertainment.—The Mechanics' Institute.—Funeral of the Town Clerk.—Departure from Majorca.—The Colony of Victoria.

THE reader will observe, from what I have above written, that life in Victoria is very much like life in England. There are the same people, the same callings, the same pleasures and pursuits, and, as some would say, the same follies and vices. There are the same religious bodies, the same political movements, the same social agencies—Teetotal Societies, Mechanics' Institutes, Friendly Societies, and such like. Indeed, Victoria is only another England, with a difference, at the Antipodes. The character, the habits of life, and tone of thought of the people are essentially English.

You have only to see the interest with which the arrival of every mail from England is watched to recognize the strength of the tie that continues to unite the people of the colony with those of the old country. A flag is hoisted over the Melbourne Post-office to announce its coming, and soon the news is flashed by telegraph all over the colony. Every local post-office is eagerly besieged by the expecters of letters and newspapers. Speaking for myself, my most exciting day in the month was that on which my home letters arrived; and I wrote at intervals all through the month against the departure of the outgoing mail.

The excitement throughout the colony became intense when the news arrived from England of the defeat of the French before Metz. The first news came by the "Point de Galle," and then, six days later, intelligence was received *viâ* San Francisco, of the disaster at Sedan. Crowds besieged the office of the local paper at Talbot when the mail was telegraphed, and the doors had to be shut to keep them out until the telegram could be set up in type and struck off. At first the news was not believed, it was so extraordinary and unexpected; but the Germans in the town accepted it at once as true, and began their rejoicings forthwith. The Irish at Talbot were also very much excited, and wished to have a fight, but they did not exactly know with whom.

There are considerable numbers of Germans settled throughout the colony, and they are a very useful and industrious class of settlers. They are, for the most part, sober and hard-working men. I must also add that they minister in no small degree to the public amusement. At Maryborough they give very good concerts. Here, the only band in the town is furnished by the German settlers, and, being a very good one, it is in request on all public occasions. The greater number of the Germans live at M'Cullum's Creek, about a mile distant, where they have recently opened a Verein or Club, celebrating the event, as usual, by a dance. It was a very gay affair. The frantic Deutschers and their fraus danced like mad things — Tyrolese waltzes and old-fashioned quadrilles.

There was a great deal of singing in praise of Vaterland and Freundschaft, with no end of "Hochs!" They kept it up, I was told, until broad daylight, dispersing about eight o'clock in the morning.

The Germans also give an annual picnic, which is a great event in the place. There is a procession in the morning, headed by their band and the German tri-color flag. In the afternoon there are sports, and in the evening continuous dancing in a large marquee. One of the chief sports of the afternoon is "Shooting at the Eagle" with a cross-bow, and trying to knock off the crown or sceptre from the effigy of a bird, crowned with an eagle and holding a sceptre, stuck up on the top of a high pole. The crown or the sceptre represents a high prize, and each feather struck off represents a prize of some value or other.

The French have only one representative in the town. As I soon got to know everybody in the place, dropping in upon them in their houses, and chatting with them about the last news from home, I also made the acquaintance of the Frenchman. He had last come from Buenos Ayres, accompanied by madame. Of course the news about the defeat of the French army was all false— merely a vile *canard*. We shall soon know all. I confess I like this French couple very much, their little house is always so trim and neat. Fresh-plucked flowers are usually set out on the mantel-piece, on the arrangement and decoration of which madame evidently prides herself. Good taste is so cheap and so pleasant a thing that I wish it were possible for these French people to inoculate their neighbors with a little of it. But rough plenty seems to be sufficient for the Anglo-Saxon.

I must tell you of a few more of the doings of the place, to show how very much life here resembles life in England. The place is of course newer, the aggregation of society is more recent, life is more rough and ready, more free and easy, and that is nearly all the difference. The people have brought with them from the old country their habits of industry, their taste for holidays, their religious spirit, their desire for education, their love of home life.

Public Teas are an institution in Majorca, as at home. There being but little provision for the maintenance of religious worship, there is a constant whipping up for money, and tea-meetings are usually resorted to for the purpose of stimulating the flagging energies of the people. Speakers from a distance are advertised, provisions and hot water are provided in abundance, and after a gorge of tea and buns, speeches are fired off, and the hat goes round.

We had a great disappointment on one occasion, when the Archdeacon of Castlemaine was advertised to preach a sermon in aid of our Church Fund, and preside at the subsequent tea-meeting. Posters were stuck up; great preparatory arrangements were made; but the archdeacon did not come. Some hitch must have occurred. But we had our tea nevertheless.

The Ranters also are great at tea-meetings, but still greater at revival meetings. Matthew Burnett, "the great Yorkshire evangelist," came to our town to rouse us from our apathy, and he certainly contrived to work up many people, especially women, to a high pitch of excitement. The meetings being held in the evenings, and continued far into the nights, the howling, shouting, and groaning were by no means agreeable noises to such sinners in their immediate neighborhood as slept lightly, of whom I was one.

Burnett was, at the same time, the great star of the Teetotalers, who held him in much esteem. He was a man of a rough sort of eloquence, probably the best suited for the sort of people whom he came to address and sought to reclaim; for fine tools are useless for doing rough work. Another very good speaker at their meetings was known as Yankee Bill, whose homely appeals were often very striking, and even affecting in a degree. At intervals they sang hymns, and sang them very well. They thus cultivated some taste for music. They also kept people for the time being out of their favorite "publics." Like many teetotalers, however, they were very intolerant of non-teetotalers. Some even went so far as to say that one must be a teetotaler to get to heaven. Yet, notwithstanding all their exaggerations, the teetotalers do much good, and their rough appeals often penetrate hearts and heads that would be impervious to gentler and finer influences.

Let me not forget to mention the public entertainments got up for the benefit of the common school of the town. The existing schools being found too small for the large number of children who attend, it was proposed to erect another wing for the purposes of an infant school. With this object, active efforts were made to raise subscriptions, the understanding being that the government gives a pound for every pound collected in the district.

The difficulties in managing these common schools seem to be considerable, where members of different religious persuasions sit on the managing committee. At Majorca the principal difficulty seemed to be with the Roman Catholics, and it was said that their priest had threatened to refuse absolution to such parents as allowed their children to attend the common school. Whatever truth there might be in this story, it is certain that about thirty-six children *were* withdrawn, and instead of continuing to receive the elements of a good education, they were intrusted to the care of an old man quite incompetent for the office, but who was of the right faith.

I was enlisted as a collector for the school fund, and went round soliciting subscriptions, but I found it up-hill work. My district lay in the suburbs, and I was by no means successful. A good many of those I called upon were Ranters, and I suspect that the last sensation preacher had carried off what otherwise might have fallen to my share. I was tolerably successful with the diggers working at their claims. At least they always gave me a civil answer. One of them said, "Well, if our washing turns out well on Saturday, you shall have five shillings." And the washing must have turned out well, for on Saturday evening the digger honestly brought me the sum he had named.

Further to help the fund, a fête was held in the open air, and an entertainment was given by amateurs in the Prince of Wales's Theatre — for our little town also boasts of its theatre. The fête was held on Easter Monday, which was kept as a holiday, and it commenced with a grand procession of Odd Fellows, Foresters, German Verein, Rechabites, and other clubs, all in their Sunday clothes, and many of them wearing very gorgeous scarves. The German band headed the procession, which proceeded toward the paddock at M'Cullum's Creek used on such festive occasions. There all the contrivances usually adopted for extracting money from the pockets of the visitors were in full operation. There was a bazar, in which all manner of useless things were offered for sale, together with raffles, bowls, croquet, dancing, shooting at the eagle, tilting at the ring, and all sorts of sports—a small sum being paid on entry. I took up with a forlorn Aunt Sally, standing idle without customers, and by dint of sedulous efforts contrived to gather about a pound in an hour and a half. All did their best; and thus a pleasant day was spent, and a good round sum of money was collected for the fund.

The grand miscellaneous entertainment was also a complete success. The theatre was filled with a highly respectable audience, including many gayly-dressed ladies, and all the belles of Majorca and the neighborhood. Indeed, I wondered where they could all come from. The performances excited the greater interest, as the whole of them were by amateurs, well known in the place. The songs went off well, and several of them were encored. After the concert the seats were cleared away, and the entertainment wound up with the usual dance. And thus did we each endeavor to do our share of pleasant labor for the benefit of the common school.

The reading-room of the Mechanics' Institute is always a source of entertainment when nothing else offers. The room is small, but convenient, and it contains a fair collection of books. The Telegraph Office, the Post-office, Council Chamber, and Mechanics' Institute all occupy one building—not a very extensive one, being only a one-storied wooden erection. One of the chief attractions of the reading-room is a collection of colonial papers, with "Punch," "The Illustrated News," and the "Irish Nation." On Saturday nights, when the diggers wash up and come into town, the room is always well filled with readers. The members of the committee are also very active in getting up entertainments and popular readings; and, in short, the Mechanics' Institute may be regarded as one of the most civilizing institutions in the place.

But my time in Majorca was drawing to an end. One of the last public events in which I took part was attending the funeral of our town clerk, the first funeral I have ever had occasion to be present at. A long procession followed his remains to the cemetery. Almost all the men in the township attended, for the deceased was highly respected. The service was very solemn, held under the bright, clear, blue Australian sky. Poor old man! I knew him well. I had seen him so short a time ago in the hospital, where, three hours before he died, he gave me his blessing. He was then lying flushed and in great pain. All that is over now. "Dust to dust, and ashes to ashes." The earth sounded as it fell upon his coffin, and now the good man sleeps in peace, leaving a blessed memory behind him.

I was now under orders for home. My health was completely re-established. I might have remained, and perhaps succeeded in the colony. As it was, I carried with me the best wishes of my employers. But I had no desire to pursue the career of bank clerk farther. I was learning but little, and had my own proper business to pursue, so I made arrangements for leaving Australia.

Enough money had been remitted me from England to enable me to return direct by first-class ship, leaving me free to choose my own route. As I might never have another opportunity of seeing that great new country, the United States of America, the question occurred whether I might not be able to proceed up the Pacific to San Francisco, *viâ* Honolulu, and cross America by the Atlantic and Pacific Railway. On inquiry, I found it would be practicable, but not by first-class. So I resolved to rough it a little, and proceed by that route second-class, for which purpose my funds would be sufficient. I accordingly took my final leave of Majorca early in December, just as summer was reaching its height, and after spending three more pleasant weeks with my hospitable and kind friends in Melbourne, took my passage in the steamer for Sydney, and set sail the day after Christmas.

On looking over what I have above written about my life in Victoria, I feel how utterly inadequate it is to give the reader an idea of the country as a whole. All that I have done has merely been to write down my first impressions, unpremeditatedly and faithfully, of what I saw, and what I felt and did while there. Such a short residence in the colony, and such a limited experience as mine was, could not have enabled me — no matter what my faculty of observation, which is but moderate — to convey any adequate idea of the magnitude of the colony or its resources. To pretend to write an account of Victoria and Victorian life from the little I saw were as absurd as it would be for a native-born Victorian, sixteen years old, to come over to England, live two years in a small country town, and then write a book of his travels headed "England." And yet this is the way in which the Victorians complain, and with justice, that they are treated by English writers. Some eminent man arrives in the colony, spends a few weeks in it, perhaps rushes through it by railway, and hastens home to publish some contemptuous account of the people whom he does not really know, or some hasty, if not fallacious, description of the country which he has not really seen. I am sure that, however crude my description may be, Victorians will not be offended with what I have said of themselves and their noble colony; for, small though the sphere of my observation was, they will see that I have written merely to the extent of my knowledge, and have related, as faithfully as I was able, the circumstances that came within the range of my own admittedly limited, but actual experience of colonial life.

SYDNEY, PORT JACKSON.

CHAPTER XVIII.

ROUND TO SYDNEY.

Last Christmas in Australia.—Start by Steamer for Sydney.—The "Great Britain."—Cheap Trips to Queenscliffe.—Rough Weather at Sea.—Mr. and Mrs. C. Mathews.—Botany Bay.—Outer South Head.—Port Jackson.—Sydney Cove.—Description of Sydney.—Government House and Domain.—Great future Empire of the South.

I SPENT my last Australian Christmas with my kind entertainers in Melbourne. Christmas scarcely looks like Christmas with the thermometer at 90° in the shade; but there is the same roast beef and plum-pudding nevertheless, reminding one of home. The immense garnishing of strawberries, however, now in season—though extremely agreeable—reminds us that Christmas at the Antipodes must necessarily differ in many respects from Christmas in England.

The morning after Christmas Day saw me on board the steamer "Raugatira," advertised to start for Sydney at eleven. Casting off from our moorings at the Sandridge pier, the ship got gradually under weigh; and, waving my last adieu to friends on shore, I was again at sea.

We steamed close alongside the "Great Britain," which has for some time been the crack ship between Australia and England. She had just arrived from Liverpool with a great freight of goods and passengers, and was lying at her moorings—a splendid ship. As we steamed out into Hobson's Bay, Melbourne rose up across the flats, and loomed large in the distance. All the summits seemed covered with houses—the towers of the fine Roman Catholic Cathedral, standing on the top of a hill to the right, being the last building to be seen distinctly from the Bay.

In about two hours we were at Queenscliffe, inside the Heads—at present the fashionable watering-place of Melbourne. Several excursion steamers had preceded us, taking down great numbers of passengers, to enjoy Boxing-day by the sea-side. The place looked very pretty indeed from our ship's deck. Some of the passengers, who had taken places for Sydney, were landed here, fearing lest the sea should be found too rough outside the Heads.

There had been very little wind when we left Sandridge, and the waters of Port Phillip were comparatively smooth; but as we proceeded the wind began to rise, and our weatherwise friends feared lest they should have to encounter a gale outside. We were now in sight of the white line of breakers running across the Heads. There was still a short distance of smooth water before us, but that was soon passed, and then our ship dashed her prow into the waves, and had to fight her way as for very life against the heavy sea that rolled in through Bass's Straits from the South Pacific.

The only distinguished passengers on board are Mr. and Mrs. Charles Mathews, who have been "starring" it in Victoria to some purpose. A few nights ago Mr. Mathews took his leave in a characteristic speech, partly humorous and partly serious; but the enthusiastic audience laughed and cheered him all the way through; and it was rather comic to read the newspaper report of next morning, and to find that the actor's passages of the softest pathos had been received with "roars of laughter."

Mr. Mathews seems to be one of the most perennially juvenile of men. When he came on board at Sandridge he looked as frisky and larky as a boy. He skipped up and down the deck, and took an interest in every thing. This lasted so long as the water was smooth. When he came in sight of the broken water at the Heads, I fancy his spirit barometer went down a little; but when the ship began to put her nose into the waves freely, a total change seemed to pass over him. I very soon saw his retreating skirts. For the next three days—three long, rough, wave-tossing days—very little was seen of him; and when he at length did make his appearance on deck, alas! he seemed no longer the brisk and juvenile passenger that had come on board at Sandridge only a few days before.

Indeed, it was a very rough and "dirty" passage. The passengers were mostly prostrate during the whole of the voyage. The sea was rolling in from the east in great billows, which our little boat breasted gallantly; but it was tossed about like a cork, inclining at all sorts of angles by turns. It was not much that I could see of the coast, though at some places it is bold, at others beautiful. We passed very near to it at Ram Head and Cape Howe—a grand promontory forming the southwest point of Australia.

On the third day from Melbourne, about daybreak, I found we were steaming close along shore, under dark brown cliffs, not very high, topped with verdure. The wind had gone down, but the boat was pitching in the heavy sea as much as ever. The waves were breaking with fury and noise along the beach under the cliffs. At 9 A.M. we passed Botany Bay—the first part of New South Wales sighted by Captain Cook just a hundred years ago. It was here that he first landed, and erected a mound of stones and a flag to commemorate the event.* Banks and Solander, who were with him, found the land covered with new and beautiful flowers, and hence the name which was given it of "Botany Bay"—afterward a name of terror, associated only with crime and convict life.

We steamed across the entrance to the Bay until we

* The Hon. Thomas Holt, on whose property the landing-place is situated, last year erected an obelisk on the spot, with the inscription "Captain Cook landed here 28th April, A.D. 1770," with the following extract from Captain Cook's Journal: "At daybreak we discovered a bay, and anchored under the south shore, about two miles within the entrance, in six fathom water, the south point bearing S.E., and the north point east. Latitude 34° S., Longitude 208° 37' W.

were close under the cliffs of the outer South Head, guarding the entrance to Port Jackson. The white Macquarie light-house on the summit of the Head is seen plainly at a great distance. Steaming on, we were soon under the inner South Head, and at the entrance to the famous harbor, said to be the finest in the world.

The opening into Port Jackson is comparatively narrow; so much so, that when Captain Cook first sailed past it, he considered it to be merely a boat entrance, and did not examine it. While he was at breakfast, the lookout man at the mast-head—a man named Jackson—reported that he saw the entrance to what seemed a good anchorage; and so the captain, half in derision, named it "Port Jackson." The Heads seemed to me only about four hundred feet apart from each other, the north head somewhat overlapping the south. The rocks appear to have broken off abruptly, and stand up perpendicularly over against each other, about three hundred feet high, leaving a chasm or passage between them which forms the entrance to Port Jackson. When the Pacific rolls in full force against the Heads, the waves break with great violence on the cliffs, and the spray is flung right over the light-house on the South Head. Now that the sea has gone somewhat down, the waves are not so furious, and yet the dash of the spray half way up the perpendicular cliffs is a grand sight.

Once inside the Heads, the water becomes almost perfectly calm; the scenery suddenly changes; the cliffs subside into a prettily wooded country, undulating and sloping gently to the water's edge. Immediately within the entrance, on the south side, is a pretty little village—the pilot station in Watson's Bay. After a few minutes' more steaming the ship rounds a corner, the open sea is quite shut out from view, and neither Heads nor pilot station are to be seen.

My attention is next drawn to a charming view on the north shore—a delicious little inlet, beautifully wooded, and surrounded by a background of hills, rising gradually to their greatest height behind the centre of the little bay. There, right in among the bright green trees I observe a gem of a house, with a broad terrace in front, and steps leading down to the clear blue water. A few minutes more, and we have lost sight of the charming nook, having rounded the headland of the inlet—a rocky promontory covered with ferns and mosses.

But our attention is soon absorbed by other beauties of the scene. Before us lies a lovely island prettily wooded, with some three or four fine mansions and their green lawns sloping down to the water's edge, while on the left the hills are constantly varying in aspect as we steam along. At length, some seven miles up Port Jackson, the spires, and towers, and buildings of Sydney come into sight; at first Wooloomooloo, and then, in ten minutes more, on rounding another point, we find ourselves in Sydney Cove, alongside the wharf. Here we are in the midst of an amphitheatre of beauty—a wooded island opposite covered with villas and cottages, with headlands, coves, and bays, and beautiful undulations of lovely country as far as the eye can reach. Altogether, I think Port Jackson is one of the most charming pieces of water and landscape that I have ever seen.

After our three days' tossing at sea, I was, however, glad to be on shore again; so, having seen my boxes safely deposited in the Californian baggage dépôt, I proceeded into the town and secured apartments for the few days I was to remain in Sydney.

From what I have already said of the approach to the landing, it will be inferred that the natural situation of Sydney is very fine. It stands upon a ridge of sandstone rock, which runs down into the bay in numerous ridges or spines of land or rock, between which lie the natural harbors of the place, and these are so deep that vessels of almost any burden may load and unload at the projecting wharves. Thus Sydney possesses a very large extent of deep-water frontage, and its wharfage and warehouse accommodation is capable of enlargement to almost any extent. Of the natural harbors formed by the projecting spines of rock into the deep water, the most important are Wooloomooloo Bay, Farm Cove, Sydney Cove, and Darling Harbor.

From the water-side, the houses, ranged in streets, rise like so many terraces up to the crown of the ridges, the main streets occupying the crests and flanks of two or three of the highest. One of these, George Street, is a remarkably fine street, about two miles long, containing many handsome buildings.

My first knowledge of Sydney was acquired in a stroll up George Street. We noticed the original old market-place, bearing the date of 1793; a quaint building, with queer old-fashioned domes, all shingle-roofed. A little farther on we came to a large building in course of erection—the new Town Hall, built of a yellowish sort of stone. Near it is the English Cathedral, a large and elegant structure. Farther on is the new Roman Catholic Cathedral, the original Cathedral in Hyde Park having been burnt down some time ago.

Altogether, Sydney has a much older look than Melbourne. It has grown up at longer intervals, and does not look so spic-and-span new. The streets are much narrower and more irregular—older-fashioned, and more English in appearance — occasioned, doubtless, by its slower growth and its more hilly situation. But it would also appear as if there were not the same go-ahead spirit in Sydney that so pre-eminently characterizes her sister city. Instead of the splendidly broad, well-paved, and well-watered streets of Melbourne, here they are narrow, ill paved, and dirty. Such a thing as the miserable wooden hut which serves for a post-office would not be allowed to exist for a day at Melbourne. It is the original office, and has never been altered or improved since it was first put up. I must, however, acknowledge that a new post-office is in course of erection; but it shows the want of public spirit in the place that the old shanty should have been allowed to stand so long.

The railway terminus at the end of George Street is equally discreditable. It is, without exception, the shabbiest, dirtiest shed of the kind I have ever seen. They certainly need a little of the Victorian spirit in Sydney. The Melbourne people, with such a site for a city, would soon have made it one of the most beautiful places in the world. As it is, nothing can surpass its superb situation, the view over the harbor from some of the higher streets being unequaled—the numerous ships lying still, as if asleep on the calm waters of the bay beneath, while the rocky promontories all round it, clothed with verdure, are dotted with the villas and country mansions of the Sydney merchants.

One of the busiest parts of Sydney is down by the

quays, where a great deal of shipping business is carried on. There are dry docks, patent slips, and one floating dock; though floating docks are of minor importance here, where the depth of water along shore is so great, and the rise and fall of the tide is so small. Indeed, Sydney Harbor may be regarded as one immense floating dock. The Australasian Steam Navigation Company have large ship-building and repairing premises at Pyrmont, which give employment to a large number of hands. Certainly the commanding position of Sydney, and the fact of its being the chief port of a great agricultural and pastoral country in the interior, hold out the promise of great prosperity for it in the future.

Every visitor to Sydney of course makes a point of seeing the Government House and the Domain, for it is one of the principal sights of the place. The government buildings and park occupy the double-headed promontory situated between Wooloomooloo Bay and Sydney Cove. The Government House is a handsome and spacious castellated building, in every way worthy of the colony, the views from some parts of the grounds being of almost unparalleled beauty. There are nearly four miles of drives in the park, through alternate cleared and wooded grounds, sometimes opening upon cheerful views of the splendid harbor, then skirting the rocky shores, or retreating inland amid shadowy groves and grassy dells. The grounds are open to the public, and the entrances being close upon the town and suburbs, this public park of Sydney is one that for convenience and beauty perhaps no capital in the world surpasses.

The Botanical Gardens are situated in what is called the outer Domain. We enter the grounds under a long avenue of acacias and sycamores, growing so close together as to afford a complete shade from the noonday heat. At the end of the avenue we came upon a splendid specimen of the Norfolk Island pine, said to be the largest and finest tree out of the island itself. After resting for a time under its delicious shade, we strolled on through other paths overhung with all sorts of flowering plants. Then, passing through an opening in the wall, a glorious prospect of the bay suddenly spread out before us. The turf was green down to the water's edge, and interspersed with nicely-kept flower-beds, with here and there a pretty clump of trees.

Down by the water-side is a broad esplanade—the most charming of promenades—running all round the beautiful little bay which it incloses. Tropical and European shrubs grow in profusion on all sides, an English rose-tree in full bloom growing alongside a bamboo, while at another place a banana throws its shade over a blooming bunch of sweet pea, and a bell-flowered plant overhangs a Michaelmas daisy. A fine view of the harbor and shipping is obtained from a part of the grounds where Lady Macquarie's chair—a hollow place in a rock—is situated—itself worth coming a long way to see. Turning up the gardens again we come upon a monkey-house, an aviary, and—what interested me more than all—an inclosed lawn in which were numerous specimens of the kangaroo tribe, from the "old boomer" standing six feet high, down to the rock kangaroo not much bigger than a hare. We hung about, watching the antics of the monkeys and the leapings of the kangaroos until it was time to take our departure.

The country inland, lying to the south of Sydney, is

by no means picturesque. Much of it consists of sandy scrub, and it is by no means fertile except in the valleys. But nothing can surpass the beauty of the shores of the bay as far up as Paramatta, about twenty miles inland. The richest land of the colony lies well into the interior, but the time at my disposal was too short to enable me to do more than visit the capital, with which the passing stranger can not fail to be greatly pleased.

Altogether, it seems a wonderful thing that so much should have been done within so short a time toward opening up the resources of this great country; and most wonderful of all, that the people of a small island like Britain, situated at the very opposite side of the globe, some sixteen thousand miles off, should have come hither, and within so short a time have built up such cities as Sydney and Melbourne—planted so large an extent of territory with towns, and villages, and farmsteads—covered its pastures with cattle and sheep—opened up its mines—provided it with roads, railroads, and telegraphs, and thereby laid the firm foundations of a great future empire in the south. Surely these are things of which England, amid all her grumblings, has some reason to be proud!

AUCKLAND, NEW ZEALAND.

CHAPTER XIX.

TO AUCKLAND, IN NEW ZEALAND.

Leaving Sydney.—Anchor within the Heads.—Take in Mails and Passengers from the "City of Adelaide."—Out to Sea again.—Sight New Zealand.—Entrance to Auckland Harbor.—The "Galatea."—Description of Auckland.—Founding of Auckland due to a Job.—Maori Men and Women.—Drive to Onehunga.—Splendid View.—Auckland Gala.—New Zealand Delays.—Leave for Honolulu.

On the last day of December, 1870, I set out for Honolulu, in the Sandwich Islands, embarking as second-class passenger on board the " City of Melbourne." Our first destination was Auckland, in New Zealand, where we were to stop for a few days to take in passengers and mails.

I had been so fortunate as accidentally to encounter a friend, whom I knew in Maryborough, in the streets of Sydney. He was out upon his summer holiday, and when he understood that I was bound for New Zealand he determined to accompany me, and I had, therefore, the pleasure of his society during the earlier part of my voyage.

As we steamed down the harbor I had another opportunity of admiring the beautiful little bays, and sandy coves, and wooded islets of Port Jackson. The city, with its shipping, and towers, and spires, gradually receded in the distance, and as we rounded a headland Sydney was finally shut out from farther view.

We were soon close to the abrupt headlands which guard the entrance to the bay, and letting drop our anchor just inside the southern head, we lay safely sheltered from the gale which began to blow from the east. There we waited the arrival of the "City of Adelaide" round from Melbourne with the last mails and passengers for England by the California route.

But it was some time before the "Adelaide" made her appearance. Early next morning, hearing that she was alongside, I hurried on deck. The mails were speedily brought off from the inward-bound ship, together with seven more passengers. Our anchor was at once weighed, and in ten more minutes we are off. We are soon at the entrance to the Heads; and I see by the scud of the clouds, and the long line of foaming breakers driving across the entrance, that before long we shall have the spray flying over our hurricane deck. Another minute and we are outside, plunging into the waves, and throwing the water in foam from our bows.

I remain upon deck, holding on as long as I can. Turning back, I see a fine little schooner coming out of the Heads behind us, under a good press of sail. On she came, dipping her bows right under the water, but buoyant as a cork. Her men were aloft reefing a sail, her yards seeming almost to touch the water as she leaned over to leeward. Passing under our stern, she changed her course, and the plucky little schooner held up along the coast, making for one of the northern ports.

Taking a last look at the Sydney Heads, I left the farther navigation of the ship in the hands of the captain, and retired below. I was too much occupied by private affairs to see much more of the sea during the next twenty-four hours. New Year's Day though it was, there was very little jollity on board; indeed, as regarded the greater number of the passengers, it was spent rather sadly.

The weather, however, gradually moderated, until, on the third day of our voyage, the weather became fine, such wind as there was being well aft. On the fifth day the wind had gone quite down, and there only remained the long low roll of the Pacific; but the ship rolled so heavily that I suspect there must have been a very strong under-current somewhere about. Early in the forenoon we sighted the "Three Kings' Islands," off the extreme north coast of New Zealand. At first they seemed to consist of three detached rocks; but, as we neared them, they were seen to be a number of small rocky islands, with very little vegetation on them. The main land shortly came in sight, though it was still too distant to enable us to recognize its features.

Early next morning we found ourselves steaming close

in shore past Cape Brett, near the entrance to the Bay of Islands. The high cliffs along the coast are bold and grand; here and there a waterfall is seen, and occasionally an opening valley, showing the green woods beyond. In the distance are numerous conical hills, showing the originally volcanic character of the country. During the forenoon we passed a huge rock that in the distance had the appearance of being a large ship in full sail; hence its name of the "Sail Rock."

The entrance to the harbor of Auckland, though by no means equal to Port Jackson, is yet highly picturesque. On one side is the City of Auckland, lying in a hollow, and extending up the steep hills on either side; while opposite to it, on the north shore of the Frith of Thames, is a large round hill, used as a pilot signal station. Situated underneath it are many nice little villas, with gardens close to the sea. The view extends up the inlet, which widens out and terminates in a background of high blue mountains. From Auckland, as from Sydney, the open sea is not to be seen, there are so many windings in and out before the harbor is reached.

A fine queen's ship was lying at anchor in the bay, which, on inquiry, we found to be the "Galatea," commanded by the Duke of Edinburg. The "Clio" also was anchored not far off. We were soon alongside the long wooden pier, to which were also moored several fine clipper ships, and made our way into the town. As the principal street continues straight in from the pier, we were shortly enabled to see all the principal buildings of the place.

Though a small shipping town, there seems to be a considerable amount of business doing at Auckland.

There is a good market-place, some creditable bank buildings, and some three or four fine shops, but the streets are dirty and ill paved. The Supreme Court and the Post-office—both fine buildings—lie off the principal street. The governor's house, which occupies a hill to the right, commands a fine view of the bay, as well as of the lovely green valley behind it.

Auckland, like Sydney, being for the most part built upon high land, is divided by ravines, which open out toward the sea in little coves or bays, such as Mechanics' Bay, Commercial Bay, and Official Bay. The buildings in Mechanics' Bay, as the name imports, are principally devoted to ship-building, boat-building, and rope-making. The shore of Commercial Bay is occupied by the store and shop-keeping people, while Official Bay is surrounded by the principal official buildings, the government store-houses, and such like.

I have been told here that Auckland is completely out of place as the capital of the colony, being situated at the narrowest part of the island, far away from the principal seats of population, which are in Cook's Straits, and even farther south. The story is current that Auckland is due to an early job of government officials, who combined to buy up the land about it, and when it had been fixed upon as the site of the capital, sold out their lots at fabulous prices, to the feathering of their own nests.

A great many natives, or Maoris, are hanging about the town. It seems that they are here in greater numbers than usual, their votes being wanted for the passing or confirmation of some land measure. Groups of them stand about the streets talking and gesticulating; a still greater number are hanging round the public houses, which they enter from time to time to have a drink. I can not say I like the look of the men; they look very ugly customers indeed—beetle-browed and down-looking, "with foreheads villainous low." Their appearance is all the more revolting by reason of the large blue circles of tattoo on their faces. Indeed, when the New Zealander is fully tattooed, which is the case with the old aristocrats, there is very little of his original face visible, excepting perhaps his nose and his bright black eyes.

Most of the men were dressed in the European costume, though some few were in their native blankets, which they wear with grace and even dignity. The men were of fine physique—tall, strong, and well made—and, looking at their keen fierce eyes, I do not wonder that they have given our soldiers so much trouble. I could not help thinking, as I saw them hanging about the drinking-shops, some half drunk, that English drink will in the long run prove their conquerors far more than English rifles.

There were many Maori women mingled with the men. Some of them were good looking. Their skin is of a clear dark olive; their eyes dark brown or black; their noses small, and their mouths large. But nearly all of them have a horrid blue tattoo mark on their lips, that serves to give them—at least to European eyes—a repulsive look.

Many of the women, as well as the men, wear a piece of native greenstone hanging from their ears, to which is attached a long piece of black ribbon. This stone is supposed by the Maoris to possess some magical virtue.

Others of them—men as well as girls—have sharks' teeth hanging from their ears and dangling about their faces, the upper part of the teeth being covered with bright red wax.

Mixed with the Maoris were the sailors of the "Galatea," rolling about the streets, and, like them, frequent customers of the public houses. In fact, the sailors and the Maoris seemed to form a considerable proportion of the population of the place.

The landlord of the hotel at which we staid—the "Waitemata"—having recommended us to take a drive into the interior, we set out at midday by stage-coach for Onehunga. Auckland being situated at the narrowest part of the North Island, Onehunga, which is on the west coast, is only seven miles distant by land, though five hundred by water.

The coach started at noon, and it was hard work for the four horses to drag the vehicle up the long steep hill at the back of the town. Nice country houses stood on both sides of the road, amid fresh green gardens, the houses almost buried in foliage.

From the high ground a magnificent landscape stretched before us. It reminded me very much of a particular view of the Lake of Geneva, though this was even more grand and extensive. The open sea was at such a distance, and so shut out by intervening high land, that it was scarcely visible. The lovely frith or bay, with its numerous inlets, islands, and surrounding bright green hills, lay at our feet. The blue water wound in and out among the hills on our right for a distance of about fifteen miles. There was a large open stretch of water, surrounded by high mountains, toward the west. Right before us was the entrance to the bay, with the pilot-station hill on one side and Mount Victoria on the other. Between these two hills high land stood up in the distance, so that the whole gave one the impression of a beautiful inland lake rather than of a sea view. It was, without exception, the most magnificent prospect I had ever looked upon; yet they tell me this is surpassed by the scenery in other parts of New Zealand, in which case it must indeed be an exceedingly picturesque country.

We drove along through a pretty green country, with fine views of the plains toward the right, bounded by distant blue mountains. In about another quarter of an hour, after passing through the village of Epsom, we came in sight of the sea on the west coast, and were shortly set down at Onehunga, on the shore of Manukau Bay. Onehunga is a small township containing a few store-houses, besides dwelling-houses, with a hotel or two. The view here was also fine, but not so interesting as that on the eastern side of the island. Plains, bounded by distant mountains, extended along the coast on one side, and high broken cliffs ran along the shore and bounded the sea in front of us. After an hour's rest at Onehunga we returned to Auckland, enjoying the drive back very much, in spite of the inconveniently-crowded coach.

There was a sort of gala in Auckland that evening. A promenade concert was given on the parade-ground at the barracks, at which the band of the "Galatea" played to the company. The prince himself, it was announced, would perform on the occasion. It was a fine moonlight night, and the inhabitants of Auckland turned out in force. There must have been at least two thousand well-dressed people promenading about, listening to the music. The prince's elephant was there too, and afforded a good deal of amusement. How the poor brute was slung out of the "Galatea," got on shore, and got back on shipboard again, was to me a mystery.

I went down to the steamer at the appointed time of sailing, but found that the "City" was not to leave for several hours after time. The mail express was to wait until Mr. and Mrs. Bandmau—who had been acting in Auckland—had received some presentation from the officers of the "Galatea!" It seemed odd that a mail steamer should be delayed some hours to suit the convenience of a party of actors. But there are strange doings connected with this mail line. Time is of little moment here, and in New Zealand I suspect time is even less valued than usual. They tell me that few mails leave New Zealand without having to wait on some pretext or another. There does not seem to be the same activity, energy, and business aptitude that exists in the Australian colonies. The Auckland people seem languid and half asleep. Perhaps their soft, relaxing, winterless climate has something to do with it.

Having nothing else to occupy me before the ship sailed, I took leave of my Australian friend, gave him my last messages for Maryborough and Majorca, and went on board. I was wakened up about midnight by the noise of the anchor coming up, and in a few minutes more we were off and on our way to Honolulu, up the Pacific.

CHAPTER XX.

UP THE PACIFIC.

Departure for Honolulu.—Monotony of a Voyage by Steam.—Desagrémens.—The "Gentlemen" Passengers.—The one Second-class "Lady."—The Rats on Board.—The Smells.—Flying Fish.—Cross the Line.—Treatment of Newspapers on Board.—Hawaii in Sight.—Arrival at Honolulu.

When I went on deck next morning we had left New Zealand far behind us; not a speck of land was to be seen, and we were fairly on our way to Honolulu. We have before us a clear run of about four thousand miles, and if our machinery and coal keep good, we know that we shall do it easily in about seventeen days.

Strange though it may seem, there is much greater monotony in a voyage on board a steamer than there is on board a sailing vessel. There is nothing like the same interest felt in the progress of the ship, and thus one unfailing topic of conversation and speculation is shut out. There are no baffling winds, no sleeping calms, alternating with a joyous and invigorating run before the wind, such as we had when coming out, from Plymouth to the Cape. We only know that we shall do our average ten miles an hour, be the weather what it may. If the wind is blowing astern, we run before it; if ahead, we run through it. Fair or foul, it matters but little.

A voyage by a steamer, compared with one by sailing ship, is what a journey by railway train is to a drive across country in a well-horsed stage-coach. There is, however, this to be said in favor of the former. We know that, monotonous though it be, it is very much sooner over; and on a voyage of some thousands of miles, we can calculate to a day, and almost to an hour, when we shall arrive at our destination.

But to be set against the shorter time consumed on the voyage there are numerous little *desagrémens*. There is the dismal, never-ending grind, grind of the screw, sometimes, when the ship rolls, and the screw is out of the water, going round with a horrible *birr*. At such times the vessel has a double motion, pitching and rolling, and thereby occasioning an inexpressibly sickly feeling. Then, when the weather is hot, there is the steam of heated oil wafted up from the engine-room, which, mingled with the smell of bilge, and perhaps cooking, is any thing but agreeable or appetizing. I must also acknowledge that a second-class berth, which I had taken, is not comparable in point of comfort to a first, not only as regards the company, but as regards smells, food, and other surroundings.

There are not many passengers at my end, and the few there are do not make themselves very agreeable. First, there are two German Jews, grumbling and growling at every thing. They are a couple of the most cantankerous fellows I ever came across—never done knagging, swearing, grunting, and bellowing. They keep the steward, who is an obliging sort of fellow, in a state of constant "wax," which, when I want any thing done for me, I have to remedy by tipping; so that they are likely to prove somewhat costly companions, though in a peculiar way.

Next there is a German-Yankee, a queer old fellow, who came on board at Auckland. He seems to have made some money at one of the New Zealand goldfields called "The Serpentine," somewhere near Dunedin. This old fellow and I cotton together very well. He is worth a dozen of the other two Germans. He had been all through the American War under Grant, and spins some long yarns about the Northerners and the "cussed rebs."

As there are twenty-seven bunks in our cabin and only four passengers, there is, of course, plenty of room and to spare; but there is also a "lady" passenger at our end of the ship, and she has all the fifteen sleeping-places in her cabin to herself. It might be supposed that, there being only one lady, she would be in considerable demand with her fellow-passengers; but it was quite the contrary. Miss Ribbids, as I will call her, proved to be a most uninteresting individual. I am sorry to have to confess to so much ungallantry; but the only effort which I made, in common with the others, was to avoid her—she was so hopelessly dense. One night she asked me, quite seriously, "If that was the same moon they had at Sydney!" I am sure she does not know that the earth is round. By stretching a hair across the telescope glass, I made her look in and showed her the Line, but she did not see the joke. She gravely asked if we should not land at the Line: she understood there was land there! Her only humor is displayed at table, when any thing is spilled by the rolling of the ship, when she exclaims, "Over goes the apple-cart!" But enough of the awful Miss Ribbids.

There are, however, other passengers aboard that must not be forgotten—the rats! I used to have a horror of rats, but here I soon became used to them. The first night I slept on board I smelt something very disgusting as I got into my bunk, and at last I discovered that it arose from a dead rat in the wainscot of the ship. My nose being somewhat fastidious as yet, I moved to the other side of the cabin. But four kegs of strong-smelling butter sent me quickly out of that. I then tried a bunk next to the German Jews, but I found proximity to them was the least endurable of all; and so, after many changes, I at last came back and slept contentedly beside my unseen and most unsavory companion, the dead rat.

But there are plenty of living and very lively rats too. One night a big fellow ran over my face, and in a fright I cried out. But use is every thing, and in the course of a few more nights I got quite rid of my childish astonishment and fear at rats running over my face. Have you ever heard rats sing? I assure you they sing in a very lively chorus, though I confess I have heard much pleasanter music in my time.

Amid all these little troubles the ship went steadily on. During the second night after leaving Auckland the wind began to blow pretty fresh, and the hatch was closed. It felt very close and stuffy below that night. The light went out, and the rats had it all their own way. On the following day it was impossible to go on deck without getting wet through, so we were forced to stick down below. The rolling of the ship was also considerable.

Next day was fine, but hot. The temperature sensibly and even rapidly increases as we approach the Line. We see no land, though we have passed through among the Friendly Islands, with the Samoa or Navigator's Islands lying to the west. It is now a clear course to Honolulu. Not being able to go on deck in the heat of the day at risk of sunstroke, I wait until the sun has gone down, and then slip on deck with my rug and pillow, and enjoy a siesta under the stars. But sometimes I am disturbed by a squall, and have to take refuge below again.

As the heat increases, so do the smells on board. In passing from the deck to our cabin I pass through seven distinct perfumes: 1st, the smell from the galley smoke;

2d, the perfume of decaying vegetables stored on the upper deck; 3d, fowls; 4th, dried fish; 5th, oil and steam from the engine-room; 6th, meat undergoing the process of cooking; 7th, the galley by which I pass; until I finally enter No. 8, our own sweet cabin, with the butter, the rats, and the German Jews.

We are again in the midst of the flying fish, but they interest me nothing like so vividly as they did when I first saw them in the Atlantic. Some of them take very long flights, as much as thirty or forty yards. Whole shoals of them fly away from the bows of the ship as she presses through the water.

On the 19th of January we crossed the Line, in longitude about 160°. We continue on a straight course, making an average of about 240 miles a day. It already begins to get cooler, as we are past the sun's greatest heat. It is a very idle, listless life, and I lie about on the hen-coops all day, reading, or sitting down now and then to write up this log, which has been written throughout amid discomfort and under considerable difficulties.

One of my fellow-passengers is enraged at the manner in which newspapers are treated while in transit. If what he says be true, I can easily understand how it is that so many newspapers miscarry—how so many numbers of "Punch" and the "Illustrated News" never reach their destination. My informant says that when an officer wants a newspaper, the mail-bag is opened, and he takes what he likes. He might just as well be permitted to have letters containing money. Many a poor colonial who can not write a letter buys and dispatches a newspaper to his friends at home to let them know he is alive, and this is the careless and unfaithful way in which the missive is treated by those to whom its carriage is intrusted. I heard many complaints while in Victoria of newspapers containing matter of interest never reaching their address, from which I infer that the same practice more or less prevails on the Atlantic route. It is really too bad.

As we steam north the weather grows fine, and we begin to have some splendid days and glorious sunsets; but we are all longing eagerly to arrive at our destination. At length, on the morning of the 24th of January, we discerned the high land of the island of Hawaii about seventy miles off, on our beam. That is the island where Captain Cook was murdered by the natives in 1779. We saw distinctly the high, conical volcanic mountain of Mauna Loa, 14,000 feet high, its peak showing clear above the gray clouds.

We steamed on all day, peering ahead, looking out for the land. Night fell, and still our port was not in sight. At length, at about ten, the light-house on the reef which stretches out in front of Honolulu shone out in the darkness. Then began a little display of fire-works, and rockets and blue-lights were exchanged between our ship and the shore. A rocket also shot up from a steamer to seaward, and she was made out to be the "Moses Taylor," the ship that is to take us on to San Francisco.

At about one in the morning we take our pilot on board, and shortly after my German friends rouse me with the intelligence that we are alongside the wharf. I am now, however, getting an "old bird;" my enthusiasm about novelty has gone down considerably, and I decline the pleasure of accompanying them on shore at this early hour. Honolulu will doubtless wait for me until morning.

HONOLULU, SANDWICH ISLANDS.

CHAPTER XXI.

HONOLULU AND THE ISLAND OF OAHU.

The Harbor of Honolulu.—Importance of its Situation.—The City.—Churches and Theatres.—The Post-office.—The Suburbs.—The King's Palace.—The Nuuanu Valley.—Poi.—People coming down the Valley.—The Pali.—Prospect from the Cliffs.—The Natives (Kanakas).—Divers.—The Women.—Drink Prohibition.—The Chinese.—Theatricals.—Musquitoes.

WHEN I came on deck in the early morning the sun was rising behind the mountains which form the background of Honolulu as seen from the harbor, tipping them with gold and red, and bathing the landscape in beauty. I could now survey at leisure the lovely scene.

I found we had entered a noble harbor, round which

the town of Honolulu is built, with its quays, warehouses, and ship-yards. Looking seaward, I observe the outer bay is nearly closed in at its lower extremity by the long ridge-like hill called Diamond Head. Nearer at hand, behind the town, is a remarkable eminence called Punchbowl Hill, evidently of volcanic origin, crowned with a battery, and guarding the entrance to the smaller bay which forms the harbor.

The entrance to the harbor is through a passage in one of the coral reefs which surround the island, the coral insects building upward from the submerged flanks of the land until the reefs emerge from the waves more or less distant from the shore. As the water at the shallowest part of the entrance is only about twenty-two feet, vessels of twenty-feet draught and over have to remain outside, where, however, there is good anchorage and shelter, unless when the wind blows strong from the south. The water inside the reefs is usually smooth, though the waves outside may be dashing themselves to foam on their crests.

A glance at the situation of the Sandwich Islands on the map will serve to show the important part they are destined to play in the future commerce of the Pacific. They lie almost directly in the course of all ships passing from San Francisco and Vancouver to China and Japan, as well as to New Zealand and Australia. They are almost equidistant from the coasts of Russia and America, being rather nearer to the American coast, from which they are distant about 2100 miles. They form, as it were, a stepping-stone on the great ocean highway of the Pacific between the East and the West—between the Old World and the New—as well as between the

newest and most prosperous settlements in the western states of America and Australia; and it is because Honolulu — the principal town in the island of Oahu, and the capital of the Sandwich Islands—possesses by far the best, most accessible, and convenient harbor, that it is a place likely to become of so much importance in the future. It has not been unusual to see as many as from a hundred to a hundred and fifty sail riding securely at anchor there.

As seen from the harbor, Honolulu is an extremely pretty place. It lies embowered in fresh green foliage, the roofs of the houses peeping up here and there from among the trees, while the waving fronds of the cocoanut palms rise in some places majestically above them, contrasting strangely with the volcanic crags and peaks which form the distant background. In the older part of the town, to the right, the houses are more scattered about; and from the first appearance of the place, one would scarcely suppose that it contained so large a population as twelve thousand, though many of the houses are doubtless hidden by the foliage and the undulations of the ground on which the place is built.

Behind the town, a plain of about two miles in width extends to the base of the mountain range which forms its background. The extraordinary shapes of the mountains—their rugged ravines and precipitous peaks—unmistakably denote the volcanic agencies that have been at work in forming the islands, and giving to the scenery its most marked features. Just at the back of the town, a deep valley, or rather gorge, runs through a break in the hills, the sides of which are covered with bright green foliage. The country, which rises gradually up this break in the mountains, is exceedingly picturesque. Altogether, the first sight of the place came fully up to my anticipations of the beauty of a tropical town in the Pacific.

I proceeded to take my first walk through Honolulu at half past five in the morning. It was the 25th of January—the dead of winter; but there is no winter in Honolulu. It is as warm as August is in England; and the warmth of the place all the year through is testified by the fact that there is not a dwelling-house chimney in the town. I walked along the shady streets up to the market-place, and there I found a number of the natives squatted on their haunches, selling plantains, oranges, bananas, fruits, and vegetables. I invested sixpence in an enormous bunch of bananas, which I carried back with me to the ship for the use of our party, very much to their enjoyment, for the fruit was in perfection.

In the course of the forenoon I proceeded to explore Honolulu at greater leisure. I found the central portion of the town consisted of regularly laid-out streets, many of the houses inclosed within gardens. The trees, standing here and there among the shops and warehouses, give them a fresh and primitive look. I pass several places of worship in going to the Post-office—the English Cathedral, chapels of American Congregationalists, Wesleyan Methodists, and Roman Catholics. There is also the Royal Hawaiian Theatre, and an Equestrian

Circus, as well as a Police-office. Police? "Yes; bless you, sir, we are civilized!"

I could see the Post-office a long way off before I reached it, standing in a small square at the head of one of the principal streets. It was easily known by the crowd of people, both natives and foreigners, on the steps; for the mail had just come in by the "Moses Taylor," and every body was anxious to know what had been the upshot of the European war and the siege of Paris. That war even threatens to disturb the peace of Honolulu itself; for there is now a French man-of-war at anchor in the harbor, the "Hamelin," watching a fine German merchant ship, the "Count Bismarck," that arrived a few days before the Frenchman. The Germans have taken the precaution to paint "Honolulu" on the stern of their vessel, and to place themselves under the protection of the Hawaiian government. So the commander of the French ship, finding he can make no capture here, has weighed anchor and steamed out of port, doubtless to lie in wait for the German vessel outside should she venture to put to sea.

I found the Post-office a sort of joint post-office and stationer's shop, the principal business consisting in the sale of newspapers. I was amazed to find that, though a steamer runs regularly from Honolulu to Australia, there is no postal communication with Victoria except *viâ* America and England! This is on account of the Victorian government refusing to subsidize the new Californian and Australian mail line. Should such a line become established and prosper, the Victorians fear that an advantage would be given to Sydney, and that Melbourne, instead of being on the main line of mail communication, as it now is, would be shunted on to a branch. But surely there is room enough for a mail line by both the Atlantic and Pacific routes, without occasion for jealousy either on the part of Sydney or Melbourne.

After settling my business at the Post-office, accompanied by my German-Yankee fellow-passenger, I took a stroll round the town and suburbs; though it is so open and green that it seems *all* suburbs. We invested a small sum in oranges, which we found in perfection, and sucked them as we went along in the most undignified way possible. We directed our steps to that part of the town where the better class seemed to reside, in cool, shady lanes, the houses embowered in large-leaved tropical trees, cocoanut, banana, bread-fruit, calabash, and other palms, with cycas and tree-ferns with stems some fifteen feet high. Flower-bearing shrubs also abounded, such as the hibiscus, mairi, of which the women make wreaths, and gardenia, with the flowers of which they also adorn themselves. In some of the gardens water was laid on, and pretty fountains were playing, from which it would appear that the water supply is good, and that there is a good head of it in some mountain reservoir above.

We strolled along to the right of the town, toward the high volcanic mountain on which the fort is situated, the long-extinct crater showing plainly on its summit. Some years since, when a French ship bombarded the town, the Kanakas who manned the fort threw down their sponges, rammers, and all, directly the first shot was fired, leaving the fort to take care of itself.

We returned to the harbor by way of the king's palace, which is in the centre of the town, and may be known

K

by the royal flag floating over it. The palace is built of coral stone, and is an unpretending building, reminding one of a French *maison de campagne*. It stands in about an acre of ground, ornamented with flowers, shrubs, and an avenue of kukui and koa trees. A native sentry stood at the gate in his uniform of blue coat and white trowsers, and with his musket duly shouldered in regulation style.

On the following day I made an excursion with an American gentleman, who is something of a naturalist, to the remarkable valley, or gorge, in the mountains at the back of the town, which had so attracted my notice when I first saw it from the deck of our ship. It is called the Nuuanu Valley, and is well worthy of a visit. The main street of the town leads directly up to the entrance to the valley; and on the road we passed many pretty low-roofed houses surrounded by beautifully-kept gardens, the houses being those of the chief merchants and consuls of the port. They looked quite cool and pleasant, embowered in green papyrus, tamarind, and palm trees, which shaded them from the hot tropical sun with their large-leaved foliage. I find the sun now, in winter time, so hot that it is almost intolerable. What must it be in summer?

As we proceed we reach the fertile land, which nearly all lies at the foot of the mountains, the long disintegration of the high ground having left a rich deposit for vegetable growth. Some patches of arrowroot lie close to the road, irrigated by the streams that run down from the mountain above. But the principal crop is the taro plant (*Arum esculentum*), from which the native food of *poi* is made. Let me say a few words about this *poi*, as it forms the main staple of Hawaiian food. The taro is grown in pits or beds, kept very wet; in which case, urged by the natural heat of the climate, it grows with immense rapidity and luxuriance. It is the succulent root which is used for food. It is pounded into a semi-fluid mess, after which it is allowed to stand a few days and ferment; it is then worked about with the hands until it acquires the proper consistency for eating, when it is stored in gourds and calabashes. It must be of a certain thickness, neither too soft nor too firm, something of the consistency of thick flour-paste, though glutinous, and it is eaten in the following manner. Two fingers are dipped into the pot containing the *poi*, and turned rapidly round until a sufficient quantity of the paste adheres to them; then, by a rapid motion, the lot is wriggled out of the pot, conveyed into the mouth, and the fingers are sucked clean. Young girls dip in only one finger at a time, the men two fingers. I was frequently invited to dip my fingers into the *poi* and try it, being told that it was very good, but I had not the courage.*

But to proceed on my walk up the Nuuanu Valley. About two miles from the town we came to a very pretty villa on one side of the road, with some large native huts, in a shady garden, on the other. We find that this villa is the country residence of Queen Emma. Looking in through the gate of the garden opposite, who should I see but our quondam lady passenger from Sydney, Miss

* The poi is said to grow so abundantly and with so little labor in the Sandwich Islands, that it tends to encourage the natural indolence of the people. A taro pit no bigger than an ordinary drawing-room will keep a man in food a whole year. Nature is so prolific that labor is scarcely requisite in these hot climates. Thus the sun may be a great demoralizer.

Ribbids, reclining on a bank in the most luxurious fashion! She had walked up the valley alone, she informed us, and the natives had been most kind to her, giving her fruits, and wreaths of flowers for her adornment.

Proceeding up the valley, we find ourselves on high ground, our road having been for the most part up hill. Looking back, a charming view lies spread before us. The sky is brilliant and unclouded. Below us lies the town and harbor, the blue sea as smooth as a mirror, shipping dotting the bay, and a silvery line of water breaking along the distant reef. We begin to catch the breeze blowing from the upper part of the valley, and it feels fresh and invigorating after toiling under the noon-day sun.

As we ascend the road we meet several of the native girls coming down on horseback. They seem to have quite a passion for riding in the island, and have often to be prevented racing through the streets of Honolulu. The horses are of a poor breed; but the women, who sit astride like the men, seem plucky riders, their long, flowing dresses making respectable riding-habits. Most of the girls wore garlands of *ohelo* and other flowers round their heads, being very fond of ornament.

Shortly after meeting the girls a man passed us, at the usual jog canter, with a coffin slung on the saddle in front of him, and after him followed another rider with the lid. We remarked upon the strange burden, and I asked of the first man who was going to be buried. "My wife," he replied; "me pay seventy-five dollars for um coffin." He grinned, and seemed quite pleased with his coffin, which was really a handsome one.

As we ascend, we seem to get quite into the bush.

Thick vegetation spreads up the steep hills on each side of us. I can now understand how difficult it must be to travel through a tropical forest. The brushwood grows so close together, and is so intertwined, that it would appear almost impossible to force one's way through it. The mountains rise higher and higher as we advance, and are covered with lovely light green foliage. The hills seem to have been thrown up evenly in ridges, each ridge running up the mountain side having its separate peak. Here and there a small cataract leaps down the face of a rock, shining like a silver thread, and disappearing in the brushwood below until it comes down to swell the mountain torrent running by our side close to the road.

At a turn of the road we suddenly encountered a number of men coming down from some cattle ranch in the hills, mounted *à la Mexicaine*, with lassos on their saddles and heavy whips in their hands, driving before them a few miserable cattle. There seemed to be about eighteen men to a dozen small beasts. I guess that a couple of Australian stockmen, with their whips, could easily have driven before them the whole lot—men, horses, and cattle.

We were now about seven miles from Honolulu, and very near the end of our up-hill journey. After walking up a steeper ascent than usual, the scenery becoming even more romantic and picturesque, we pass through a thicket of hibiscus and other trees, when suddenly, on turning round a small pile of volcanic rocks, we emerge on an open space, and the grand precipice, or Pali, of the Nuuanu Valley bursts upon us with startling effect.

Here, in some tremendous convulsion of Nature, the

mountain ridge seems to have been suddenly rent and burst through toward its summit, and we look down over a precipice some five hundred feet deep. It is possible to wind down the face of the rock by a narrow path, but, having no mind to make the descent, we rest and admire the magnificent prospect before and below us. Under the precipice is a forest, so near to the foot of the rock that one might easily pitch a stone into it. Over the forest stretches a lovely country, green and fresh, dotted with hills and woods. The sea, about seven miles off, bounds the view, with its silver line of breakers on the outer reef. The long line of white looks beautiful on the calm blue sea, with the sun shining on it. The country before us did not seem to be much cultivated. Here and there, below us, a native hut might be discerned amid the trees, but no large dwelling or village was in sight.

The rent in the mountain through which we have passed is torn and rugged. Immense masses of black rock, several hundred feet in height, and nearly perpendicular, form the two sides of the rift. On one side the mountain seems to rise straight up into the air until it is lost in a white cloud; on the other side the rock is equally precipitous, but not quite so high. From this last the range stretches away in a semicircle, ending along the coast some twenty miles distant.

A few more words about the natives, whom I have as yet only incidentally alluded to. Of course I saw a good deal of them, in one way or another, during my brief stay at Honolulu. We had scarcely got alongside the wharf ere the Kanakas—as they are called—came aboard, popping their heads in and out of the cabins, some selling bananas and oranges, others offering coral and curiosities, but most of them to examine the ship out of mere curiosity. From what I observed, I should say that the Kanakas are of the same stock as the Maoris, not so much tattoo-marked, much more peacefully inclined, and probably more industrious. Some of the men are tall and handsome, which is more than I can say of the women. The men do not work very heartily on day-wages, but well enough when paid by the piece. Here, on the wharf, they get a dollar for a day's work, and a dollar and a half for night-work. They are employed in filling the coal-bunkers and unloading the ship.

The Kanakas are capital divers, and work almost as well in the water as out of it. I saw one of them engaged in repairing the bottom of the "Moses Taylor," by which I am to sail for San Francisco. He is paid three dollars for a general inspection, or five dollars for a day's work. I saw him go down to nail a piece of copper-sheathing on the bottom, where it had been damaged in grounding upon a rock when last coming out of San Francisco harbor. He took down about thirty copper nails in his mouth, with the hammer and sheet of copper in his hand, coming up to breathe after each nail was knocked in. I could hear the loud knocking as he drove the nails into the ship's side. At the same time, some Kanaka boys were playing about in the water near at hand, diving for stones or bits of money. The piece was never allowed to sink more than a few feet before a boy was down after it and secured it. They never missed the smallest silver bit. It seemed to me as if some of them could swim before they could walk.

As for the women, although travelers have spread abroad reports of their beauty, I was unable to see it. While the "Moses Taylor" lay in the harbor, the saloon was sometimes full of native girls, who came down from the country to see the ship and admire themselves in the two large saloon mirrors, before which they stood laughing and giggling. Their usual dress consists of a long, loose gown, reaching down to the ankles, with no fastening round the waist; and their heads and necks are usually adorned with leaves or flowers of some sort. They seemed to me very like the Maori women, but without the blue tattoo-mark on the lips; nor are their features so strongly marked, though they had the same wide faces, black eyes, full nostrils, and large lips. Their skins are of various hues, from a yellow to a dusky brown. Their feet and hands are usually small and neat.

I am told that the race is degenerating and dying out fast. The population of the islands is said to be little more than one tenth of what it was when Captain Cook visited them, and this falling off is reported to be mainly due to the unchaste habits of the women. The missionaries have long been trying to make a salutary impression on them, but, though the natives profess Christianity in various forms, it is to be feared that it is a profession, and little more. The king, also, has tried to make them more moral by putting in force a sort of Maine liquor-law; but every ship that enters the harbor is beset by natives wanting drink, and they adopt various methods of evading the law. The license charged by the government to a retailer of spirits is a thousand dollars a year; but he must not sell liquor to any foreigner on Sunday, nor to any native at any time, under a penalty of five hundred dollars. This penalty is rigidly exacted; and if the spirit-dealer is unable to pay the fine, he is put on to the coral-reefs, to work at twenty-five cents a day until he has worked off the amount. Accordingly, the liquor-trade is followed by very few persons, and the consumption of drink by the natives is very much curtailed, compared, for instance, with what it is among the drink-consuming natives of New Zealand, who are allowed to swallow the "fire-water," to the great profit of the publicans and to their own demoralization, without any restriction whatever.

I find the government here also levies a very considerable sum from the Chinese for the privilege of selling opium. It is put up annually to auction, and in some years as much as forty-five thousand dollars have been paid for the monopoly, though this year it has brought considerably less, in consequence of the dullness of trade. From this circumstance it will be inferred that there is a considerable Chinese population in the place. Indeed, some of the finest stores in Honolulu are kept by Chinamen. I did not at first observe many of these people about; but afterward, when exploring, I found whole back streets full of Chinamen's huts and houses.

From the announcements of theatrical and other entertainments I see about, the people here must be very fond of amusement. Indeed, Honolulu seems to be one of the great centres of pleasure in the Pacific. All wandering "stars" come hither. When I was at Auckland, in New Zealand, I went to the theatre to see a troupe of Japanese jugglers. I had seen the identical troupe in London, and "All Right" was among them. They were on their way to Honolulu, to star it here before returning to Japan. Charles Mathews, with whom I made the voyage from Melbourne to Sydney, is also advertised to appear, "for a few nights only," at the Royal Hawaiian Theatre.* And now here is The Bandman, my fellow-passenger from Auckland, advertised, in big placards, as "The World-renowned Shakspearian Player," etc., who

* I find in a Californian paper the following amusing account, by Mr. Mathews himself, of his appearance before a Honolulu audience:

"At Honolulu, one of the loveliest little spots upon earth, I acted one night 'by command, and in the presence of his majesty Kamehameha V., King of the Sandwich Islands' (not Hoky Poky Wonky Fong,' as erroneously reported), and a memorable night it was. On my way to the quaint little Hawaiian theatre, situated in a rural lane, in the midst of a pretty garden, glowing with gaudy tropical flowers, and shaded by cocoa-trees, bananas, banyans, and tamarinds, I met the play-bill of the evening. A perambulating Kanaka (or native black gentleman), walking between two boards (called in London, figuratively, 'a sandwich man,' but here, of course, literally so), carried aloft a large illuminated white lantern, with the announcement in the Kanaka language to catch the attention of the colored inhabitants: 'Charles Mathews: Keaka Keia Po (Theatre open this evening). Ka uku o Ke Komo ana (reserved seats, dress circle), $2 50; Nohi mua (Parquette), $1; Noho ho (Kanaka pit), 75 cents.' I found the theatre (to use the technical expression) 'crammed to suffocation,' which merely means 'very full,' though, from the state of the thermometer on this occasion, 'suffocation' was not so incorrect a description as usual. A really elegant-looking audience (tickets 10s. each), evening dresses, uniforms of every cut and every country. 'Chieftesses' and ladies of every tinge, in dresses of every color, flowers and jewels in profusion, satin play-bills, fans going, windows and doors all open, an outside staircase leading straight into the dress-circle, without lobby, check-taker, or money-taker. Kanaka women in the garden below selling bananas and pea-nuts by the glare of flaring torches on a sultry tropical moonlight night. The whole thing was like nothing but a midsummer night's dream. And was it nothing to see a pit full of Kanakas, black, brown, and whitey-brown (till lately cannibals), showing their white teeth, grinning and enjoying 'Patter v. Clatter' as much as a few years ago they would have enjoyed the roasting of a missionary or the baking of a baby? It was certainly a page in one's life never to be forgotten."

is about to give a series of such and such representations at the same place.

Beautiful though the island of Oahu may be, I soon found that I could not live there. Even in winter it was like living in a hot-house. The air was steamy with heat, and frightfully relaxing. At intervals my nose streamed with blood, and I grew sensibly thinner. Then I suffered terribly from the musquitoes; my ankles were quite swollen with their bites, and in a day or two more I should have been dead-lame. There are, besides, other tormentors—small flies, very like the Victorian sand-flies, that give one a nasty sting. I was very glad, therefore, after four days' stay at Honolulu, to learn that the "Moses Taylor" was ready to sail for San Francisco.

CHAPTER XXII.

HONOLULU TO SAN FRANCISCO.

Departure from Honolulu. — Wreck of the "Saginaw." — The "Moses Taylor."—The Accommodation.—The Company on Board.—Behavior of the Ship.—Death of a Passenger.—Feelings on Landing in a new Place.—Approach the Golden Gate.—Close of the Pacific Log.—First Sight of America.

The departure of the "Moses Taylor" was evidently regarded as a great event at Honolulu. At the hour appointed for our sailing a great crowd had assembled on the wharf. All the notabilities of the place seemed to be there. First and foremost was the king of the Sandwich Islands himself, Kamehameha V.— a jolly-looking, portly old fellow, standing about six feet high, and weighing over five-and-twenty stone — every inch and ounce a king. Then there were the chief ministers of his court, white, yellow, and dusky. There were also English, Americans, and Chinese, with a crowd of full-blooded Kanakas, all very orderly and admiring; and round the outskirts of the throng were several carriages filled with native ladies.

Punctually at half past 4 P.M. we got away from our moorings, with "three cheers for Honolulu," which were raised by a shipwrecked crew we had on board. Leaving the pier, we shortly passed through the opening in the reef which forms the entrance to the harbor, and steamed steadily eastward in the direction of San Francisco.

I must explain how it was that the "three cheers for Honolulu" were raised. The "Saginaw" was an American war-ship that had been sent with a contract party to Midway Island, in the North Pacific—some fifteen hundred miles west-northwest of the Sandwich Islands—to blast the coral reef there, in order to provide a harborage for the line of large steamers running between San Francisco and China. The money voted for the purpose by the government having been spent, the "Saginaw" was on its return voyage from the island, when the captain determined to call at Ocean Island to see if there were any shipwrecked crews there; but, in a fog, the ship ran upon a coral reef, and was itself wrecked. The men, to the number of ninety-three, contrived to reach the island, where they remained sixty-nine days, during which they lived mostly on seal-meat and the few stores they had been able to save from their ship. The island itself is entirely barren, containing only a few bushes and a sort of dry grass, with millions of rats, supposed to have bred from rats landed from shipwrecked vessels. Strict military discipline was preserved by the officers, and the men, as a body, behaved remarkably well.

At length, no vessel appearing in sight, four of the sailors volunteered to row in an open boat to the Sandwich Islands—more than a thousand miles distant—for the purpose of reporting the wreck of the ship, and sending relief to those on the island. The boat departed, reached the reef which surrounds Kauai, an island to the northwest of Oahu, and was there wrecked, only one of the men succeeding in reaching the shore. So soon as the intelligence of the wreck of the "Saginaw" reached Honolulu, the government immediately dispatched a steamer to take the men off the desert island, and hence the enthusiastic cheers for Honolulu raised by the rescued officers and men of the American ship, who are now all on board the "Moses Taylor," on their way back to San Francisco.

I must now describe my new ship. She is called the "Rolling Moses," but with what justice I am as yet unable to say. She certainly looks singularly top-hampered—altogether unlike any British ship that I have ever seen. She measures twice as much in the beam as the "City of Melbourne;" is about 2000 tons register; is flat bottomed, and draws about fourteen feet of water when laden. She looks like a great big house afloat, or rather a row of houses more than thirty feet high. The decks seemed piled one atop of the other quite promiscuously. First there is the dining saloon, with cabins all round it; above is the drawing-room, with more cabins; then above that is the hurricane deck, with numerous deck-houses for the captain and officers; and then, towering above all, there is the large beam-engine right between the paddle-boxes. Altogether it looks a very unwieldy affair, and I would certainly much rather trust myself to such a ship as the "City of Melbourne." It strikes me that, in a heavy sea, "Moses's" hull would run some risk of parting company with the immediate structure above.

The cabin accommodation is, however, greatly superior to that of my late ship—there is so much more room, and the whole arrangements for the comfort of the passengers are all that could be desired. The Americans certainly do seem to understand comfort in traveling.

The stewards and people about are civil and obliging, and don't seem to be always looking for a "tip," as is so customary on board an English boat. This ship also is cleaner than the one I have left—there are none of those hideous smells that so disgusted me on board "The City." The meals are better, and there is much greater variety—lots of different little dishes—of meat, stews, mashed potatoes, squashes, hominy or corn-cake, and such like. So far as the living goes, therefore, I think I shall get on very well on board the "Moses Taylor."

The weather is wet, and what sailors call "dirty," and it grows sensibly colder. As there is no pleasure in remaining on deck, I keep for the most part below. I like my company very much—mostly consisting of the ship-wrecked men of the "Saginaw." They are nice, lively fellows; they encourage me to talk, and we have many a hearty laugh together. Some of them give me no end of yarns about the late war, in which they were engaged; and they tell me (whether true or not, I have no means of knowing) that the captain of the ship we are in was first lieutenant of the "pirate" ship "Florida." I have not found among my companions as yet any of that self-assertion or pride of nationality said to distinguish the Yankee, nor have I heard a word from them of hostility to John Bull. Indeed, for the purpose of drawing them out, I began bragging a little about England, but they let me have my own way without contradiction. They say nothing about politics, or, if they allude to the subject, express very moderate opinions. Altogether, I get on with them, and like them very much.

The "Moses Taylor" proves a steadier sea-boat than I expected from her built-up appearance. She certainly gives many a long, steady roll, but there is little pitching or tossing. When the sea strikes her she quivers all over in a rather uncomfortable way. She is rather an old ship; she formerly ran between Vancouver and San Francisco, and is certainly the worse for wear. The huge engine-shafts shake the beams which support them; the pieces of timber tremble under the heavy strokes of the engine, and considerable apertures open from time to time in the deck as she heaves to and fro. The weather, however, is not stormy, and the ship will doubtless carry us safely to the end of our voyage, going steadily, as she does, at the rate of about eight knots an hour; and as the distance between Honolulu and the American coast is about 2100 miles, we shall probably make the voyage in about ten days.

On the eighth day after leaving Honolulu an incident occurred which made a startling impression on me. While we were laughing and talking in the cabin—kept down there by the rain—we were told that a poor man who had been ailing since we left port had breathed his last. It seemed that he had some affection of the gullet which prevented his swallowing food. The surgeon on board did not possess the necessary instrument to enable him to introduce food into his stomach, so that he literally died of starvation. He occupied the berth exactly opposite mine, and, though I knew he was ill, I had no idea that his end was so near. He himself, however, had been aware of it, and anxiously wished that he might survive until he reached San Francisco, where his wife was to meet him at the landing. But it was not to be, and his sudden decease gave us all a great shock.

We had our breakfast and dinner that day while the

body was lying in the cabin. We heard the carpenter busy on the main deck knocking together a coffin for its reception. Every time he knocked a nail in, I thought of the poor dead fellow who lay beside us. I began to speculate as to the various feelings with which passengers land in a new place. Some are mere passing visitors like myself, bent on seeing novel sights; some are going thither, full of hope, to make a new settlement in life; some are returning home, expecting old friends waiting on the pier-head to meet and welcome them. But there are sad meetings too; and here there will be an anxious wife waiting at the landing-place only to receive the dead body of her husband.

But a truce to moralizing, for we are approaching the Golden Gate. I must now pack up my things and finish my log. I have stuck to it at all hours and in all weathers; jotted down little bits from time to time in the intervals of sea-sickness, toothache, and tic douloureux; written under a tropical burning sun, and amid the drizzle and downpour of the North Pacific; but I have found pleasure in keeping it up, because I know that it will be read with pleasure by those for whom it is written, and it will serve to show that amid all my wanderings I have never forgotten the Old Folks at Home.

At half past four on the morning of the tenth day from our leaving Honolulu we sighted the light-house at the Golden Gate, which forms the entrance to the spacious bay or harbor of San Francisco. Suddenly there is a great scampering about of the passengers, a general packing up of baggage, a brushing of boots, hats, and clothes, and a dressing up in shore-going "togs." The steward comes round to look after his perquisites, and every one is in a bustle about something or other.

I took a last rest in my bunk—for it was still early morning—until I was told that we were close alongshore, and then I jumped up, went on deck, and saw America for the first time.

CHAPTER XXIII.

SAN FRANCISCO TO SACRAMENTO.

Landing at San Francisco.—The Golden City.—The Streets.—The Business Quarter.—The Chinese Quarter.—The Touters.—Leave San Francisco.—The Ferry-boat to Oakland.—The Bay of San Francisco.—Landing on the Eastern Shore.—American Railway Carriages.—The Pullman's Cars.—Sleeping Berths.—Unsavory Chinamen.—The Country.—City of Sacramento.

WE have passed in from the Pacific through the Golden Gate, swung round toward the south, and then, along the eastern margin of the peninsula which runs up to form the bay, the City of San Francisco lies before me! A great mass of houses and warehouses, fronted by a long line of wharves, extends along the water's edge. Masses of houses, tipped with occasional towers and spires, rise up on the high ground behind, crowning the summits of Telegraph, Russian, and Clay Street Hills.

But we have little time to take note of the external features of the city, for we are already alongside the pier. Long before the gangways can be run out and laid between the ship and the wharf, there is a rush of hotel runners on board, calling out the names of their respective hotels and distributing their cards. There is a tremendous hurry-scurry. The touters make dashes at the baggage and carry it off, sometimes in different directions, each hoping to secure a customer for his hotel. Thus, in a very few minutes, the ship was cleared, all the passengers were bowling along toward their several destinations, and in a few minutes I found myself safely deposited in "The Brooklyn," a fine large hotel in Bush Street, situated in the business part of the town, with dwellings interspersed among the business houses.

It is not necessary to describe San Francisco. Travelers have done that over and over again. Indeed, there is not much about it that is of any great interest except to business men. One part of the city is very like another. I was told that some of the finest buildings were of the Italian order, but I should say that by far the greater number were of the Ramshackle order. Although the first house in the place was only built in 1835, the streets nearest to the wharves look already old and worn out. They are, for the most part, of wood, and their paint is covered with dirt. But, though prematurely old, they are by no means picturesque. Of course, in so large a place, with a population of 150,000, and already so rich and prosperous though so young, there are many fine buildings and some fine streets. The hotels carry away the palm as yet, the Grand Hotel at the corner of Market and New Montgomery Streets being the finest. There are also churches, theatres, hospitals, markets, and all the other appurtenances of a great city.

I had not for a long time seen such a bustle of traffic as presented itself in the streets of San Francisco. The whole place seemed to be alive. Foot-passengers jostled each other; drays and wagons were rolling about; business men were clustered together in some streets, apparently "on change;" with all the accompaniments of noise, and bustle, and turmoil of a city full of life and traffic. The money-brokers' shops are very numerous in the two finest streets—Montgomery and California

Streets. Nearly every other shop there belongs to a money-broker or money-changer. Strange to see the piles of glistening gold in the windows—ten to twenty dollar pieces, and heaps of greenbacks.

John Chinaman is here, I see, in great force. There are said to be as many as 30,000 in the city and neighborhood. I wonder these people do not breed a plague. I went through their quarter one evening, and was surprised and disgusted with what I saw. Chinese men and women of the lowest class were swarming in their narrow alleys. Looking down into small cellars, I saw from ten to fifteen men and women living in places which two white men would not sleep in. The adjoining streets smelt most abominably. The street I went through must be one of the worst, and I was afterward told that it was "dangerous" to pass through it. I observed a large wooden screen at each end of it, as if for the purpose of shutting it off from the white people's quarter.

One of the nuisances we had to encounter in the streets was that of railway touters. No sooner did we emerge from the hotel door than men lying in wait pounced upon us, offering tickets by this route, that route, and the other route to New York. I must have had a very "new-chum" sort of look, for I was accosted no less than three times one evening by different touting gentlemen. One wished to know if I had come from Sydney, expressing his admiration of Australia generally. Another asked if I was "going East," offering to sell me a through ticket at a reduced price. The third also introduced the Sydney topic, telling me, by way of inducement to buy a ticket of him, that he had "worked there." I shook them all off, knowing them to be dangerous customers. I heard some strange stories of young fellows making friends with such strangers, and having drinks with them. The drink is drugged, and the Sydney swell, on his way to New York, finds himself next morning in the streets, minus purse, watch, and every thing of value about him.

There is only one railway route as yet across the Rocky Mountains, by the Western, Central, and Union

Pacific, as far as Omaha, but from that point there are various lines to New York, and it was to secure passengers by these respective routes that the touters were so busily at work. All the hotels, bars, and stores are full of their advertisements: "The shortest route to the East" — "Pullman's Palace cars run on this Line"— "The Route of all Nations"— "The Grand Route, *viâ* Niagara" —such are a few specimens of these urgent announcements. I decided to select the route *viâ* Chicago, Detroit, Niagara, and down the Hudson River to New York, and made my arrangements accordingly.

I left San Francisco on the morning of the 8th of February. The weather was cold compared with that of the Sandwich Islands, yet there were few signs of winter. There was no snow on the ground, and at midday it was agreeable and comparatively mild. I knew, however, that as soon as we left the shores of the Pacific, and ascended the western slopes of the Rocky Mountains, if not before, we should encounter thorough winter weather, and I prepared myself with coats and wrappers as a defense from the cold.

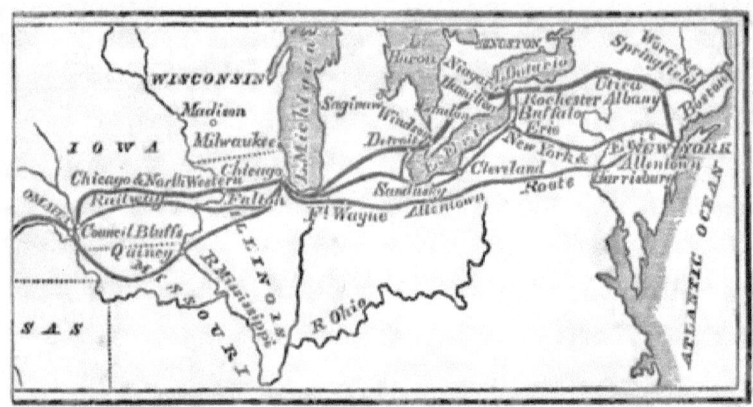

My fellow-voyager from New Zealand, the German-American of whom I have spoken above, and who seemed to take quite a liking for me, accompanied me down to the wharf, where we parted with mutual regret. It was necessary for me to cross the bay by a ferry-boat to Oakland, where the train is made up and starts for Sacramento. There was a considerable crowd round the baggage-office, where I gave up my trunks, and obtained, in exchange, two small brass checks, which will enable me to reclaim them on the arrival of the train at Omaha. I proceeded down the pier and on to the ferry-boat. Indeed, I was on it before I was aware. It looked so like a part of the wharf, and was so surrounded by piles and wooden erections, that I did not know I was on its deck, and was inquiring about its arrival to take us off, when I found the huge boat gradually moving away from the pier!

It was a regular American ferry-boat, of the same build fore and aft, capable of going alike backward or forward, and with a long bridge at each end, ready to be let down at the piers on either side of the bay, so as to enable carts or carriages to be driven directly on to the main deck, which was just like a large covered yard, standing level with the wharf. Over this was an upper deck with a nice saloon, where I observed notices stuck up of "No spitting allowed," showing that there was a greater consideration for ladies here than there was on board the "Moses Taylor," where spittle and quids were constantly shooting about the decks, with very little regard for passers-by, whether ladies or gentlemen.

Steaming away from the pier, we obtained a splendid view of the city behind us. The wharves along its front were crowded with shipping of all sorts, among which we could observe the huge American three-decker river steamers, Clyde-built clippers, brigs, schooners, and a multitude of smaller craft. Down the bay we see the green hills rising in the distance, fading away in the gray of the morning. Close on our left is a pretty island, about half way across the bay, in the centre of which is a green hill—what seemed to Australian eyes good pasture-land; and I could discern what I took to be a station or farm-house.

In about an hour we found ourselves nearing the land on the eastern shore of the bay, where we observe the railway comes out to meet us. The water on this side is so shoal for a distance from the shore that no ships of any considerable burden can float in it, so that the railway is carried out on piles into the deep water for a distance of nearly a mile. Here we land, and get into the train waiting alongside; then the engine begins to snort, and we are away. As we move off from the waters of San Francisco Bay, I feel I have made another long stride on the road toward England.

We continue for some time rolling along the rather shaky timber pier on which the rails are laid. At last we reach the dry land, and speed through Oakland—a pretty town—rattling through the streets just like an omnibus or tramway car, ringing a bell to warn people of the approach of the cars. We stop at nearly every station, and the local traffic seems large. Farm-land and nice rolling country stretches away on either side of the track.

From looking out of the carriage windows, I begin to take note of the carriage itself—a real American railway carriage. It is a long car with a passage down the middle. On each side of this passage are seats for two persons, facing the engine; but, the backs being reversible, a party of four can sit as in an English carriage, face to face. At each end of the carriage is a stove, and a filter of iced water. The door at each end leads out on to a platform, enabling the conductor to walk through the train from one end to the other.

This arrangement for the conductor, by the way, is rather a nuisance. He comes round six or seven times during the twenty-four hours, often during the night, perhaps at a time when you are trying to snatch a few

L

minutes' nap, and you find your shoulder tapped, and a bull's eye turned full upon you, with a demand for "tickets." This, however, is to be avoided by affixing a little card in your hat, which the conductor gives you, so that by inspection he knows at once whether his passenger is legitimate or not.

I did not travel by one of "Pullman's Silver Palace Drawing-room Cars," though I examined them, and admired their many comforts. By day they afford roomy accommodation, with ample space for walking about, or for playing at cards or chess on the tables provided for the purpose. At night a double row of comfortable-looking berths are made up, a curtain being drawn along their front to render them as private as may be, and leaving only a narrow passage along the centre of the car. At the end of the car are conveniences for washing, iced water, and the never-failing stove.

The use of the sleeping-car costs about three or four dollars extra per night. I avoided this expense, and contrived a very good substitute in my second-class car. Fortunately we were not very full of passengers; and by making use of four seats, or two benches, turning one of the seat-backs round, and placing the seat bottoms lengthwise, I arranged a tolerably good sleeping-place for the night; but, had the carriage been full, and the occupants been under the necessity of sitting up during the six days the journey lasted, I should imagine that it must have become almost intolerable by the time we reached Omaha.

There were some rather unpleasant fellow-travelers in my compartment—several unsavory Chinamen, smoking very bad tobacco; and other smoking gentlemen, who make the second-class compartments their rendezvous.

But for the thorough draft we obtained from time to time on the passage of the conductor, the atmosphere would be, as indeed it often was, of a very disagreeable character.

About forty-two miles from San Francisco, I find we are already in among the hills of a range, and winding in and out through pretty valleys, where all available land is used for farming purposes. We round some curves that look almost impossible, and I begin to feel the oscillation of the carriages, by no means unlike the rolling of a ship at sea. I often wished that it had been summer instead of winter, that I might better have enjoyed the beauty of the scenery as we sped along. As it was, I could see that the country must be very fine under a summer sky. We have met with no snow at present, being still on the sunny slopes of the Pacific; nor have we as yet mounted up to any very high elevation.

We were not long in passing through the range of hills of which I have spoken, and then we emerged upon the plains, which continued until we reached Sacramento, the capital of the state. The only town of any importance that we have yet passed was Stockton, a place about midway between San Francisco and Sacramento, where we now are. Down by the river-side I see some large lumber-yards, indicative of a considerable timber trade. The wharves were dirty, as wharves generally are, but they were busy with traffic. The town seemed well laid out in broad streets, the houses being built widely apart, each with its garden about it, while long lines of trees run along most of the streets. Prominent among the buildings is the large new Senate House or Capitol, a really grand feature of the city. The place having been originally built of wood, it has been liable to conflagrations, which have more than once nearly destroyed it. Floods have also swept over the valley, and carried away large portions of the town; but, having been rebuilt on piles ten feet above the original level, it is now believed to be secure against injury from this cause.

Sacramento is the terminus of the Western Pacific Railway, from which the Central Pacific extends east toward the Rocky Mountains. The railway work-shops of the Company are located here, and occupy a large extent of ground. They are said to be very complete and commodious.

Many of the passengers by the train, whom we had brought on from San Francisco or picked up along the road, descended here, and I was very glad to observe that among them were the Chinamen, who relieved us from their farther most disagreeable odor. After a short stoppage and rearrangement of the train, we were off again, toiling up the slopes of the Sierra Nevada—the Switzerland of California.

CHAPTER XXIV.

ACROSS THE SIERRA NEVADA.

Rapid Ascent.—The Trestle-bridges.—Mountain Prospects.—"Placers."—Sunset.—Cape Horn.—Alta.—The Sierras by Night.—Contrast of Temperatures.—The Snow-sheds.—The Summit.—Reno.—Breakfast at Humboldt.—The Sage Brush.—Battle Mount.—Shoshonie Indians.—Ten-mile Cañon.—Elko Station.—Great American Desert.—Arrival at Ogden.

We had now begun the ascent of the difficult mountain country that separates the eastern from the western states of the Union, and through which the Central Pacific Railway has been recently constructed and completed—one of the greatest railway works of our time. As we advance the scenery changes rapidly. Instead of the flat and comparatively monotonous country we have for some time been passing through, we now cross deep gullies, climb up steep ascents, and traverse lovely valleys. Sometimes we seem to be inclosed in mountains with an impenetrable barrier before us; but, rushing into a tunnel, we shortly emerge on the other side, to find ourselves steaming along the edge of a precipice.

What struck me very much was the apparent slimness of the trestle-bridges over which we were carried across the gullies, in the bottom of which mountain torrents were dashing some fifty or a hundred feet below us. My first experience of such a crossing was quite startling. I was standing on the platform of the last car, looking back at the fast vanishing scene—a winding valley shut in by pine-clad mountains which we had for some time been ascending—when, glancing down on the track, instead of solid earth, I saw the ground, through the open timbers of the trestle-bridge, at least sixty feet below me! The timber road was only the width of the single iron track, so that any one looking out of the side carriage-windows would see sixty feet down into space. The beams on which the trestle-bridge is supported are, in some cases, rested on stone, but oftener they are not. It is not easy to describe the sensation first felt on rattling over one of these trembling viaducts, with a lovely view down some mountain gorge, and then, perhaps, suddenly plunging into a dark cutting on the other side of the trestle. But use is every thing, and before long I got quite accustomed to the sensation of looking down through the open wood-work of the line on to broken ground and mountain torrents rushing a hundred feet or more below me.

We left Sacramento at 2 P.M., and evening was coming on as we got into the mountains. Still, long before sunset we saw many traces of large "placers," where whole sides of the hills had been dug out and washed away in the search for gold, the water being brought over the hill-tops by various ingenious methods. Sometimes, too, we came upon signs of active mining, in the water-courses led across valleys at levels above us, consisting of wooden troughs supported on trestles similar to those we are so frequently crossing. In one place I saw a party of men busily at work along the mountain side, preparatory to letting the water in upon the auriferous ground they were exploring.

I stood for more than two hours on the platform at the rear of the train, never tired of watching the wonderful scenery that continually receded from my gaze—sometimes the track suddenly disappearing as we rounded a curve, and then, looking ahead, I would find that an entirely new prospect was opening into view.

Never shall I forget the lovely scene that evening when the golden sun was setting far away on the Pacific coast. The great red orb sank slowly behind a low hill at the end of the valley which stretched away on our right far beneath us. The pine-trees shone red in the departing sunlight for a short time; then the warm, dusky glimmer gradually faded away on the horizon, and all was over. The scene now looked more dreary, the mountains more rugged, and every thing more desolate than before.

Up we rushed, still ascending the mountain slopes, winding in and out, higher and higher, the mountains becoming more rugged and wild, and the country more broken and barren looking. Crossing slowly another trestle-bridge seventy-five feet high, at the upper part of a valley, we rounded a sharp curve, and found ourselves on a lofty mountain side along which the road is cut, with a deep glen lying 2500 feet below us wrapped in the shades of evening. It seems to be quite night down there, and the trees are so shrouded in gloom that I can scarcely discern them in the bottom of that awful chasm. I can only clearly see defined against the sky above me the rugged masses of overhanging rock, black-looking and terrible.

I find, on inquiry, that this part of the road is called "Cape Horn." The bluffs at this point are so precipitous, that when the railroad was made, the workmen had to be lowered down the face of the rock by ropes, and held on by men above, until they were enabled to blast for themselves a foothold on the side of the precipice. We have now ascended to a height of nearly 3200 feet above the level of the sea, and, as may be inferred, the night air grows sharp and cold. As little more can be seen for the present, I am under the necessity of taking shelter in the car.

At half past six we stopped for tea at Alta, 207 miles from San Francisco, at an elevation of 3600 feet above the sea. Here I had a good meal for a dollar—the first since leaving 'Frisco. Had I known of the short stoppages and the distant refreshing-places along the route, I would certainly have provided myself with a well-stored luncheon-basket before setting out; but it is now too late.

After a stoppage of twenty minutes, the big bell tolled, and we seated ourselves in the cars again, and away we went as before, still toiling up hill. We are really climbing now. I can hear it by the strong snorts of the engine, and see it by the steepness of the track. I long to be able to see around me, for we are passing some of the grandest scenery of the line. The stars are now shining brightly overhead, and give light enough to show the patches of snow lying along the mountain side as we proceed. The snow becomes more continuous as we mount the ascent, until only the black rocks and pine-trees stand out in relief against their white background.

I was contrasting the sharp cold of this mountain region with the bright summer weather I had left behind me in Australia only a few weeks ago, and the much more stifling heat of Honolulu only some ten days since, when the engine gave one of its loud whistles, like the blast of a fog-horn, and we plunged into darkness. Looking through the car window, I observed that we were passing through a wooden frame-work—in fact, a snow-shed, the roof sloping from the mountain side, to carry safely over the track the snow and rocky *débris* which shoot down from above. I find there are miles upon miles of these snow-sheds along our route. At the summit we pass through the longest, which is 1700 feet in length.

We reached the summit at ten minutes to 10, having ascended 3400 feet in a distance of only thirty-six miles. We are now over 7000 feet above the level of the sea, traveling through a lofty mountain region. In the morning I was on the warm shores of the Pacific, and now, at night, I am amid the snows of the Sierras. After passing the summit we had some very tortuous traveling; going very fast during an hour, but winding in and out, as we did, following the contour of the hills, I found that we had only gained seven geographical miles in an hour. We then reached the "City" of Truckee, principally supported by lumbering. It is the last place in California, and we shall very soon be across the state boundary into the Territory of Nevada.

After passing this station I curled up on my bench, wrapped myself in my rugs, and had a snatch of sleep. I was wakened up by the stoppage of the train at the Reno Station, when I shook myself up, and went out to have a look round me. As I alighted from the train, I had almost come to the ground through the slipperiness of the platform, which was coated with ice. It was a sharp frost, and the ground was covered with snow. At the end of the platform, the snow was piled up in a drift about twenty feet high on the top of a shed outside the station. I find there are two kinds of snow-sheds—one sort used on the plains, with pointed roofs, from which the snow slides down on either side, thereby preventing the blocking of the line; the other, used along the mountain sides, sloping over the track, so as to carry the snow-shoots clear over it down into the valley below.

I soon turned in again, wrapped myself up, and slept soundly for some hours. When I awoke it was broad daylight; the sun was shining in at the car windows; and on looking out, I saw that we were crossing a broad plain, with mountains on either side of us. The conductor, coming through the car, informs us that we shall soon be at Humboldt, where there will be twenty minutes' stoppage for breakfast. I find that we are now 422 miles on our way, and that during the night we have crossed the great sage-covered Nevada Desert, on which so many travelers left their bones to bleach in the days of the overland journey to California, but which is now so rapidly and safely traversed by means of this railway. The train draws up at Humboldt at seven in the morning, and on descending, I find a large, well-appointed refreshment-room, with the tables ready laid, and a tempting array of hot tea and coffee, bacon, steaks, eggs, and other eatables. "I guess" I had my full dollars' worth out of that Humboldt establishment—a "regular square meal," to quote the language of the conductor.

We mount again, and are off across the high plains. The sage-brush is the only vegetation to be seen, interspersed here and there with large beds of alkali, on which not even sage-brush will grow. The sage country extends from Wadsworth to Battle Mount Station, a distance of about two hundred miles. Only occasionally, by the river sides, near the station, small patches of cultivated land are to be seen; but, generally speaking, the country is barren, and will ever remain so. We are still nearly 5000 feet above the level of the sea. There is no longer any snow on the ground alongside us, but the mountains within sight are all covered. Though the day is bright and sunshiny, and the inside of the car warm, with the stove always full of blazing wood or coke, the air outside is cold, sharp, and nipping.

At Battle Mount—so called because of a severe engagement which occurred here some years since between the Indians and the white settlers—the plains begin to narrow, and the mountains to close in again upon the track. Here I saw for the first time a number of Shoshonie Indians—the original natives of the country—their faces painted red, and their coarse black hair hanging down over their shoulders. Their squaws, who carried their papooses in shawls slung over their backs, came alongside the train to beg money from the passengers. The Indian men seemed to be of a very low type —not for a moment to be compared with the splendid Maoris of New Zealand. The only fine tribe of Indians left are said to be the Sioux, and these are fast dying out. In the struggle of races for life, savages nowhere seem to have the slightest chance when they come in contact with what are called "civilized" men. If they are not destroyed by our diseases or our drink, they are by our weapons.

We are now running along the banks of the sluggish Humboldt River up to almost its source in the mountains near the head of the Great Salt Lake. We cross the winding river from time to time on trestle-bridges, and soon we are in among the mountains again, penetrating a gorge, where the track is overhung by lofty bluffs; and, climbing up the heights, we shortly leave the river foaming in its bed far beneath us. Steeper and higher rise the sides of the gorge, until suddenly, when we round a curve in the cañon, I see the Devil's Peak, a large, jagged mass of dark brown rock, which, rising perpendicularly, breaks up into many points, the highest towering majestically to a height of 1400 feet above the level of the track. This is what is called the "Ten-mile Cañon;" and the bold scenery continues until we emerge from the top of the gorge. At last we are in the open sunlight again, and shortly after we draw up at the Elko Station.

We are now evidently drawing near a better-peopled district than that we have lately passed through. Two heavy stage-coaches are drawn up alongside the track, to take passengers to Hamilton and Treasure City, in the White Pine silver-mining district, about 126 miles distant. A long team of mules stand laden with goods, destined for the diggers of the same district. Elko is "not much of a place," though I should not wonder if it is called a "city" here. It mostly consists of what in Victoria would be called shanties—huts built of wood and canvas—some of the larger of them being labeled "Saloon," "Eating-house," "Drug-store," "Paint-shop," and such like. If one might judge by the number of people thronging the drinking-houses, the place may be pronounced prosperous.

Our course now lies through the valleys, which look more fertile, and are certainly much more pleasant to pass along than those dreary Nevada plains. The sun goes down on my second day in the train as we are traversing a fine valley with rolling hills on either side. The ground again becomes thickly covered with snow, and I find we are again ascending a steepish grade, rising a thousand feet in a distance of about ninety miles, where we again reach a total altitude of 6180 feet above the sea.

At six next morning I found we had reached Ogden, in the Territory of Utah. During the night we had passed "The Great American Desert," extending over an area of sixty square miles—an utterly blasted place—so that I missed nothing by passing over it wrapped in sleep and rugs. The country about Ogden is well cultivated and pleasant looking. Ogden itself is a busy place, being the terminus of the Central Pacific Railroad, and the junction for trains running down to Salt Lake City. From this point the Union Pacific commences, and runs eastward as far as Omaha.

CHAPTER XXV.

ACROSS THE ROCKY MOUNTAINS.

Start by Train for Omaha.—My Fellow-passengers.—Passage through the Devil's Gate.—Weber Cañon.—Fantastic Rocks.—"Thousand-mile Tree."—Echo Cañon.—More Trestle-bridges.—Sunset amid the Bluffs. —A Wintry Night by Rail.—Snow-fences and Snow-sheds.—Laramie City.—Red Buttes.—The Summit at Sherman.—Cheyenne City.—The Western Prairie in Winter.—Prairie Dog City.—The Valley of the Platte.—Grand Island.—Cross the North Fork of the Platte.—Arrival in Omaha.

I DECIDED not to break the journey by visiting Utah—about which so much has already been written—but to go straight on to Omaha, and I accordingly took my place in the train about to start eastward. Here I encountered quite a new phase of American railroad society. One of my fellow-passengers was a quack doctor, who contemplated depositing himself in the first populous place he came to on the track-side for the purpose of picking up some "'tarnal red cents." A colonel and a corporal in the American army were on their way home from some post in the Far West, where they had been to keep the Indians in order. There were several young commercial travelers, some lucky men returning from the silver-mines in Idaho, a steward of one of the Pacific mail steamers returning to England, and an iron-moulder with his wife and child on their way to Chicago.

The train soon started, and for some miles we passed through a well-cultivated country, divided into fields and orchards, looking pretty even under the thick snow, and reminding me of the vales of Kent. But we very soon left the cultivated land behind us, and were again in among the mountain gorges. I got out on to the platform to look around me, and though the piercing cold rather chilled my pleasure, I could not help enjoying the wonderful scenery that we passed through during the next three hours. We are now entering the Wahsatch Mountains by the grand chasm called the Devil's Gate. We cross a trestle-bridge fifty feet above the torrent which boils beneath, and through the black, frowning rocks that guard the pass I catch the last glimpse of the open sunlit plain below.

We are now within the wild Weber Cañon, and the scene is changing every moment. On the right we pass a most wonderful sight, the Devil's Slide. Two ridges of gray rock stand some ten feet out from the snow and brushwood, and they run parallel to each other for about 150 feet, right away up the mountain side. For a distance of thirty-five miles we run along the dark, deep cleft, the rocks assuming all sorts of fantastic shapes, and the River Weber running almost immediately beneath us, fretting and raging against the obstacles in its course. Sometimes the valley widens out a little, but again to force us against a cliff, where the road has been hewn out of the solid bluff. In the cañon we pass a pine-tree standing close to the track, with a large board hung upon it bearing the words "1000 miles from Omaha." It is hence named the "Thousand-mile Tree." We have all that long way before us to travel on this Union Pacific Railway.

At last we emerge from Weber Cañon and pull up at

Echo City, a small place, chiefly inhabited by railway employés. We start again, and are soon plunged amid red, rocky bluffs, more fantastic than any we have yet passed. We pass the Mormon fortifications at a place where a precipitous rock overhangs the narrowing cañon. Here, on the top of the rock, a thousand feet above us, are piled huge stones, placed close to the brink of the precipice, once ready to be hurled down upon the foes of Mormonism—the army sent out against them in 1857. The stones were never used, and are to be seen there yet. The rocks in the cañon are of a different color from those we passed an hour ago. The shapes that they take are wonderful. Now I could fancy that I saw a beautiful cathedral, with spires and windows; then a castle, battlements and bastions all complete; and more than one amphitheatre fit for a Cæsar to have held his sports in. What could be more striking than these great rugged masses of red rock, thrown one upon another, and mounting up so high above us? Such fantastical and curious shapes the weather-worn stone had taken! Pillars, columns, domes, arches, followed one another in quick succession. Rounding a corner, a huge circle of rocks comes into sight, rising story upon story. There, perched upon the top of the rising ground is a natural castle, complete with gateway and windows. Indeed, the hour passed quickly in spite of the cold, and I felt myself to have been in fairy-land for the time. The whole seemed to be some wild dream. But dream it could not be. There was the magnificence of the solid reality—pile upon pile of the solid rock frowning down upon me; great boulders thrown together by some giant force; perpendicular heights, time-worn and battered by the elements. All combined to produce in me a feeling of the utmost wonder and astonishment.

Emerging from Echo Cañon and the Castle Rocks, we enter a milder valley, where we crawl over a trestle-bridge 450 feet long and 75 feet high. Shortly after passing Wahsatch Station we cross the Aspen Summit and reach an opener country. Since we left Ogden, we have, in a distance of ninety-three miles, climbed an ascent of 2500 feet, and are now in a region of frost and snow. After another hour's traveling the character of the scenery again changes, and it becomes more rugged and broken. The line crosses the Bear River on another long trestle-bridge 600 feet long, and, following the valley, we then strike across the higher ground to the head of Ham's Fork, down which we descend, following the valley as far as Bryan or Black's Fork, 171 miles from Ogden.

As the day is drawing to a close, I take a last look upon the scene outside before turning in for the night. The sun is setting in the west, illuminating with its last rays the red sandstone bluffs, the light contrasting with the deep blue sky overhead, and presenting a novel and beautiful effect. We are now traversing a rolling desert, sometimes whirling round a bluff in our rapid descent, or crossing a dry water-course on trestles, the features of the scene every moment changing. Then I would catch a glimpse of the broken, rolling prairies in the distance, covered with snow, and anon we were rounding another precipitous bluff. The red of the sunlight grows dull against the blue sky, until night gradually wraps the scene in her mantle of gray. Then the moon comes out with her silvery light, and reveals new features of wondrous wildness and beauty. I stood for hours leaning on the rail of the car, gazing at the fascinating vision, and was only reminded by the growing coldness of the night that it was time to re-enter the car and prepare for my night's rest.

After warming myself by the stove, I arranged my extemporized couch between the seats as before, but was wakened up by the conductor, who took from me a cushion more than was my due; so I had to spend the rest of the night nodding on a box at the end of the car. However, even the longest and most comfortless night will come to an end; and when at last the morning broke, I went out to ascertain whereabouts we were. I found that it had snowed heavily during the night, and we now seemed to be in a much colder and more desolate country. The wind felt dreadfully keen as I stood on the car platform and looked about, the dry snow whisking up from the track as the train rushed along. The fine particles somehow got inside the thickest comforter and wrapper, and penetrated every where. So light and fine were the particles that they seemed to be like thick hoar-frost blowing through the air.

We have, I observe, a snow-plow fixed on the front of the engine, and, from the look of the weather, it would appear as if we should have abundant use for it yet. Snow-fences and snow-sheds are numerous along the line we are traversing, for the purpose of preventing the cuts being drifted up by the snow. At first I could not quite make out the nature of these fences, standing about ten yards from the track, and in some parts extending for miles. They are constructed of wood-work, and are so made as to be capable of being moved from place to place, according as the snow falls thick or is drifting. That is where the road is on a level, with perhaps an opening amid the rolling hills on one side or the other; but when we pass through a cutting we are protected by a snow-shed, usually built of boards supported on poles.

At Laramie City we stop for breakfast. The name of "city" is given to several little collections of houses along the line. I observe that the writer of the "Trans-continental Guide-book" goes almost into fits when describing the glories of these "cities," which, when we come up to them, prove to be little more than so many clusters of sheds. I was not, therefore, prepared to expect much from the City of Laramie, and the more so as I knew that but a few years since the original Fort Laramie consisted of only a quadrangular inclosure inhabited by trappers, who had established it for trading purposes with the Indians. I was accordingly somewhat surprised to find that the modern Laramie had suddenly shot up into a place of some population and importance. The streets are broad and well laid out; the houses are numerous, and some of them large and substantial. The place is already provided with schools, hotels, banks, and a newspaper. The Railway Company have some good substantial shops here, built of stone; and they have also provided a very commodious hospital for the use of their employés when injured or sick—an example that might be followed with advantage in places of even greater importance.

After a stoppage of about half an hour we were again careering up hill past Fort Saunders and the Red Buttes, the latter so called from the bold red sandstone bluffs, in some places a thousand feet high, which bound the track on our right. Then still up hill to Harney, beyond which we cross Dale Creek bridge—a wonderful structure, 650 feet long and 126 feet high, spanning the creek from bluff to bluff. Looking down through the interstices of the wooden road, what a distance the thread of water in the hollow seemed to be below us!

At Sherman, some two hours from Laramie, we arrived at the summit of the Rocky Mountain ridge, where we reached the altitude of about 8400 feet above the sea-level. Of course it was very cold, hill and dale being covered with snow as far as the eye could reach. Now we rush rapidly down hill, the breaks screwed tightly down, the cars whizzing round the curves, and making the snow fly past in clouds. We have now crossed the back-bone of the continent, and are speeding on toward the settled and populous country in the East.

At Cheyenne we have another stoppage for refreshment. This is one of the cities with which our guide-book writer falls into ecstasies. It is "The Magic City of the Plains"—a place of which it "requires neither a prophet nor the son of a prophet to enumerate its resources or predict its future!" Yet Cheyenne is already a place of importance, and likely to become still more so, being situated at the junction with the line to Denver, which runs along the rich and lovely valley of the Colorado. Its population of 8000 seems very large for a place that so short a time ago was merely the haunt of Red Indians. Already it has manufactories, warehouses, wharves, and stores of considerable magnitude, with all the usual appurtenances of a place of traffic and business.

Before leaving Cheyenne I invested in some hung buffalo steak for consumption at intervals between meals. It is rather tough and salt, something like Hamburg beef; but, seasoned with hunger, and with the appetite sharpened by the cold and frost of these high regions, the hung buffalo proved useful and nutritious.

For several hundred miles our track lay across the prairie — monotonous and comparatively uninteresting now in its covering of white, but in early summer clad in lively green and carpeted with flowers. I read that this fine, cultivable, well-watered country extends seven hundred miles north and south, along the eastern base of the Rocky Mountains, with an average width of two hundred miles. It is said to be among the finest grazing land in the world, with pasturage for millions of cattle and sheep.

Shortly after passing Antelope Station the track skirts the "Prairie Dog City," which I knew at once by its singular appearance. It consists of hundreds of little mounds of soil, raised about a foot and a half from the ground. There were, however, no dogs about at the time. The biting cold had doubtless sent them within doors. Indeed, I saw no wild animals on my journey across the continent excepting only some black antelopes with white faces that I saw on the plains near this Prairie Dog City.

For a distance of more than five hundred miles—from leaving Cheyenne until our arrival in Omaha—the railway held along the left bank of the Lodge Pole Creek, then along the South Fork or Platte River, and finally along the main Platte River down to near its junction with the Missouri. When I went to sleep on the night of the 11th of February—my fourth night in the railway train—we were traveling through the level prairie, and when I woke up on the following morning I found we were on the prairie still.

At seven in the morning we halted at the station of Grand Island, so called from the largest island in the Platte River, near at hand. Here I had breakfast, and a good wash in ice-cold water. Although the snow is heavier than ever, the climate seems already milder; yet it is very different indeed from the sweltering heat of Honolulu only some twelve days ago. At about 10 A.M. we bid adieu to the uninhabited prairie—though doubtless, before many years are over, it will be covered with farms and homesteads—and approached the fringe of the settled country, patches of cultivated land and the log huts of the settlers beginning to show themselves here and there alongside the track.

Some eighty miles from Omaha we cross the north fork of the Platte River over one of the usual long timber bridges on piles, and continue to skirt the north bank of the Great Platte, certainly a very remarkable river, being in some places three quarters of a mile broad, with an average depth of only six inches! At length, on the afternoon of the fifth day, the engine gives a low whistle, and we find ourselves gliding into the station at Omaha.

CHAPTER XXVI.

OMAHA TO CHICAGO.

Omaha Terminus.—Cross the Missouri.—Council Bluffs.—The Forest.—Cross the Mississippi.—The cultivated Prairie.—The Farmsteads and Villages.—Approach to Chicago.—The City of Chicago.—Enterprise of its Men.—The Water Tunnels under Lake Michigan.—Tunnels under the River Chicago.—Union of Lake Michigan with the Mississippi.—Description of the Streets and Buildings of Chicago.—Pigs and Corn.—The Avenue.—Sleighing.—Theatres and Churches.

I HAVE not much to tell about Omaha, for I did not make any long stay in the place, being anxious to get on and finish my journey. It was now my fifth day in the train, having come a distance of 1912 miles from San Francisco, and I had still another twenty-four hours' travel before me to Chicago. There was nothing to detain me in Omaha. It is like all places suddenly made by a railway, full of bustle and business, but by no means picturesque. How can it be? The city is only seventeen years old. Its principal buildings are manufactories, breweries, warehouses, and hotels.

Omaha has been made by the fact of its having been fixed upon as the terminus of the Union Pacific Railroad, and by its convenient position on the great Missouri River. It occupies a sloping upland on the right bank, about fifty feet above the level of the stream, and behind it stretches the great prairie country we have just traversed. On the opposite bank of the Missouri stands Council Bluffs, from which various railroad lines diverge north, south, and east, to all parts of the Union. It is probable, therefore, that before many years have passed, big though Omaha may now be—and it already contains 20,000 inhabitants—the advantages of its position will tend greatly to swell its population, and perhaps to render it, in course of time, one of the biggest cities of the West.

Having arranged to proceed onward to Chicago by the Northwestern line, I gave up my baggage in ex-

change for the usual check, and took my place in the train. We rolled down a steepish incline on to the "mighty Missouri," which we crossed upon a bridge of boats. I should not have known that I was upon a deep and rapid river but for the huge flat-bottomed boats that I saw lying frozen in along the banks. It was easy to mistake the enormous breadth of ice for a wide field covered with snow. As we proceeded across we met numbers of sledges, coaches, and omnibuses driving over the ice along a track made in the deep snow not far from our bridge.

After passing through Council Bluffs we soon lost sight of the town and its suburbs, and were again in the country. But how different the prospect from the car window, compared with the bare and unsettled prairies which we had traversed for so many hundred miles west of Omaha! Now, thick woods extend on both sides of the track, with an occasional cleared space for a township, where we stop to take up and set down passengers. But I shall not proceed farther with my description of winter scenery as viewed from a passing railway train.

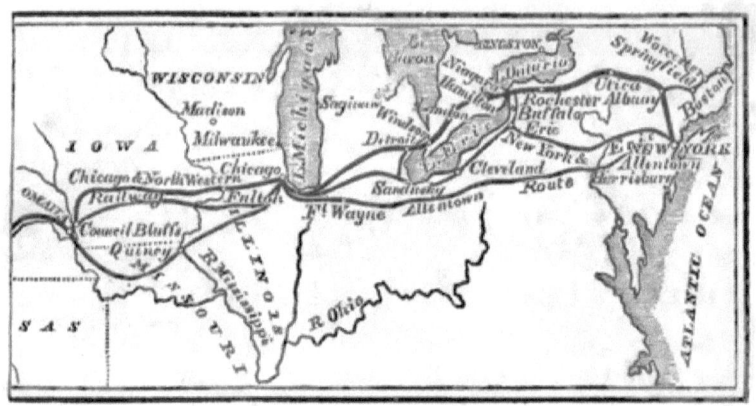

Indeed, I fear that my descriptions heretofore, though rapid, must be felt somewhat monotonous, for which I crave the reader's forgiveness.

I spent my fifth night in the train pretty comfortably, having contrived to make up a tolerable berth. Shortly after I awoke we crossed the Mississippi on a splendid bridge at Fulton. What a noble river it is! Here, where it must be fifteen hundred miles from its mouth, it seemed to me not less than a mile across. Like the Missouri, however, it is now completely frozen over and covered with thick snow.

M

We are again passing through a prairie country, the fertile land of upper Illinois, all well settled and cultivated. We pass a succession of fine farms and farmsteads. The fields are divided by rail fences, and in some places stalks of maize peep up through the snow. The pretty wooden houses are occasionally half hidden by the snow-laden trees amid which they stand. These Illinois clusters of country houses remind one very much of England, they look so snug and home-like; and they occupy a gently undulating country—lovely, no doubt, in summer time. But the small towns we passed could never be mistaken for English. They are laid out quite regularly, each house with its little garden surrounding it, the broad streets being planted with avenues of trees.

The snow is lying very heavy on the ground, and there are drifts we pass through full twenty feet deep on either side of the road. But the day is fine, the sky is clear and blue, the sun shines brightly, and the whole scene looks much more cheerful than the Rocky Mountain region in the west.

Very shortly, evidences appear of our approach to a considerable place; in fact, we are nearing Chicago. But long before we reach it we pass a succession of pretty villas and country houses, quite in the English suburban style, with gardens, shrubberies, and hot-houses. These are the residences of the Chicago merchants. The houses become more numerous, and before long we are crossing streets and thoroughfares, the engine snorting slowly along, and the great bell ringing to warn all foot-passengers off the track.

What an immense smoky place we have entered, so different from the pure snow-white prairie country we have passed! It looks just like another Manchester. But I suspect we have as yet traversed only the manufacturing part of the city, as the only buildings heretofore visible are small dwelling-houses and manufactories. At length we pull up in the station, and find ourselves safely landed in Chicago.

Oh, the luxury of a good wash after a continuous journey of two thousand four hundred miles by rail! What a blessing cold water is, did we but know it. The luxury, also, of taking off one's clothes to sleep in a bed after 'five nights' rolling about in railway cars—that, also, is a thing to be enjoyed once in a lifetime! But, for the sake of the pleasure, I confess I have no particular desire to repeat the process.

And now for the wonders of Chicago. It is really a place worth going a long way to see. It exhibits the enterprise of the American people in its most striking light. Such immense blocks of buildings forming fine broad streets, such magnificent wharves and warehouses, such splendid shops, such handsome churches, and such elegant public buildings! One can scarcely believe that all this has been the work of little more than thirty years.

It is true, the situation of Chicago at the head of Lake Michigan, with a great fertile country behind it, has done much for the place, but without the *men* Chicago would have been nothing. It is human industry and energy that have made it what it is. Nothing seems too bold or difficult for the enterprise of Chicago men. One of their most daring but successful feats was in altering the foundation level of the city. It was found that the business quarter was laid too low—that it was damp, and could not be properly drained. It was determined to raise the whole quarter bodily from six to eight feet higher! And the extraordinary feat was accomplished, with the help of jack-screws, safely and satisfactorily.

With the growth of population—and its increase was most rapid (from 4000 persons in 1837 to about 350,000 at the present time)—the difficulty of obtaining pure water steadily increased. There was pure water enough in the lake outside, but along shore it was so polluted by the sewage that it could not be used with safety.* Two methods were adopted to remedy this evil. One was, to make Artesian wells 700 feet deep, which yield about a million gallons of pure water per day; but another, and much bolder scheme, was undertaken, that of carrying a tunnel under the bed of the lake, two miles out, into perfectly pure water, and this work was successfully accomplished and completed on the 25th of March, 1867, when the water was let into the tunnel to flow through the pipes and quadrants of the city. Thus 57 million gallons of water per day could be supplied to the inhabitants.

Another important and daring work was that involved in carrying the traffic of the streets from one side of the Chicago River (which flows through the city) to the other without the interference of bridges. This was accomplished by means of tunnels constructed beneath the bed of the river. The first tunnel was carried across from Washington Street to the other side some years since; it was arched with brick, floored with timber, and lighted with gas. The second, lower down the same river, was still in progress at the period of my visit to the city in March last (1871), and is not yet completed. By means of these tunnels the traffic of the streets will be sufficiently accommodated, without any interruption by the traffic of the river, large ships proceeding directly up to the wharves above to load and unload their cargoes.

But the boldest project of all remains to be mentioned. It is neither more nor less than the cutting down of the limestone ridge which intervenes between the head waters of the River Chicago and those of the River Illinois, which flows into the Mississippi. The water-supply being still found insufficient, the carrying out of a second tunnel into deep water under the bed of the lake was projected. It then occurred to the Chicago engineers that a more simple method would be, instead of going out into the lake for the pure water, to make the pure water come to them. The sewage-laden stream of the Chicago River now flowed north into the lake; would it not be practicable, by cutting down the level inland, to make it flow south, and thus bring the pure water of the lake in an abundant stream past their very doors?

This scheme has actually been carried out! The work was in progress while I was there, and I observe that it has since been completed. The limestone plateau to the south of Chicago has been cut down at a cost of about three millions of dollars, and an abundant supply of pure water has thus been secured to the town forever. But the cutting of this artificial river for the purpose of water-supply has opened up another and a much larger question. It is, whether, by sufficiently deepening the bed, a channel may not be formed for large ocean-going ships, so that Chicago may be placed in direct water communication with the Gulf of Mexico, as it now is with the Gulf of St. Lawrence. Should this project, which was freely spoken of when I was at Chicago, be carried out, it may lead to very important consequences. While it may have the effect of greatly promoting the prosperity of Chicago, it may also have an altogether different result. "The letting out of waters" is not always a safe thing; and the turning of the stream, or any considerable part of the stream which now passes over the Falls of Niagara, into the bed of the Mississippi —whose swollen waters are sometimes found sufficiently unmanageable as it is—might have a very extraordinary and even startling effect upon the low-lying regions at the mouth of that great river. But this is a point that must be left for geologists and engineers to speculate about and to settle.

Shortly after my arrival in Chicago I went out for a wander in the streets. I was accompanied by the hotel "tout," who soon gave me his history. He had been a captain in the English army, had run through all his money, and come here to make more. He had many reminiscences to relate of his huntings in Leicestershire, of his life in the army, of his foolish gamblings, of his ups and downs in America, and his present prospects. Nothing daunted by his mishaps, he was still full of hope. He was an agent for railways, agent for a billiard-table manufacturer and for several patents, and believed he should soon be a rich man again. But no one, he said, had any chance in Chicago unless he was prepared to work, and to work hard. "A man," he observed, "must have his eyes peeled to make money; as for the lazy man, he hasn't the ghost of a chance here."

My guide took me along the principal streets, which were full of traffic and bustle, the men evidently intent upon business, pushing on, looking neither to the right hand nor the left. The streets are mostly stone-paved, and, in spite of the heavy snow which has fallen, they are clean and well kept. We passed the City Hall, the Chamber of Commerce, and the Post-office—all fine buildings. In the principal streets the houses are five stories high, with handsome marble fronts. The office of the "Chicago Tribune," situated at the corner of one of the chief thoroughfares, is a splendid pile, with a spacious corner entrance. The Potter Palmer block, chiefly occupied as a gigantic draper's shop—here called a Dry Goods Store—is an immense pile of buildings, with massive marble front handsomely carved. But the building which promises shortly to overtop all others in Chicago is the Pacific Hotel, now in course of erection—an enormous structure, covering an acre and a half of ground, with a frontage of 325 feet, and a height of 104 feet. It is expected to be the largest and finest building in the city, until something else is projected to surpass and excel it.

In my progress through the streets I came upon two huge steam cranes at work, hoisting up stuff from a great depth below. I was told that this was the second tunnel in course of construction under the bed of the river to enable the traffic to pass across without the necessity for bridges. The stream over the tunnel was busy with shipping. In one street I passed a huge pile of dead pigs in front of a sausage shop. They go in pigs and come out sausages. Pork is one of the great staples of the place, the number of pigs slaughtered in Chicago being something enormous. The pig-butcheries and pork stores are among the largest buildings in the city. My guide assures me that at least a pig a second is killed and dressed in Chicago all the year through. Another street was occupied by large stores of grain, fruit, and produce of all kinds. The pathways were filled with farmers and grain-brokers, settling bargains and doing business. And yet it was not market-day, when the streets are far more crowded and full of bustle.

Some idea of the enormous amount of business in grain done in Chicago may be formed from the fact that in one year, 1868, sixty-eight million bushels of grain were shipped from its wharves. It is the centre of the grain-trade of the States; lines of railway concentre upon it from all parts of the interior; and, by means of shipping, the produce is exported to the Eastern States, to Great Britain, or to any other part of the world where it is needed.

The street-cars go jingling along with their heavy loads of passengers. A continual stream of people keeps coming and going. There are many young ladies afoot, doing their shopping, enveloped in furs, and some with white scarves — or "clouds" as they are called — round their heads. Loud advertisements, of all colors, shapes, and sizes, abound on every side. Pea-nut sellers at their stands on the pavement invite the passers-by to purchase, announcing that they roast fresh every half hour. What amused me, in one of the by-streets from which the frozen snow had not been removed, was seeing a number of boys skating along at full speed.

Fronting the lake is the fashionable avenue of the city. Here, nice detached houses range along the broad

road for miles. Trees shade the carriage-way, which in summer must look beautiful. Now all is covered with hard-frozen snow, over which the sleigh-bells sound merrily as the teams come dashing along Here comes a little cutter with a pretty black pony, which trots saucily past, and is followed by a grand double-seated sleigh drawn by three splendid grays. Other sleighs, built for lightness and speed, are drawn by fast-trotting horses, in which the Americans take so much delight. The object of most of the young men who are out sleighing seems to be to pass the sleigh in front of them, so that some very smart racing is usually to be seen along the Avenue drive.

As might be expected from the extent and wealth of its population, Chicago is well supplied with places of amusement. I observe that Christine Nilsson is here at present, and she is an immense favorite. There are also many handsome stone churches in the city, which add much to the fine appearance of the place. But I had neither time to visit the theatres nor the churches, as my time in Chicago was already up, and I accordingly made arrangements for pursuing my journey eastward.*

* It will be observed that the above summary description applies to Chicago as it was seen by the writer in February last. While these sheets are passing through the press, the appalling intelligence has arrived from America that the magnificent city has been almost entirely destroyed by fire!

NIAGARA FALLS—AMERICAN SIDE.

CHAPTER XXVII.

CHICAGO TO NEW YORK.

Leave Chicago.—The Ice Harvest.—Michigan City.—The Forest.—A Railway Smash.—Kalamazoo.—Detroit.—Crossing into Canada.—American Manners.—Roebling's Suspension Bridge.—Niagara Falls in Winter.—Goat Island.—The American Fall.—The Great Horse-shoe Fall.—The Rapids from the Lovers' Seat.—American Cousins.—Rochester.—New York.—A Catastrophe.—Return Home.

For some distance out of Chicago the railway runs alongside the fine avenue fronting Lake Michigan. We pass a long succession of villas amid their gardens and shrubberies, now white with snow and frost. Then we cross an inlet on a timber viaduct laid on piles driven into the bed of the lake. The ice at some parts is thrown up irregularly in waves, and presents a strange aspect. It looks as if it had been frozen solid in one moment at a time when the wind was blowing pretty hard.

At another part, where the ice is smoother, men were getting in the ice harvest between us and the shore. The snow is first cleared from the surface by means of a snow plane. Then the plow, drawn by a horse, with a man guiding the sharp steel cutter, makes a deep groove into the ice. These grooves are again crossed by others at right angles, until the whole of the surface intended to be gathered in is divided into sections of about four feet square. When that is done, several of the first blocks taken out are detached by means of hand-saws, after which the remainder are easily broken off with crowbars. The blocks are then stored in the large ice-houses on shore, several of which are so large as to be each capable of holding some 20,000 tons of ice.

The consumption of ice in the States is enormous. Every one takes ice in their water in winter as well as in summer. Even the commonest sort of people consume it largely; and they send round to the store for ten cents' worth of ice, just as our people send round to the nearest public for sixpenny worth of beer. I have heard Americans who have been in London complain of the scarcity of ice with us, and the parsimonious way in which it is used; but then we have not the enormous natural stores of ice close to our doors, as they have at Chicago and many other of the large American towns.

Meanwhile we have skirted the shores of the lake and shot into the country, the snow lying deep in the fields, in some places quite covering the tops of the fences. After passing through a rather thickly-wooded country, we come to Michigan City, which stands close to the lake, with a river flowing past it, on which large barges piled high with timber are now completely frozen up.

What a pretty place this Michigan must be in summer time, when the trees which line the streets, and all the shady gardens about it, are clad in green! Even now the town has a brisk, cheerful look. The sleighs are running merrily over the snow, and the omnibuses glide smoothly along the streets on their "runners."

Taking one last look of the great inland sea, we struck across the broad peninsula formed by Lake Michigan on one side and Lake Huron on the other, to the town of Detroit. The country was very thickly wooded in some places, apparently the remains of the old primeval forest; yet there were towns and villages at frequent intervals along the route. The deer have not yet been extirpated, for often and again I saw their tracks in the snow along the banks of the railway.

At one part of the road the speed of the train slackened, and the engine moved along slowly, whistling as it went. What was wrong? I got out on to the platform to see. We soon came up to a smashed train; frames of cars, wrecks of cases, wheels, axles, and *débris*, laying promiscuously tumbled together. I asked the conductor what had happened. He answered quite coolly, "Guess the express ran into goods train!" It looked very like it.

In the course of the day we passed several small manufacturing towns. It seemed so odd, when we appeared as if traveling through the back woods, to see above the trees, not far off, a tall red chimney, where not long before we had passed the track of the wild deer. There was one very large manufactory—so large that it had a special branch to itself connecting it with the main track—at a place called Kalamazoo, reminding one of Red Indians and war trails over this ground not so very long ago. The town of Kalamazoo itself is a large and busy place: who knows but that it may contain the embryo of some future Leeds or Manchester?

It was dark when the train reached Detroit, where we had to cross the river which runs betwen Lake St. Clair and Lake Erie by ferry-boat into Canada. The street being dark, I missed my way, and at last found myself on the edge of the water when I least expected it. I got on board just as the last bell was sounding before the boat put off from the quay. I then had my baggage checked on to Niagara, a custom-house officer on board marking all the pieces intended only to pass through Canada, thereby avoiding examination. All the arrangements of the American railways with respect to luggage seem to me excellent, and calculated greatly to promote the convenience of the traveling public.

We were not more than a quarter of an hour on board the ferry-boat, during which I found time to lay in a good supper in the splendid saloon occupying the upper story of the vessel. Arrived at the Canadian side, there was a general rush to the train, and the carriages were soon filled. There were great complaints among some of the passengers that the Pullman's cars were all full, and that no beds were to be had; there being usually a considerable run upon these convenient berths, especially in the depth of winter.

My next neighbor during the night was a very pleasant gentleman—an American. I must here confess to the agreeable disappointment I have experienced with respect to the Americans I have hitherto come in contact with. I have as yet met with no specimens of the typical Yankee depicted by satirists and novelists. In my innocence, I expected to be asked in the cars such questions as "I guess you're a Britisher, sir?" "Where do you come from, stranger?" "Where are you going to, sir?" "What are you going to do when you get there?" and such like. It is true that at San Francisco I encountered a few of such questions, but the persons who put them were for the most part only hotel touters. Among the Americans of about my own condition with whom I traveled I met with nothing but politeness and civility. I will go farther, and say, that the generality of Americans are more ready to volunteer a kindness than is usual in England. They are always ready to answer a question, to offer a paper, to share a rug, or perhaps tender a cigar. They are generally easy in manner, yet unobtrusive. I will also add, that, so far as my experience goes, the average intelligence of young men in America is considerably higher than it is in England. They are better educated and better informed; and I met few or none who were not able to enter into any topic of general conversation, and pursue it pleasantly.

I saw but little of Canada, for I passed through what is called the "London district" of it in the night. It was about four in the morning when the train reached the suspension bridge which crosses from Canada into the States, about a mile and a half below the Falls of Niagara. We were soon upon the bridge—a light, airy-looking structure, made principally of strong wire—and I was out upon the carriage platform looking down into the gorge below. It was bright moonlight, so that I could see well about me. There were the snow-covered cliffs on either side, and the wide rift between them two hundred and fifty feet deep, in the bottom of which ran the river at a speed of about thirty miles an hour. It almost made the head dizzy to look down. But we were soon across the bridge, and on solid land again. We were already within hearing of the great roar of the Falls, not unlike the sound of an express train coming along the track a little distance off. Shortly after we reached our terminus and its adjoining hotel, in which for a time I forgot the Falls and every thing else in a sound sleep.

The first thing that struck me on wakening was the loud continuous roar near at hand. I was soon up and out, and on my way to the Falls, seated in a grand sleigh drawn by a pair of fine black horses. Remember it was the dead of winter, the 15th of February, not by any means the time of the year for going about sight-seeing, and yet I fancy the sight of Niagara in midwinter must be quite as astonishing, and perhaps even more picturesque, than at any other season.

Over the crisp snow, and through the clean little town, the sleigh went flying, the roar of the water growing louder as we neared the Falls. Soon we are at the gates of a bridge, where a toll is charged for admission to the island from which the great Falls are best seen. Crossing the bridge, we reach the small island, on which a large paper-mill has been erected; and I am pointed to a rock to which last winter a poor fellow—beyond the reach of safety, though in sight—clung for hours, until, unable to hold on any longer, he was finally swept away down the torrent.

We cross another small bridge, and are on the celebrated Goat Island, which divides the great Canadian from the smaller American fall. My driver first took me to a point on the American side of this island from which a fine view is to be obtained. The sight is certainly most wonderful. I walked down a steep pathway slippery with ice, with steps cut here and there in the rock, and suddenly found myself on the brink of the precipice. Close to my left the water was pouring down into a chasm a hundred and sixty feet below, disappearing in a great blue cavern of ice that seemed to swallow it up. By the continual freezing of the spray, this great ice-cave reaches higher and higher during winter time. Immense icicles, some fifty feet long, hang down the sides of the rock immediately over the precipice. The trees on the island above were bent down with the weight of the frozen spray, which hung in masses from their branches. The blending of the ice and water far beneath my feet was a remarkable sight. As the spray and mist from time to time cleared off, I looked deep down into the dark icy abyss, in which the water roared, and foamed, and frothed, and boiled again.

Then I went to the other side of the island, quite fairy-like as it glistened in the sunlight, gemmed with ice-drops, and clad in its garment of white, and there I saw that astounding sight, the great Horse-shoe Fall, seven hundred feet across, over which the enormous mass of water pours with tremendous force. As the water rolled over the cliff, it seemed to hang like a green curtain in front of it until it reached half way down; then gradually breaking, white streaks appeared in it, broadening as they descended, until at length the mighty mass spread out in foam, and fell roaring into the terrific gulf some hundred and fifty feet below. A great ice-bridge stretched across the river beyond the boiling water at the bottom of the Fall, rough and uneven like some of the Swiss glaciers. Clouds of spray flew about, seemingly like smoke or steam. Words fail to describe a scene of such overpowering grandeur as this.

I was next driven along Goat Island to a small suspension bridge, some distance above the Falls, where I crossed over to one of the three Sister Islands—small bits of land jutting right out into the middle of the rapids. The water passes between each of these islands. I went out to the extreme point of the farthest. The sight here is perhaps second only to the great Fall itself. The river, about a mile and a quarter wide, rushes down the heavy descent, contracting as it goes before leaping the precipice below. The water was tossing and foaming like an angry sea, reminding me of the ocean when the waves are running high and curling their white crests after a storm.

These rapids had far more fascination for me than the Falls themselves. I could sit and watch for hours the water rushing past; and it was long before I could leave them, though my feet were in deep snow. It must be very fine to sit out at that extreme point in summer time, shaded by the rich foliage of the trees, and dream away the hours. The seat is known as the Lover's Seat, but lovers would need to have strong lungs to shout their whispers to each other there, if they wished them to be heard.

At length I turned my back upon the foaming torrent, and resumed the road to my hotel. On my way back I stopped at the genuine Niagara curiosity-shop, where photographs, Indian bead and feather work, and articles manufactured out of the "real Niagara spar," are sold.

Only the photographs are really genuine and good. The bead-work is a manufacture, and probably never passed through Indian hands; while the Niagara spar is imported from Matlock, much of it doubtless returning to England in the form of curious specimens of workmanship from the Great Falls.

I have very little more to add relating to my journey through the States. I was not making a tour, but passing through America at railway speed on my way home to England, and I have merely described, in the most rapid and cursory way, the things that struck me along my route. All that remained for me to do between Niagara and New York was to call at Rochester, and pay an unheralded visit to my American cousins there. What English family has not got relations in the States? I find that I have them living in Rochester, Boston, and St. Louis. It is the same blood, after all, in both countries—in Old and New England.

After traveling through the well-cultivated, well-peopled country that extends eastward from Niagara to Rochester, I arrived at my destination about four in the afternoon, and immediately went in search of my American cousins. I was conscious of being a rather untidy sight to look at, after my long railway journey of nearly three thousand miles, and did not know what, in my rough traveling guise, my reception might be. But any misgivings on that point were soon set at rest by the cordiality of my reception. I was at once made one of the family, and treated as such. I enjoyed with my new-found relatives four delightful days of recruiting rest and friendly intercourse. To use the common American phrase, I had a "real good time."

The town of Rochester is much bigger than the English city of the same name. It is a place of considerable trade and importance, with a population of about 60,000. Some of the commercial buildings are very fine, and I was told of one place that it was "the finest fireproof establishment in the world." Possibly the American world was meant, and that is by no means a small one. Rochester is especially famous for its nurseries, where trees of all kinds are reared and sent far and near, its principal nursery firms being known all over Europe.

There are some fine waterfalls near Rochester — the Falls of the Genesee. Had I not seen Niagara, I should have doubtless wondered at their beauty. Their height is as great, but the quantity of water is wanting. After Niagara, all other falls must seem comparatively tame.

My short stay in Rochester was made most pleasant. I felt completely at home and at my ease in the American household I had so suddenly entered. I also accompanied my cousins to two evening entertainments, one a fancy dress ball, and the other a *soirée dansante*, where I made the passing acquaintance of some very agreeable American ladies and gentlemen. I was really sorry to leave Rochester; and as the carriage drove me along the pretty avenue to the station, I felt as if I were just leaving a newly-found home.

I traveled from Rochester to New York during the night, passing several large towns, and at some places iron-furnaces at work, reminding one of the "Black country" in England by night. The noble Hudson was hard bound in ice as we passed along its banks, so that I missed the beautiful sight that it presents in summer time. But it is unnecessary for me to dwell either upon the Hudson or the city of New York, about which most people are in these days well read up. As for New York, I can not say that I was particularly struck by it, except by its situation, which is superb, and by its magnitude, which is immense. It seemed to me only a greater Manchester, with larger sign-boards, a clearer atmosphere, and a magnificent river front. It contains no great buildings of a metropolitan character, unless among such buildings are to be included hotels, newspaper offices, and dry goods stores, some of which are really enormous piles. Generally speaking, New York may be described as a city consisting of comparatively insignificant parts greatly exaggerated, and almost infinitely multiplied. It may be want of taste; but, on the whole, I was better pleased with Chicago. The season of my visit was doubtless unpropitious. Who could admire the beauties of the noble Central Park in the dead of winter? Perhaps, too, I was not in a good humor to judge of New York, as it was there that I met with my first and only misfortune during my two years' absence from home—for there I was robbed.

I had been strongly urged by my friends at Rochester to go to Booth's Theatre to see Mr. Booth play in "Richelieu" as a thing not to be seen in the same perfection any where else. I went accordingly, enjoyed Booth's admirable acting, and returned to my hotel. When I reached there, on feeling my pocket, lo! my purse was gone. I had been relieved of it either in the press at the theatre exit, or in entering or leaving the tramway car on my return.

I had my ticket for Liverpool safe in my waistcoat pocket; but there was my hotel bill to pay, and several necessaries to purchase for use during the voyage home. What was I to do? I knew nobody in New York. It was too far from home to obtain a remittance from thence, and I was anxious to leave without farther delay. I bethought me of the kind friends I had left at Rochester, acquainted them with my misfortune, and asked for a temporary loan of twenty dollars. By return post an order arrived for a hundred. "A friend in need is a friend indeed."

The same post brought two letters from my Rochester friends, in one of which my correspondent said that my misfortune was one that few escaped in New York. He himself had been robbed of his purse in a Broadway stage, his father had been robbed of a pocket-book containing money, and his father-in-law of a gold watch. My other kind correspondent, who inclosed me his check, said, by way of caution, "You must bear in mind that the principal streets of New York are full of pickpockets and desperadoes. They will recognize you as a stranger, so you must be wary. You may be 'spotted' as you go into or come out of the banking office. It often happens that a man is robbed in Wall Street in open day—is knocked down, and his money 'grabbed' before his eyes; so be very careful, and trust nobody. Go alone to the banking office, or get a trusty servant from the house to go with you; but let no outsider see check or money."

Of course I took very good care not to be robbed in New York a second time, and I got away in safety next morning by the "City of Brooklyn," taking with me the above very disagreeable reminiscence of my New York experience. It is not necessary to describe the voyage home, the passage from New York to Liverpool being now as familiar an event as the journey from London to York. At Queenstown I telegraphed my arrival to friends at home, and by the time the ship entered the Mersey there were those waiting at the landing-place to give me a cordial welcome back. I ran up to town by the evening train, and was again at home. Thus I completed my Voyage Round the World, in the course of which I have gained health, knowledge, and experience, and seen and learned many things which will probably furnish me with matter for thought in all my future life.

INDEX.

Albatross, 51, 57.
Alta, Central Pacific Railway, 248.
American cousins, 282; Indians, 251; manners, 277, 278; railway cars, 241.
Amusements on board ship, 28, 33, 34, 50, 60, 62.
Arrival of home mail, Majorca, 175.
Arum esculentum, Honolulu, 218.
Atlantic and Pacific Railway, 241-262; the railway cars, 241; Sacramento City, 243; scenery of the Sierra Nevada, 245; Cape Horn, 247; snow-sheds, 249, 258; the summit, 249; the sage desert, 250, 251; Shoshonie Indians, 251; Devil's Peak, 252; Weber Cañon, 255; Laramie City, 259; Cheyenne, 260; Prairie Dog City, 261; River Platte, 261, 262; arrival at Omaha, 262.
Auckland, New Zealand, 199-204.
Aurora Australis, 129.
Australia, first sight of, 62; last, 198.
Autumn rains, Majorca, 130.
Avoca, 167.
Azores, 27.

Ballarat, visit to, 160-166.
Bank, at Majorca, 95, 130.
Bank-robbing, 156, 157.
Bar at a gold-rush, 91.
Batman, first settler in Victoria, 69.
Battle Mount, Nevada, 251.
Becalmed on the Line, 37.
Beggars, absence of, in Victoria, 70, 98.
Bell-bird, 134.
Birds in South Atlantic, 56.
Black Thursday in Victoria, 122.
"Blue Jacket," burning of, 40-47.
Bonitos, 31, 34.
Booth's Theatre, New York, 284.
Botanic Gardens, Melbourne, 76.
Botany Bay, 188.
Bourke Street, Melbourne, 66.
Brighton, 64, 76.
Brooke, the murderer, 154-156.
Bush animals: marsupials, 131, 132, 138; reptiles, 137; birds, 134-136.
Bush fires, 122.
Bush, the, 106; in summer, 119, 127; by moonlight, 173.
Bush piano, 129.

Calms on the Line, 37.
Cape Brett, 199.
Cape de Verd Islands, 30.
Cape Horn, Central Pacific Railway, 247.
Cape Leeuwin, 62.
Cape of Good Hope, 50, 53.
Cape Otway, 62, 63.
Cape pigeons, 53, 57.
Carlton Gardens, Melbourne, 71.
Castlemaine, 84.
Castle Rocks, Rocky Mountains, 256.
Cautions against robbers, 158, 285.
Central Pacific Railway, 245-253.
Channel, in the, 16-18.
Cheltenham, Australia, 76.
Cheyenne, U. S., 260.
Chicago, arrival at, 266; enterprise of, 267, 268; water-supply, 268, 269; tunnels under river, 268, 271; buildings, 271, 272; pigs and pork, 271, 272; grain-trade of, 272; sleighs, 273; departure from, 274.
Chinese, character, 71; gardens and gardeners, 96, 115, 116; music, 104; burials, 105; gold-diggers, 141-143, 146; at Honolulu, 225; at San Francisco, 237.
Christmas in Victoria, 122, 185.
"City of Melbourne," steam-ship, 196-211.
Climate of Victoria: winter, 109; spring, 117; summer, 118; autumn, 125, 130.
Clunes, 111, 112, 167.
Coach, journeys by: Castlemaine to Majorca, 85, 86; Clunes to Ballarat, 160, 161; Auckland to Onehunga, 202.
Cochon Islands, 58.
Collingwood Bank, attempt to rob, 156, 157.
Collins Street, Melbourne, 68.
Cook, Captain, in New South Wales, 188.
Corner, the, Ballarat, 164.
Council Bluffs, U. S., 264.
Crab-holes, 167.
Crozet Islands, 58.

Dale Creek Bridge, U. S., 260.
Death on board ship, 232.
Deck-bath in tropics, 32.
Descent into a gold mine, 145.
Detroit, U. S., 277; to Niagara, 277, 278.
Devil's Peak, Rocky Mountains, 252; Gate, 255.
Diggers at a gold-rush, 90-92; amateur, 143; Chinese, 141, 146; hospitality of, 100, 101.
Diggers' tales, 126, 148, 152-156.
Divers, Honolulu, 223.
Drink-license, Honolulu, 224, 225.
Drunkenness, absence of, in Majorca, 97, 98.
Dust-winds in Victoria, 120.

Echo City and Cañon, U. S., 256.
Elsternwick, 76.

INDEX.

Elko, Nevada, 252.
Epsom, New Zealand, 203.
Eucalyptus, 110.

Farms near Majorca, 125, 126, 128.
Ferry-boat, San Francisco, 239.
Fête at Talbot, 169-171; at Majorca, for school-fund, 180, 181.
Fire-brigade, Ballarat, 166.
Fires in the bush, 122.
Fitzroy Gardens, Melbourne, 71.
Flies in Majorca, 121.
Floods, about Majorca, 112-114; at Ballarat, 115, 116; at Clunes, 114.
Flowers, Majorca, 118.
Flying fish, 31, 210.
Frenchman in Majorca, 177.
Fruits, Majorca, 122.
Funeral of Majorca town clerk, 182.

"Galatea," H.M.S., 199, 204.
Genesee Falls, U. S., 283.
"George Thompson," of London, 48, 49.
Germans in Victoria, 94, 176, 177.
Goat Island, Niagara, 279.
Gold: buying, 139-143; finding, 147-150; mining, 144-150, 163, 256; purifying, 139, 140; rushing, 89-92, 151, 162.
Grain-trade, Chicago, 272.
Grapes in Victoria, 124.
"Great Britain," of Liverpool, 186.
Green sea, shipping a, 55.
Gum-tree, Australian, 87, 110.

Harvest-time, Majorca, 125.
Havelock rush, 152.
Hawaii, 211.
Heat in summer, Australia, 119.
Holystoning, 23, 24.
Honeysuckers, 134.
Honolulu: arrival at, 211; the harbor, 212; commercial importance of, 213; description of, 214, 215; churches, 215; post-office, 216; king's palace at, 217, 218; visit to the Nuuanu Valley, 218-222; Poi, 218, 219; Queen Emma's villa, 219; the Pali, 221; the natives, 222, 223; the women, 224; liquor-licenses, 224, 225; Chinese opium-license, 225; theatricals at, 225; climate of, 218, 227.
Honolulu to San Francisco, 228-234.
Horse-shoe Fall, Niagara, 280.
Hudson River, 283.
Humboldt, U. S., 250.

Ice-bird, 57.
Ice-consumption in U. S., 275.
Ice-harvest, Lake Michigan, 275.
Illinois Prairie, 266.
Irish in Majorca, 94.

Kalamazoo, U. S., 276, 277.
Kamehameha V., 228.
Kanakas, Honolulu, 223-224, 228.
Kangaroo, 138, 194.

Landing in Australia, 64, 65.
Laramie City, U. S., 259.

Leatherheads, 134.
Leeches in Victoria, 128, 129.
Les Apôtres Islands, 58, 59.
Libraries, public, in Australia: Melbourne, 72; Ballarat, 164; Majorca, 182.
Line, cross the, 38, 210.
Liquor-law, Honolulu, 224, 225.
"Lord Raglan," 35, 36.
Lovers' Seat, Niagara, 281.
Lowe Kong Meng Mine, 145.
Luggage on American railways, 277.
Lung complaints, sea-voyage in, 21.

M'Cullum's Creek, 99, 115.
Macquarie Light-house, 189.
Magpie, Australian, 134.
Mails: Victoria and Honolulu, 216; delays of New Zealand, 204; newspapers by ocean mail, treatment of, 210, 211; arrival at Majorca, 175.
Majorca, life in, 89-183.
Manukau Bay, New Zealand, 203.
Maoris, 200-202.
Marsupials, 138.
Maryborough, 86; rush at, 126.
Mathews, Mr. Charles, 187, 226.
Mauna Loa, Sandwich Islands, 211.
Melbourne, arrival at, 66; description of, 67, 68; youth of, 69; rapid growth of, 69; absence of beggars, 70; the Chinese Quarter, 71; public library, 72; visit to Pentridge Prison, 73-75; Botanic Gardens, 76; the Yarra, 76; the sea suburbs of, 76; hospitality of, 77; Christmas in, 185.
Michigan City, U. S., 275.
Michigan, Lake, 267-269, 274, 276.
Mina-birds, 135.
Mississippi River, 265.
Missouri River, 264.
Monument to Cook, 188 (note).
Moonlight in Victoria, 120, 173.
Mormon fortifications, 256.
"Moses Taylor," steam-ship, 223, 230, 231.
Mount Greenock, Australia, 123.
Musquitoes, 133, 227.

New chums, 70, 237.
New York, 284.
New Zealand, 196-204.
Niagara Falls in winter, 278-282.
Nursery Gardens, Rochester, 283.
Nuuanu Valley, Honolulu, 218.

Oahu Island, 214.
Oakland, California, 241.
Ogden, Utah, 253.
Omaha, 263.
Onehunga, New Zealand, 202, 203.
Opium-license, Honolulu, 225.
Opossum-shooting, 131-133.

Pacific, up the, 205-234.
Pali, of the Nuuanu Valley, 221.
Parliament House, Melbourne, 67.
Parroquets, 135.

INDEX. 289

"Patter *vs.* Clutter," at Honolulu, 226 (*note*).
Pentridge Prison, 73-75.
Phosphorescence, 27, 28.
Pigtail, Chinese, 71, 72.
Piping Crow, 134, 135.
Platte River, U. S., 261, **262.**
Plymouth Harbor, 19.
Poi, 218, 219.
Port Jackson, 189, 190, 197.
Port Phillip Heads, 63.
Possession Island, 58, 59.
"Pyrmont," of Hamburg, **40-47.**

Queenscliffe, Australia, 64, 186.

Race with the "George Thompson," 49.
Railway: Atlantic and Pacific, *see Atlantic*; to Castlemaine, 84; carriage, American, 241; smash, 276; touters at San Francisco, 237.
Rain in Victoria, **110-116.**
Robbed in New York, **284.**
Rochester, U. S., 282.
"Rosa," of Guernsey, abandoned, 19.
Rough life at the diggings, 151.
Rushes, gold, 89, 90, 151, 162, 163.

Sacramento, California, **244.**
Sage-bush, 250, 251.
"Saginaw," wreck of the, **229.**
Sail Rock, New Zealand, **199.**
St. Kilda, Victoria, **64, 76.**
San Antonio, 30.
Sandridge, Victoria, 64, **67, 71, 186.**
Sandwich Islands, 213.
San Francisco, 233-240; arrival at, 233; Bay of, 241; buildings, 236; Chinese Quarter, 237; ferry-boat, 240; money-brokers, 236, 237; railway touters, 237; railway terminus, 241; streets, 236.
Schools, Majorca, 179, 180.
Scotch at Majorca, 94.
Serious family, visit to a, 79.
Shipping a green sea, 55.
Shooting sea-birds, 58; opossums, **131-133.**
Shoshonie Indians, 251.
"Shouting" for drinks, **97.**
Sierra Nevada, 245-253.
Sister Islands, Niagara, **281.**
Snakes in the bush, 136, 137.
Snow-sheds and fences, Atlantic and Pacific Railway, 249, 250, **258.**
South Atlantic, 48.
Spring at Majorca, **117.**
Squatters, 107, 127.
Steam-voyage, monotony of, 205.

Stevenson on the power of waves, 55 (*note*).
Stink-pot, **57.**
Stockton, California, **243.**
Summer in Victoria, **118.**
Sunrise in the bush, **173, 174.**
Sunset in the tropics, 38.
Suspension Bridge, Niagara, 278.
Sydney, 191-195; age of, 192; animals in Botanic Gardens, 194; Botanic Gardens, 193, 194; compared with Melbourne, 192; Cove, 190, 191; description of, 191; domain, 193; harbors, 191; public buildings, 191, 193; suburbs, 195.
Sydney to New Zealand, 196-204.

Talbot, 167-171.
Taro plant, 218.
Tea-meetings, Majorca, **178.**
Teetotalers, 179.
Telegraph, Victoria, 114, 159.
Theatres: Honolulu, 215; Melbourne, 67; New York, 284.
Theatricals on board ship, **60, 62.**
Thieves, New York, **285.**
Thousand-mile Tree, 255.
Three Kings' Island, New Zealand, **198.**
Trade winds, 29.
Trestle-bridges, Atlantic and Pacific Railway, 246.

Union Pacific Railway, 254-262.

Verein, opening of, Majorca, **176.**
Victoria, when colonized, **69, 70.**
Victorian climate, *see Climate.*
Victorian life, **175, 178, 183.**
Vineyards, Australia, **125.**

Wahsatch Mountains, U. S., **255.**
Wallaby, 138.
Water-supply, Chicago, **268, 269.**
Wattle birds, 134.
Weber Cañon, **255.**
Western Pacific Railway, 241-244.
Whale-bird, 52.
Williamstown, Victoria, **64, 76.**
Wine in Victoria, 124, 125.
Winter in Majorca, **109.**
Wooloomooloo, Sydney, 190, **191.**
Work in Victoria, **70, 97.**
Wreck of the "Saginaw," 229.
Wrens, Victorian, 135.

Yarra-Yarra River, 75, 76.
"Yorkshire," **13-65.**

THE END.

By Samuel Smiles.

Character.

12mo, Cloth, $1 50.

CONTENTS:

Influence of Character.—Home Power.—Companionship.—Example.—Work.—Courage.—Self-Control.—Duty.—Truthfulness.—Temper.—Manner.—Companionship of Books.—Companionship in Marriage.—Discipline of Experience.

Self-Help.

Self-Help; with Illustrations of Character and Conduct. 12mo, Cloth, $1 25.

One of the most interesting, entertaining, and instructive books ever published, and as such should be in every family. One wonders how such a common-sense, excellent book could be made so attractive.—*Correspondence Cincinnati Chronicle.*

It enforces the wholesome lessons that genuine success in any purpose of life is to be expected or achieved only by the resolute practice of industry, patience, and perseverance, and that the continual exercise of these qualities will enable him who is most moderately endowed by nature or favored by circumstances to win the highest rewards and accomplish the noblest deeds; and that habits of exact, zealous, and unremitting application are more certain to secure their possessor the object of his desire, be it wealth, influence, or reputation, than is the strongest inherent aptitude or even genius itself. These principles are illustrated by a host of examples from the history of the most eminent men of all ranks and professions.—*Chicago Evening Post.*

Its purpose is to show how it is possible to gain honorable and brilliant success without adventitious aid, and to surmount the difficulties of "iron fortune" by patient and faithful endeavor.—*Brooklyn Eagle.*

It is a perfect magazine of encouraging facts drawn from a wide circle of biographical literature, ancient and modern, all tending to impress the truth that "Heaven helps those who help themselves." * * * Mr. Smiles tells what he has to say with such simplicity and sympathy and good cheer that it is no wonder his book is a pleasant companion for young readers.—*Examiner and Chronicle.*

Life of the Stephensons.

The Life of George Stephenson, and of his Son Robert Stephenson; comprising, also, a History of the Invention and Introduction of the Railway Locomotive. With Portraits and numerous Illustrations. 8vo, Cloth, $3 00.

It is as interesting as a romance—far more instructive than nine-tenths of the best romances. It relates one of the most wonderful stories that was ever imagined, yet a story every part of which is true.—*London Review.*

Mr. Smiles's book is one of the most attractive of biographies, both as regards the personal character of a poor man of genius, fighting out the battle of life with an exemplary valor, and, in a more general way, the history and progress of the railway system in the place where it originated. It contains every thing necessary to be known on that theme, and is as well written as it is comprehensive. It will be the popular life of the Stephensons, as Southey's book is the popular life of Nelson.—*N. Y. Times.*

Not only the lives of the two modern Titans who have waged successful war against Nature—storming its strongholds with a success denied the giants of old—but it is a history of the origin and development of one of the most wonderful and useful inventions that humanity has ever profited by.—*Albany Argus.*

History of the Huguenots.

The Huguenots: their Settlements, Churches, and Industries in England and Ireland. With an Appendix relating to the Huguenots in America. Crown 8vo, Cloth, Beveled, $1 75.

The author has given his subject the most thorough investigation. Drawing his material only from the best authenticated historic sources, he has followed the accounts of the most impartial writers in regard to the persecutions of the Huguenots on the Continent of Europe. Respecting their sojourn in England Mr. Smiles narrates much that is entirely new and of great interest.—*Philadelphia Inquirer.*

The wonderful story is told with spirit and accuracy, and in a better manner than ever before it was told. The reader is enabled to follow the course of events with pleasure, so lively and effective is the style of the exciting narrative. Seldom has so much valuable matter been placed between the covers of a single volume as we find in this; and the opinions of the author are as sound as his statements are trustworthy. The work is written in a philosophical spirit, and helps the reader to a just understanding of the bearing of the great events the history of which is told on other and later events that are even more important. As an instructive work, it would be difficult to name the equal of this.—*Boston Traveller.*

Mr. Smiles has never had a subject more intimately connecting what is greatest in the stir of mind with the establishment of new forms of industry than in this account of the settlement of the Huguenots, who left France after the Revocation of the Edict of Nantes, costing her, it is said, a million of her best subjects.—*Examiner.*

Round the World.

Round the World; including a Residence in Victoria, and a Journey by Rail across North America. By a Boy. Edited by SAMUEL SMILES. With Illustrations. 12mo, Cloth, $1 50.

How the book came to be written is as follows: The boy, whose two years' narrative forms the subject of these pages, was at the age of sixteen seized with inflammation of the lungs, from which he was recovering so slowly and unsatisfactorily that I was advised by London physicians to take him from business and send him on a long sea voyage. He was accordingly sent out to Melbourne. It will be found from his own narrative that for a period of about eighteen months he resided at Majorca, an up-country township situated in the gold-mining district of Victoria.

When his health had become re-established he was directed to return home; and he decided to make the return voyage by the Pacific route, via Honolulu and San Francisco, and from thence to proceed by railway across the Rocky Mountains to New York.

While at sea the boy kept a full log, intended for the perusal of his relatives at home. He had not the remotest idea that any thing which he saw and described during his absence would ever appear in a book. But since his return it has occurred to the Editor of these pages that the information they contain will probably be found of interest to a wider circle of readers than that to which the letters were originally addressed; and, in that belief, the substance of them is here reproduced, the Editor's work having consisted mainly in arranging the materials, leaving the writer to tell his own story as much as possible in his own way, and in his own words.—*Extract from Preface.*

PUBLISHED BY HARPER & BROTHERS, NEW YORK.

☞ HARPER & BROTHERS *will send either of the above works by mail, postage prepaid, to* any *part of the United States, on receipt of the price.*

VALUABLE AND INTERESTING

WORKS OF TRAVEL

PUBLISHED BY

HARPER & BROTHERS, New York.

☞ Harper & Brothers *will send either of the following works by mail, postage prepaid, to any part of the United States, on receipt of the price.*

KINGSLEY'S WEST INDIES. At Last: a Christmas in the West Indies. By Charles Kingsley, Author of "Alton Locke," "Yeast," &c., &c. Illustrated. 12mo, Cloth, $1 50.

ADVENTURES OF A YOUNG NATURALIST. By Lucien Biart. Edited and Adapted by Parker Gillmore. With 117 Illustrations. 12mo, Cloth, $1 75.

THE MUTINEERS OF THE BOUNTY. Some Account of the Mutineers of the Bounty and their Descendants in Pitcairn and Norfolk Islands. By Lady Belcher. Illustrated. 12mo, Cloth, $1 50.

REINDEER, DOGS, AND SNOW-SHOES. A Journal of Siberian Travel and Explorations made in the Years 1865-'67. By Richard J. Bush, late of the Russo-American Telegraph Expedition. Illustrated. Crown 8vo, Cloth, $3 00.

DIXON'S FREE RUSSIA. Free Russia. By W. Hepworth Dixon, Author of "Her Majesty's Tower," &c. With Two Illustrations. Crown 8vo, Cloth, $2 00.

DU CHAILLU'S AFRICA. Explorations and Adventures in Equatorial Africa; with Accounts of the Manners and Customs of the People, and of the Chase of the Gorilla, the Crocodile, Leopard, Elephant, Hippopotamus, and other Animals. By Paul B. Du Chaillu, Corresponding Member of the American Ethnological Society, of the Geographical and Statistical Society of New York, and of the Boston Society of Natural History. With numerous Illustrations. 8vo, Cloth, $5 00.

DU CHAILLU'S ASHANGO LAND. A Journey to Ashango Land, and Further Penetration into Equatorial Africa. By Paul B. Du Chaillu. New Edition. Handsomely Illustrated. 8vo, Cloth, $5 00.

ALCOCK'S JAPAN. The Capital of the Tycoon: a Narrative of a Three Years' Residence in Japan. By Sir Rutherford Alcock, K.C.B., Her Majesty's Envoy Extraordinary and Minister Plenipotentiary in Japan. With Maps and Engravings. 2 vols., 12mo, Cloth, $3 50.

ANDERSSON'S OKAVANGO RIVER. The Okavango River: a Narrative of Travel, Exploration, and Adventure. By Charles John Andersson. With Steel Portrait of the Author, numerous Woodcuts, and a Map showing the Regions explored by Andersson, Cumming, Livingstone, and Du Chaillu. 8vo, Cloth, $3 25.

ANDERSSON'S LAKE NGAMI. Lake Ngami; or, Explorations and Discoveries during Four Years' Wanderings in the Wilds of Southwestern Africa. By Charles John Andersson. With numerous Illustrations, representing Sporting Adventures, Subjects of Natural History, Devices for Destroying Wild Animals, &c. 12mo, Cloth, $1 75.

ATKINSON'S AMOOR REGIONS. Travels in the Regions of the Upper and Lower Amoor, and the Russian Acquisitions on the Confines of India and China. With Adventures among the Mountain Kirghis; and the Manjours, Manyargs, Toungous, Touzemts, Goldi, and Gelyaks; the Hunting and Pastoral Tribes. By Thomas Witlam Atkinson, F.G.S., F.R.G.S. With a Map and numerous Illustrations. 8vo, Cloth, $3 50.

ATKINSON'S SIBERIA. Oriental and **Western Siberia**: a Narrative of Seven Years' Explorations and Adventures **in Siberia, Mongolia,** the Kirghis Steppes, Chinese Tartary, and part **of Central Asia.** By THOMAS WITLAM ATKINSON. With a Map and **numerous Illustrations.** 8vo, Cloth, $3 50.

BECKWOURTH'S AUTOBIOGRAPHY. The Life and **Adventures of** James P. Beckwourth, Mountaineer, Soldier, and Pioneer, and **Chief of** the Crow **Indians.** Written from his own Dictation, by T. **D.** BONNER. With Illustrations. 12mo, Cloth, $1 50.

BARTH'S NORTH AND CENTRAL AFRICA. Travels and Discoveries **in North and Central** Africa. Being **a J**ournal of an Expedition under**taken under the** Auspices of H. B. M.'s Government, in the Years 1849–1855. By HENRY BARTH, Ph.D., D.C.L. Illustrated. 3 vols., 8vo, Cloth, $12 00.

BALDWIN'S AFRICAN HUNTING. African Hunting, from Natal to the Zambesi, including Lake Ngami, **the** Kalahari Desert, &c., from 1852 to 1860. By WILLIAM CHARLES BALDWIN, ESQ., F.R.G.S. With Map, Fifty Illustrations by Wolf and Zwecker, and a Portrait. **12mo,** Cloth, $1 50.

BURTON'S LAKE REGIONS OF CENTRAL AFRICA. **The Lake Re**gions of Central Africa. A Picture of Exploration. **By** RICHARD F. BURTON, Captain H. M.'s Indian Army, Fellow and Gold **Medalist of** the Royal Geographical Society. With Maps and Engravings **on Wood.** 8vo, Cloth, $3 50.

BURTON'S CITY OF THE SAINTS. The City of the Saints; and Across the Rocky Mountains to California. By Captain RICHARD F. BURTON, Fellow and Gold Medalist of the Royal Geographical Societies of France and England, H. M.'s Consul in West Africa. With Maps and numerous Illustrations. 8vo, Cloth, $3 50.

BAIRD'S MODERN GREECE. Modern Greece: a Narrative **of a Resi**dence and Travels **in that** Country. With Observations on its **Antiqui**ties, Literature, Language, Politics, and Religion. By HENRY M. **BAIRD, M.A.** Numerous Illustrations. 12mo, Cloth, $1 50.

BROWNE'S APACHE COUNTRY. Adventures in the Apache Country: a Tour through Arizona and Sonora, with Notes on the Silver Regions of Nevada. By J. Ross BROWNE. With Illustrations. 12mo, Cloth, $2 00.

BROWNE'S AMERICAN FAMILY **IN** GERMANY. An American Family in Germany. By J. Ross BROWNE. Illustrations. 12mo, Cloth, $2 00.

BROWNE'S CRUSOE'S ISLAND, CALIFORNIA, &c. Crusoe's Island: a **Ramble in** the Footsteps of Alexander Selkirk. With Sketches of Ad**venture** in California and Washoe. By J. Ross BROWNE. With Illustrations. 12mo, Cloth, $1 75.

BROWNE'S LAND OF THOR. The Land **of Thor.** By J. Ross BROWNE. Illustrations. 12mo, Cloth, $2 00.

BROWNE'S YUSEF. A Crusade in the East. A Narrative of Personal Adventures and Travels on the Shores of the Mediterranean, in Asia Minor, Palestine, and Syria. By J. Ross BROWNE. Engravings. 12mo, Cloth, $1 75.

BUFFUM'S SIGHTS AND SENSATIONS. Sights **and Sensations in** France, Germany, and Switzerland; or, Experiences **of an American** Journalist in Europe. By EDWARD GOULD BUFFUM, **Author of "Six** Months in the Gold Mines," &c. **12mo,** Cloth, $1 50.

BAKER'S CAST UP BY THE SEA. Cast Up by the Sea; or, the Adventures of Ned Grey. By Sir SAMUEL W. BAKER, M.A., F.R.G.S., Author of the "Albert N'Yanza Great Basin **of the** Nile," "The Nile Tributaries **of** Abyssinia," &c. With Ten Illustrations by Huard. 12mo, Cloth, 75 cents.

BELLOWS'S TRAVELS. The Old **World** in its New Face: Impressions of Europe in 1867, 1868. By HENRY **W.** BELLOWS. In Two Volumes. 12mo, Cloth, $3 50.

CURTIS'S THE HOWADJI IN **SYRIA. By** GEORGE WILLIAM CURTIS. 12mo, Cloth, $1 50.

Valuable and Interesting Works of Travel. 3

CURTIS'S NILE NOTES OF A HOWADJI. By GEORGE WILLIAM CURTIS. 12mo, Cloth, $1 50.

CUMMING'S HUNTER'S LIFE IN AFRICA. Five Years of a Hunter's Life in the far Interior of South Africa. With Notices of the Native Tribes, and Anecdotes of the Chase of the Lion, Elephant, Hippopotamus, Giraffe, Rhinoceros, &c. With Illustrations. By R. GORDON CUMMING. 2 vols., 12mo, Cloth, $3 00.

DURBIN'S OBSERVATIONS IN EUROPE. Principally in France and Great Britain. By Rev. J. P. DURBIN, D.D. Engravings. 2 vols., 12mo, Cloth, $3 00.

DURBIN'S OBSERVATIONS IN THE EAST. Chiefly in Egypt, Palestine, Syria, and Asia Minor. By Rev. J. P. DURBIN, D.D. 2 vols., 12mo, Cloth, $3 00.

DARWIN'S VOYAGE OF A NATURALIST. Journal of Researches into the Natural History and Geology of the Countries visited during the Voyage of H. M. S. *Beagle* round the World, under the command of Captain Fitzroy, R. N. By CHARLES DARWIN, M.A., F.R.S. 2 vols., 12mo, Cloth, $2 00.

DAVIS'S CARTHAGE. Carthage and her Remains: being an Account of the Excavations and Researches on the Site of the Phœnician Metropolis in Africa and other Adjacent Places. Conducted under the Auspices of Her Majesty's Government. By Dr. N. DAVIS, F.R.G.S. Profusely Illustrated with Maps, Woodcuts, Chromo-Lithographs, &c. 8vo, Cloth, $4 00.

DILKE'S GREATER BRITAIN. Greater Britain: a Record of Travel in English-speaking Countries during 1866 and 1867. By CHARLES WENTWORTH DILKE. With Maps and Illustrations. 12mo, Cloth, $1 00.

DOOLITTLE'S CHINA. Social Life of the Chinese; with some Account of their Religious, Governmental, Educational, and Business Customs and Opinions. With special but not exclusive Reference to Fuhchau. By Rev. JUSTUS DOOLITTLE, Fourteen Years Member of the Fuhchau Mission of the American Board. Illustrated with more than 150 characteristic Engravings on Wood. 2 vols., 12mo, Cloth, $5 00.

EWBANK'S BRAZIL. Life in Brazil; or, a Journal of a Visit to the Land of the Cocoa and the Palm. With an Appendix, containing Illustrations of Ancient and South American Arts, in recently discovered Implements and Products of Domestic Industry, and Works in Stone, Pottery, Gold, Silver, Bronze, &c. By THOMAS EWBANK. With over 100 Illustrations. 8vo, Cloth, $3 00.

ELLIS'S MADAGASCAR. Three Visits to Madagascar, during the Years 1853, 1854, 1856. Including a Journey to the Capital, with Notices of the Natural History of the Country, and of the Present Civilization of the People. By the Rev. WILLIAM ELLIS, F.H.S. Illustrated by a Map and Woodcuts from Photographs, &c. 8vo, Cloth, $3 50.

GERSTAECKER'S TRAVELS ROUND THE WORLD. Narrative of a Journey round the World. Comprising a Winter Passage across the Andes to Chili; with a Visit to the Gold Regions of California and Australia, the South Sea Islands, Java, &c. By F. GERSTAECKER. 12mo, Cloth, $1 50.

GIRONIERE'S PHILIPPINE ISLANDS. Twenty Years in the Philippines. By PAUL DE LA GIRONIERE. Revised and Extended by the Author expressly for this Translation. Engravings. 12mo, Cloth, $1 50.

GREENWOOD'S REUBEN DAVIDGER. The Adventures of Reuben Davidger, Seventeen Years and Four Months Captive among the Dyaks of Borneo. By JAMES GREENWOOD. With Engravings. 8vo, Cloth, $1 75.

GREENWOOD'S WILD SPORTS OF THE WORLD. Wild Sports of the World: a Book of Natural History and Adventure. By JAMES GREENWOOD. With 147 Illustrations. Crown 8vo, Cloth, $2 50.

HALL'S ARCTIC RESEARCHES. Arctic Researches and Life among the Esquimaux: being the Narrative of an Expedition in Search of Sir John Franklin, in the Years 1860, 1861, and 1862. By CHARLES FRANCIS HALL. With Maps and 100 Illustrations. 8vo, Cloth, Beveled, $5 00.

4   *Valuable and Interesting Works of Travel.*

HERODOTUS, LIFE AND TRAVELS **OF.** **The Life and** Travels of Herodotus in the Fifth Century before Christ: an Imaginary Biography founded on Fact, illustrative of the History, Manners, Religion, Literature, Arts, and Social Condition of the Greeks, Egyptians, Persians, Babylonians, Hebrews, Scythians, and other Ancient **Nations, in** the Days of Pericles and Nehemiah. By J. TALBOYS WHEELER, F.R.G.S. Map. 2 vols., 12mo, Cloth, $3 50.

HOLTON'S NEW GRANADA: Twenty Months in the Andes. **By I. F.** HOLTON. Illustrations and Maps. 8vo, Cloth, $3 00.

HUC'S TRAVELS THROUGH **THE** CHINESE EMPIRE. A Journey through the Chinese Empire. **By M.** HUC. With a Map. 2 vols., 12mo, Cloth, $3 00.

LAMONT'S SEASONS WITH THE SEA-HORSES. Seasons with the Sea-Horses; or, Sporting Adventures in the Northern Seas. By JAMES LAMONT, Esq., F.G.S. With Map and Illustrations. **8vo,** Cloth, $3 00.

LIVINGSTONE'S SOUTH AFRICA. Missionary Travels and Researches in South Africa; including a Sketch of Sixteen Years' Residence in the Interior of Africa, and a Journey from the Cape of Good Hope to Loando on the West Coast; thence across the Continent, down the River Zambesi, to the Eastern Ocean. By DAVID LIVINGSTONE, LL.D., D.C.L. With Portrait, Maps by Arrowsmith, and numerous Illustrations. 8vo, Cloth, $4 50.

LIVINGSTONE'S EXPEDITION TO THE ZAMBESI. Narrative of an Expedition to the Zambesi and its Tributaries; and of the Discovery of the Lakes Shirwa and Nyassa. 1858–1864. By DAVID and CHARLES LIVINGSTONE. With Map and Illustrations. 8vo, Cloth, $5 00.

LAYARD'S NINEVEH. A Popular Account of the Discoveries at **Nineveh.** By AUSTEN HENRY LAYARD. Abridged by him from his larger **Work.** With numerous Wood Engravings. 12mo, Cloth, $1 75.

LAYARD'S FRESH DISCOVERIES AT NINEVEH. Fresh Discoveries at Nineveh and Babylon; with Travels in Armenia, Kurdistan, and the Desert. Being the Result of a Second Expedition undertaken for the Trustees of the British Museum. By AUSTEN HENRY LAYARD, M.P. With all the Maps and Engravings in the English Edition. 8vo, Cloth, $4 00.

MADEIRA, PORTUGAL, AND THE ANDALUSIAS. Sketches and Adventures in Madeira, Portugal, and the Andalusias of Spain. By the **Author of** "Daniel Webster and his Contemporaries." With Illustrations. 12mo, Cloth, $1 50.

MARCY'S ARMY LIFE ON THE BORDER. Thirty Years of Army Life **on the** Border. Comprising Descriptions of the Indian Nomads of the **Plains;** Explorations of New Territory; a Trip across the Rocky Mountains **in** the Winter; Descriptions of the Habits of Different Animals found **in** the West, and the Methods of Hunting them; with Incidents in **the Life** of different Frontier Men, &c., &c. By Brevet Brig.-General R. B. MARCY, U. S. A. **8vo,** Cloth, Beveled Edges, $3 00.

MOENS'S ENGLISH TRAVELERS AND ITALIAN BRIGANDS. **A Narrative** of Capture **and** Captivity. By W. J. C. MOENS. With **Illustrations.** 12mo, Cloth, $1 75.

MOWRY'S ARIZONA AND SONORA. Arizona and Sonora. The Geography, History, and Resources of the Silver Region of North America. By SYLVESTER MOWRY, of Arizona, Graduate of the U. S. Military Academy at West Point, late Lieutenant Third Artillery, U. S. A., Corresponding Member of the American Institute, **late U. S.** Boundary Commissioner, **&c., &c.** 12mo, Cloth, $1 50.

MACGREGOR'S ROB ROY ON THE JORDAN. The Rob Roy on the Jordan, Nile, Red Sea, and Gennesareth, &c. A Canoe Cruise in Palestine and Egypt, and the Waters of Damascus. By J. MACGREGOR, M.A. With Maps and Illustrations. Crown 8vo, Cloth, $2 50.

OLIN'S (DR.) TRAVELS. Travels in Egypt, Arabia Petræa, and the Holy Land. Engravings. 2 vols., 8vo, Cloth, $3 00.

Valuable and Interesting Works of Travel.

NEVIUS'S CHINA. China and the Chinese: a General Description of the Country and its Inhabitants; its Civilization and Form of Government; its Religious and Social Institutions; its Intercourse with other Nations; and its Present Condition and Prospects. By the Rev. JOHN L. NEVIUS, Ten Years a Missionary in China. With a Map and Illustrations. 12mo, Cloth, $1 75.

NEWMAN'S FROM DAN TO BEERSHEBA. From Dan to Beersheba; or, the Land of Promise as it now appears. Including a Description of the Boundaries, Topography, Agriculture, Antiquities, Cities, and Present Inhabitants of that Wonderful Land. With Illustrations of the Remarkable Accuracy of the Sacred Writers in their Allusions to their Native Country. By Rev. J. P. NEWMAN, D.D. Maps and Engravings. 12mo, Cloth, $1 75.

OLIPHANT'S CHINA AND JAPAN. Narrative of the Earl of Elgin's Mission to China and Japan, in the Years 1857, '58, '59. By LAURENCE OLIPHANT, Private Secretary to Lord Elgin. Illustrations. 8vo, Cloth, $3 50.

ORTON'S ANDES AND THE AMAZON. The Andes and the Amazon; or, Across the Continent of South America. By JAMES ORTON, M.A., Professor of Natural History in Vassar College, Poughkeepsie, N. Y., and Corresponding Member of the Academy of Natural Sciences, Philadelphia. With a New Map of Equatorial America and numerous Illustrations. Crown 8vo, Cloth, $2 00.

PAGE'S LA PLATA. La Plata, the Argentine Confederation, and Paraguay. Being a Narrative of the Exploration of the Tributaries of the River La Plata and adjacent Countries during the Years 1853, '54, '55, and '56, under the Orders of the United States Government. New Edition, containing Farther Explorations in La Plata during 1859 and 1860. By THOMAS J. PAGE, U. S. N., Commander of the Expeditions. With Map and numerous Engravings. 8vo, Cloth, $5 00.

PFEIFFER'S SECOND JOURNEY. A Lady's Second Journey round the World: from London to the Cape of Good Hope, Borneo, Java, Sumatra, Celebes, Ceram, the Moluccas, &c., California, Panama, Peru, Ecuador, and the United States. By IDA PFEIFFER. 12mo, Cloth, $1 50.

PFEIFFER'S LAST TRAVELS AND AUTOBIOGRAPHY. The Last Travels of Ida Pfeiffer: inclusive of a Visit to Madagascar. With an Autobiographical Memoir of the Author. Translated by H. W. DULCKEN. Steel Portrait. 12mo, Cloth, $1 50.

PRIME'S (S. I.) TRAVELS IN EUROPE AND THE EAST. Travels in Europe and the East. A Year in England, Scotland, Ireland, Wales, France, Belgium, Holland, Germany, Austria, Italy, Greece, Turkey, Syria, Palestine, and Egypt. By Rev. SAMUEL IRENÆUS PRIME, D.D. Engravings. 2 vols., large 12mo, Cloth, $3 00.

PRIME'S (W. C.) BOAT-LIFE IN EGYPT. Boat-Life in Egypt and Nubia. By WILLIAM C. PRIME. Illustrations. 12mo, Cloth, $2 00.

PRIME'S (W. C.) TENT-LIFE IN THE HOLY LAND. By WILLIAM C. PRIME. Illustrations. 12mo, Cloth, $2 00.

READE'S SAVAGE AFRICA. Western Africa: being the Narrative of a Tour in Equatorial, Southwestern, and Northwestern Africa; with Notes on the Habits of the Gorilla; on the Existence of Unicorns and Tailed Men; on the Slave Trade; on the Origin, Character, and Capabilities of the Negro, and on the Future Civilization of Western Africa. By W. WINWOOD READE, Fellow of the Geographical and Anthropological Society of London, and Corresponding Member of the Geographical Society of Paris. With Illustrations and a Map. 8vo, Cloth, $4 00.

SQUIER'S CENTRAL AMERICA. The States of Central America: their Geography, Topography, Climate, Population, Resources, Productions, Commerce, Political Organization, Aborigines, &c., &c. Comprising Chapters on Honduras, San Salvador, Nicaragua, Costa Rica, Guatemala, Belize, the Bay Islands, the Mosquito Shore, and the Honduras Inter-Oceanic Railway. By E. G. SQUIER, formerly Chargé d'Affaires of the United States to the Republics of Central America. With numerous Original Maps and Illustrations. 8vo, Cloth, $4 00.

SQUIER'S NICARAGUA. Nicaragua: its People, Scenery, Monuments, Resources, Condition, and Proposed Canal. With One Hundred Maps and Illustrations. By E. G. SQUIER. 8vo, Cloth, $4 00.

SQUIER'S WAIKNA. Waikna; or, Adventures on the Mosquito Shore. By E. G. SQUIER. With a Map and upward of Sixty Illustrations. 12mo, Cloth, $1 50.

SMITH'S ARAUCANIANS. The Araucanians; or, Notes of a Tour among the Indian Tribes of Southern Chili. By EDMUND REUEL SMITH, of the U. S. N. Astronomical Expedition in Chili. 12mo, Cloth, $1 50.

SPEKE'S AFRICA. Journal of the Discovery of the Source of the Nile. By Captain JOHN HANNING SPEKE, Captain H. M.'s Indian Army, Fellow and Gold Medalist of the Royal Geographical Society, Hon. Corresponding Member and Gold Medalist of the French Geographical Society, &c. With Maps and Portraits and numerous Illustrations, chiefly from Drawings by Captain Grant. 8vo, Cloth, $4 00.

STEPHENS'S TRAVELS IN CENTRAL AMERICA. Travels in Central America, Chiapas, and Yucatan. By J. L. STEPHENS. With a Map and 88 Engravings. 2 vols., 8vo, Cloth, $6 00.

STEPHENS'S TRAVELS IN YUCATAN. Incidents of Travel in Yucatan. By J. L. STEPHENS. 120 Engravings, from Drawings by F. Catherwood. 2 vols., 8vo, Cloth, $6 00.

STEPHENS'S TRAVELS IN EGYPT. Travels in Egypt, Arabia Petræa, and the Holy Land. By J. L. STEPHENS. Engravings. 2 vols., 12mo, Cloth, $3 00.

STEPHENS'S TRAVELS IN GREECE. Travels in Greece, Turkey, Russia, and Poland. By J. L. STEPHENS. Engravings. 2 vols., 12mo, Cloth, $3 00.

THOMSON'S LAND AND BOOK. The Land and the Book; or, Biblical Illustrations drawn from the Manners and Customs, the Scenes and the Scenery of the Holy Land. By W M. THOMSON, D.D., Twenty-five Years a Missionary of the A.B.C.F.M. in Syria and Palestine. With two elaborate Maps of Palestine, an accurate Plan of Jerusalem, and *several Hundred Engravings*, representing the Scenery, Topography, and Productions of the Holy Land, and the Costumes, Manners, and Habits of the People. Two large 12mo Volumes, Cloth, $5 00.

VÁMBÉRY'S CENTRAL ASIA. Travels in Central Asia: being the Account of a Journey from Teheran across the Turkoman Desert, on the Eastern Shore of the Caspian, to Khiva, Bokhara, and Samarcand, performed in the Year 1863. By ARMINIUS VÁMBÉRY, Member of the Hungarian Academy of Pesth, by whom he was sent on this Scientific Mission. With Map and Woodcuts. 8vo, Cloth, $4 50.

VIRGINIA ILLUSTRATED: containing a Visit to the Virginian Canaan, and the Adventures of Porte Crayon and his Cousins. Illustrated from Drawings by PORTE CRAYON. 8vo, Cloth, $3 50.

WALLACE'S MALAY ARCHIPELAGO. The Malay Archipelago: the Land of the Orang-Utan and the Bird of Paradise. A Narrative of Travel, 1854–'62. With Studies of Man and Nature. By ALFRED RUSSEL WALLACE. With Maps and numerous Illustrations. Crown 8vo, Cloth, $3 50.

WELLS'S EXPLORATIONS IN HONDURAS. Explorations and Adventures in Honduras; comprising Sketches of Travel in the Gold Regions of Olancho, and a Review of the History and General Resources of Central America. By WILLIAM V. WELLS. With Original Maps and numerous Illustrations. 8vo, Cloth, $3 50.

WHYMPER'S ALASKA. Travel and Adventure in the Territory of Alaska, formerly Russian America—now Ceded to the United States—and in various other Parts of the North Pacific. By FREDERICK WHYMPER. With Map and Illustrations. Crown 8vo, Cloth, $2 50.

WILKINSON'S ANCIENT EGYPTIANS. A Popular Account of the Ancient Egyptians. Revised and abridged from his larger Work. By Sir J. GARDNER WILKINSON, D.C.L., F.R.S., &c. Illustrated with 500 Woodcuts. 2 vols., 12mo, Cloth, $3 50.

www.ingramcontent.com/pod-product-compliance
Lightning Source LLC
Chambersburg PA
CBHW030820230426
43667CB00008B/1305